IMAGES
of America

BROOKSVILLE

IMAGES
of America

BROOKSVILLE

Robert G. Martinez

ARCADIA
PUBLISHING

ISBN 978-0-7385-1652-3

Published by Arcadia Publishing
Charleston, South Carolina

Printed in the United States of America

Library of Congress Catalog Card Number: 2004102680

For all general information contact Arcadia Publishing at:
Telephone 843-853-2070
Fax 843-853-0044
E-mail sales@arcadiapublishing.com
For customer service and orders:
Toll-Free 1-888-313-2665

Visit us on the Internet at www.arcadiapublishing.com

Contents

ACKNOWLEDGMENTS

I would like to thank the Heritage Museum and Virginia Jackson for their support in providing us with many photos over the years. I also give deepest thanks to the contributions of the late Alfred McKethan, who donated many photos to us before his death in 2002, and the late Bob Griffith, who also donated many photos and news articles over the years. Also thanks to Dr. Roger Landers, Lynn Endsley Bruce, Myra Varn, Margaret Rogers Ghiotto, Murray Grubbs, A.W. Arick, and Kenneth Allman for their contributions over the years, and especially to Bobby Snow, who ably assists our magazine research with his archival work along with numerous photographs. The magazine we produce, *Old Brooksville In Photos and Stories*, has become a community effort, with hundreds of individuals over the years contributing photos, stories, newspaper clippings, etc. We deeply appreciate all these efforts from so many who love local history as much as I do.

Sincerely,
Robert G. Martinez

INTRODUCTION

Brooksville is located about 45 miles north of Tampa in Hernando County on Florida's west coast. It is one of the highest points in the state of Florida at approximately 225 feet above sea level. The area's history began with a strong tribe of Native Americans known as Timucua, who Spanish explorer Ponce de Leon first encountered in 1513 around this area. In 1528, Panfilo de Narvaez, another Spanish explorer, visited this area, but many of his men were lost to a storm or hurricane. Hernando de Soto, the next Spanish visitor, came to the area around 1539 and proceeded northward to other states as well. It was during the period of 1540 through 1830 that the Native Americans were the main inhabitants of this area. The United States purchased Florida from Spain in 1821. A new tribe, the Seminoles, branched off from the Creek nation around 1767. Gradually, their warlike efforts eliminated all other tribes in the area. The real beginnings of Hernando County stretch back to the days of the Second Seminole War (1835–1842). The first white inhabitants settled close to what is now Brooksville around 1835. The county was known as Benton County for a brief period after 1840 before being renamed Hernando County. There were early struggles with the natives, and in 1842 Charlotte Crum was the first white victim, killed just southeast of Brooksville.

One of the earliest settlers was William Hope, who recalled in an 1893 newspaper interview first coming to the area in 1835. Before being called "Brooksville," the community was called Melendez and Pierceville during the 1840s and 1850s. In 1856, Sen. Charles Sumner of Massachusetts delivered a harangue against slavery and accused the absent Sen. Andrew Butler of South Carolina as "The Don Quixote of slavery" and referred to slavery as "the ugly harlot of the South." The outburst angered the chivalrous core of many southerners, especially Rep. Preston Brooks of South Carolina. A few days later, Brooks approached Senator Sumner on the Senate floor and began beating him with a cane. The beating severely injured Sumner and put the Massachusetts senator out of commission for several months. This act propelled Brooks to hero status throughout the South. In Hernando County, where many of the folks hailed from South Carolina, the assault was considered a noble deed, so that same year their new county seat was named Brooksville in his honor. Hernando County also saw in 1856 the last big attack from the Seminoles, which killed two children and injured a few adults in Darby, a town about 15 miles south of Brooksville. In 1858 the Seminoles were sent out of the area to Oklahoma.

During the Civil War (1861–1865), Hernando County provided the South with a vital port in Bayport, about 18 miles west of Brooksville. Brooksville and Hernando County represented the Confederate Army with hundreds of soldiers. In 1864, a famous skirmish called the Brooksville

Raid occurred between Brooksville and Bayport, and it now has become a very popular annual reenactment. After the war, the South was broke; most families around Brooksville depended on farming as a source of income. Many African Americans who were slaves remained as sharecroppers or workers. Hernando County's population would grow from 1,200 in 1860 to 4,248 in 1880. The experience of Reconstruction, plus the bond of hard work and poverty among all races, provided a melting pot of shared fears, religions, and cultures. The City of Brooksville was incorporated in 1880, and the county was split in 1887 into two other counties, Citrus to the north and Pasco to the south. Citrus, turpentine, and timber were some of the key industries for the area during this period. A devastating freeze in 1894–1895 hurt the citrus industry, but it eventually recovered. A city west of Brooksville based on the lumber and timber industry was called Centralia, which had as many as 2,000 inhabitants during 1910–1920. All the trees were cut down by 1922 and it became a ghost town. Small hamlets around the county seat of Brooksville had their own churches, schools, and small businesses. Villages named Add, Spring Lake, Lake Lindsey, Wiscon, Masaryktown, Nobleton, and Istachatta were part of the landscape. Into the 20th century, the two key industries were citrus and tourism. Brooksville was known as the "Home of the Tangerine"; Brooksville and Hernando County at one time provided more tangerines to the New York–Philadelphia area than anyone. Unfortunately, the last big freeze of 1983 ended the role of citrus as a major player. The natural pristine beauty and close proximity to the Gulf would help the area become a magnet for tourism. Hunters and fishermen, including Yankee legend Babe Ruth, visited the area for Gulf fishing trips out of Bayport or Aripeka. The Weeki Wachee mermaid attraction was at one time one of the world's most popular tourist destinations. Rogers' Christmas House, the original Christmas store concept, has lured visitors from all points of the globe since the early 1970s.

There are many beautiful golf courses, including World Woods, northwest of Brooksville, which has been hailed as one of the world's finest and features an international clientele. Today, Brooksville's downtown has undergone a beautiful restoration and its streets offer a wide variety of classic Victorian homes with huge oaks welcoming you and wearing "that Spanish moss look" along brick streets, a charming and gracious reminder of classic, small-town Southern living.

One

1850–1900

The first census in Hernando County was conducted in 1850, largely around the area of what would soon be called Brooksville. In 1850, the city was known as Pierceville and counted 722 souls. Not until the 1870 census were African Americans counted because, before the Civil War, they were designated as slaves and listed as collateral only. During the later 1860s and 1870s, local industry began to take off, especially with citrus and cattle. Cattle empires would be built and cattle drives as early as 1862 would weave their way up to South Carolina. At about the same time, large amounts of cattle were shipped from here to Cuba via Tampa. There was no electricity, newspapers, or much of anything except hard work on the farm. During the 1880s, there began to be seen the semblance of a city with more schools, churches, shops, and more citizens moving to Brooksville. In 1885, the Plant Railroad connected Brooksville with Tampa and all points north. It was the beginning of a new civilization and just part of this area's industrial revolution, along with electricity, running water, the telephone, the phonograph, and something new and strange just around the corner: "a horseless carriage."

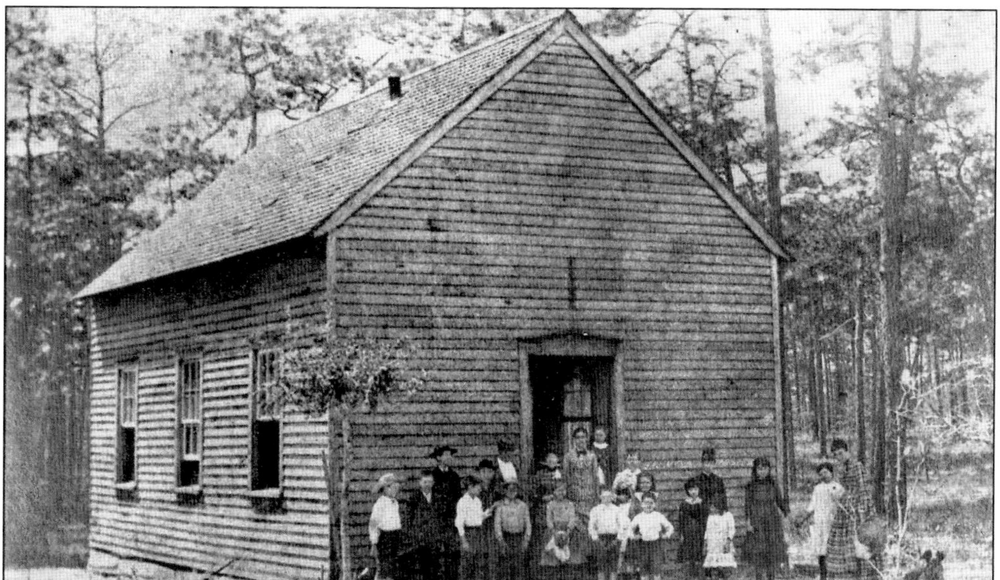

The first school in Hernando County, in 1852, was located in the small community of Spring Hill, about four miles west of Brooksville.

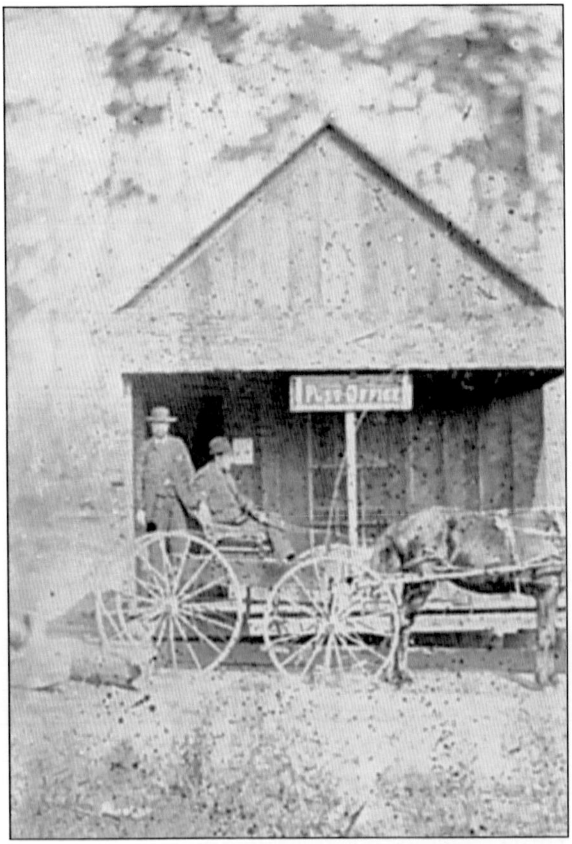

The Add General Store and Post Office, seen here in 1884 and originally built in 1853, was the focal point for the tiny hamlets of Lake Lindsey and Add, about five miles north of Brooksville. Addison McKeown, on the front porch, was the postmaster and store manager.

In 1856, Rep. Preston Brooks of South Carolina administers a vicious cane-whipping to Sen. Charles Sumner of Massachusetts on the Senate floor after Sumner's harsh harangue against the absent and aging pro-slavery Sen. Andrew Butler from South Carolina. Sumner referred to slavery as "an ugly mistress . . . a harlot." Brooks's outburst was seen at the time as a chivalrous and heroic act. Many residents from Hernando County hailed originally from South Carolina and the whipping was viewed as a noble deed, so in his honor the city's name was soon changed to "Brooksville."

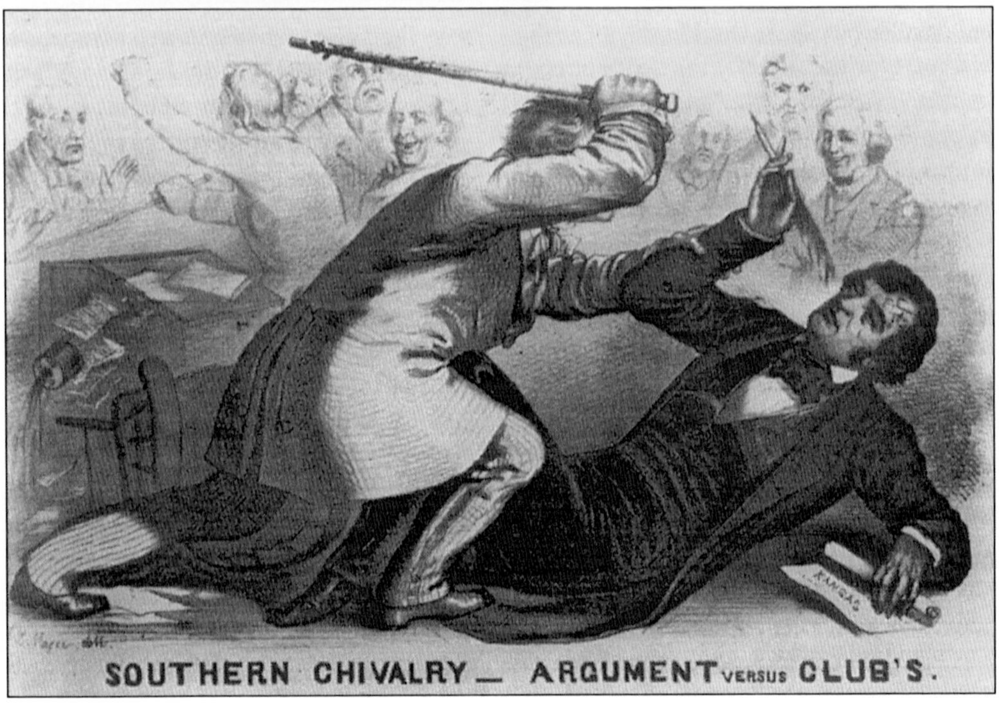

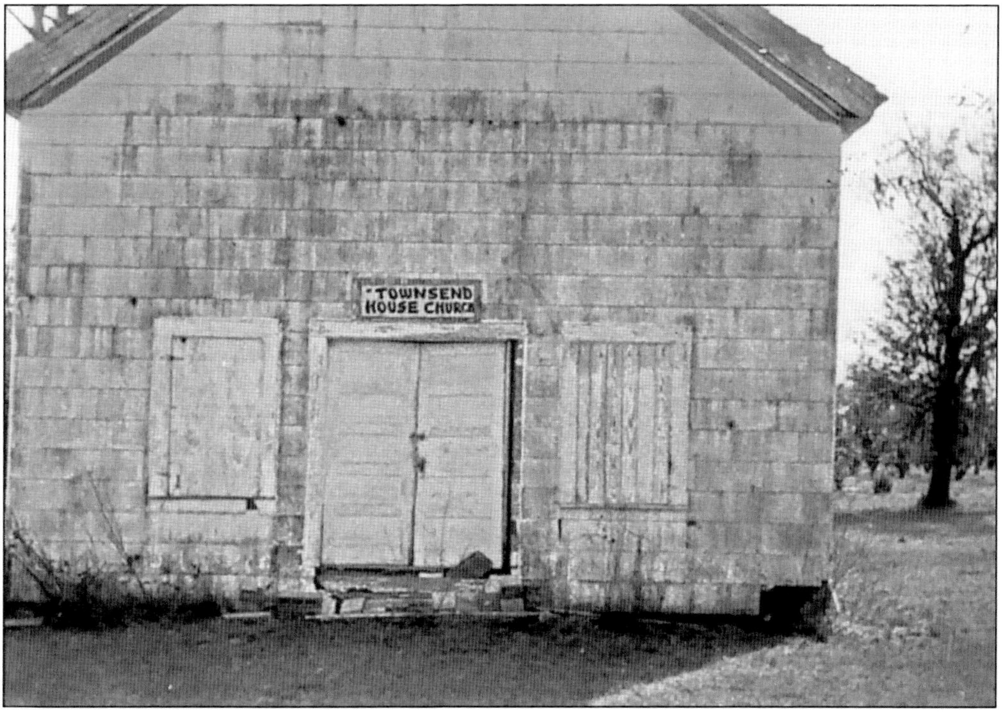

The Townsend House Baptist Church, 1856, was one of the first churches in Hernando County.

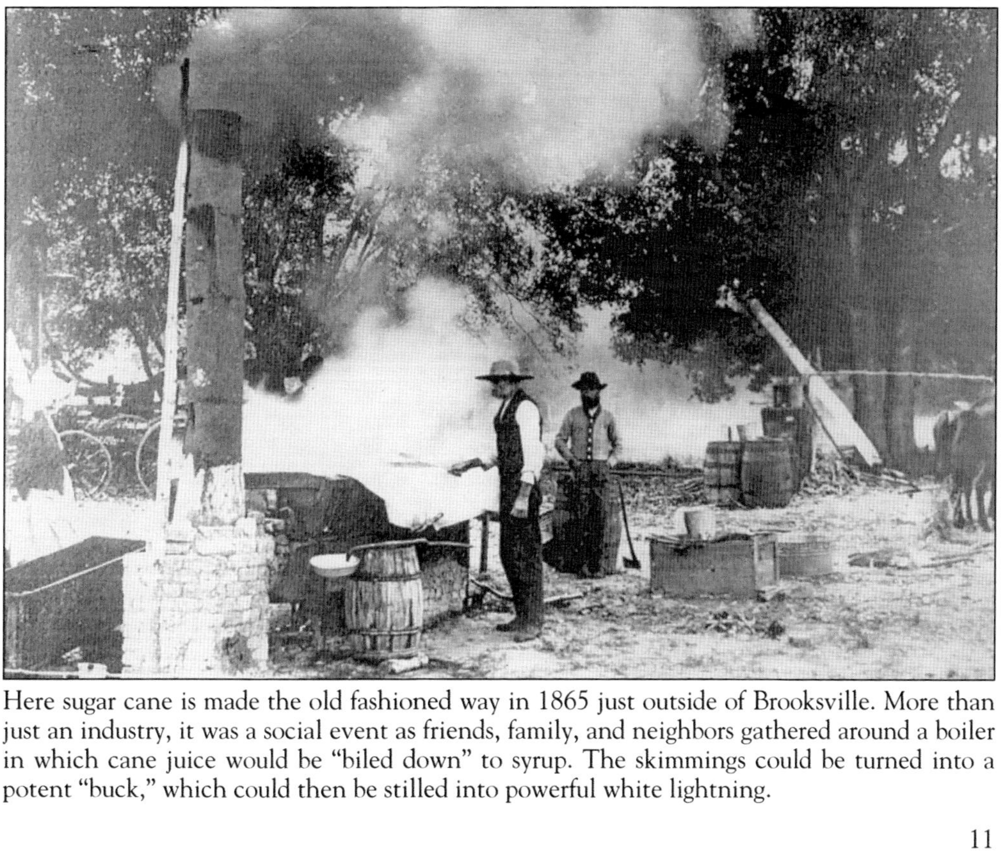

Here sugar cane is made the old fashioned way in 1865 just outside of Brooksville. More than just an industry, it was a social event as friends, family, and neighbors gathered around a boiler in which cane juice would be "biled down" to syrup. The skimmings could be turned into a potent "buck," which could then be stilled into powerful white lightning.

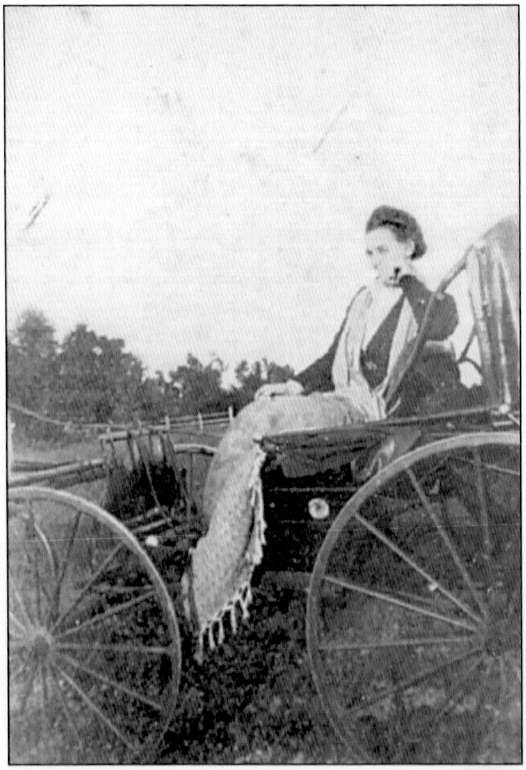

Annie Mayo, wife of Anderson Mayo, waits in a carriage in 1865. The Mayos resided north of Brooksville near Lake Lindsey and first came to the area in 1851.

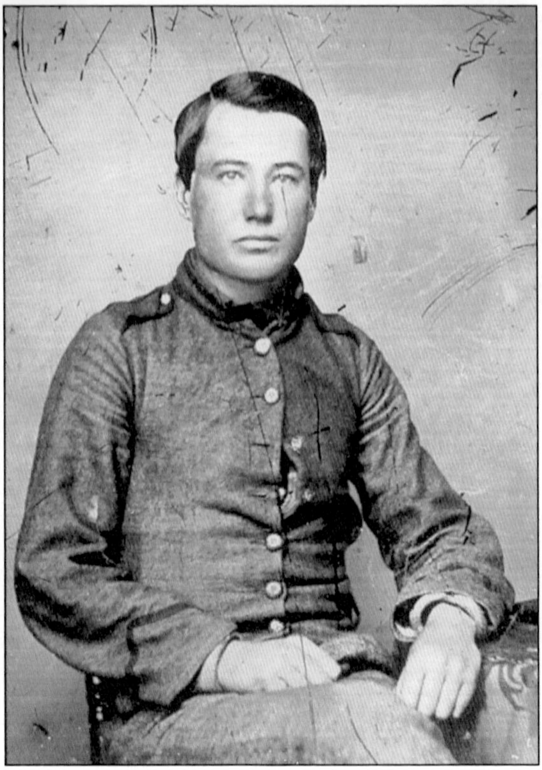

A Civil War soldier from Istachatta is pictured in 1865. Brooksville and Hernando County provided hundreds of soldiers for the Confederate Army. The port of Bayport, 18 miles west of Brooksville, was considered a vital port for soldiers' supplies and imports. A bitter skirmish in 1864 occurred along the route from Bayport to Brooksville. It has become one of the nation's most popular annual reenactments, "The Brooksville Raid."

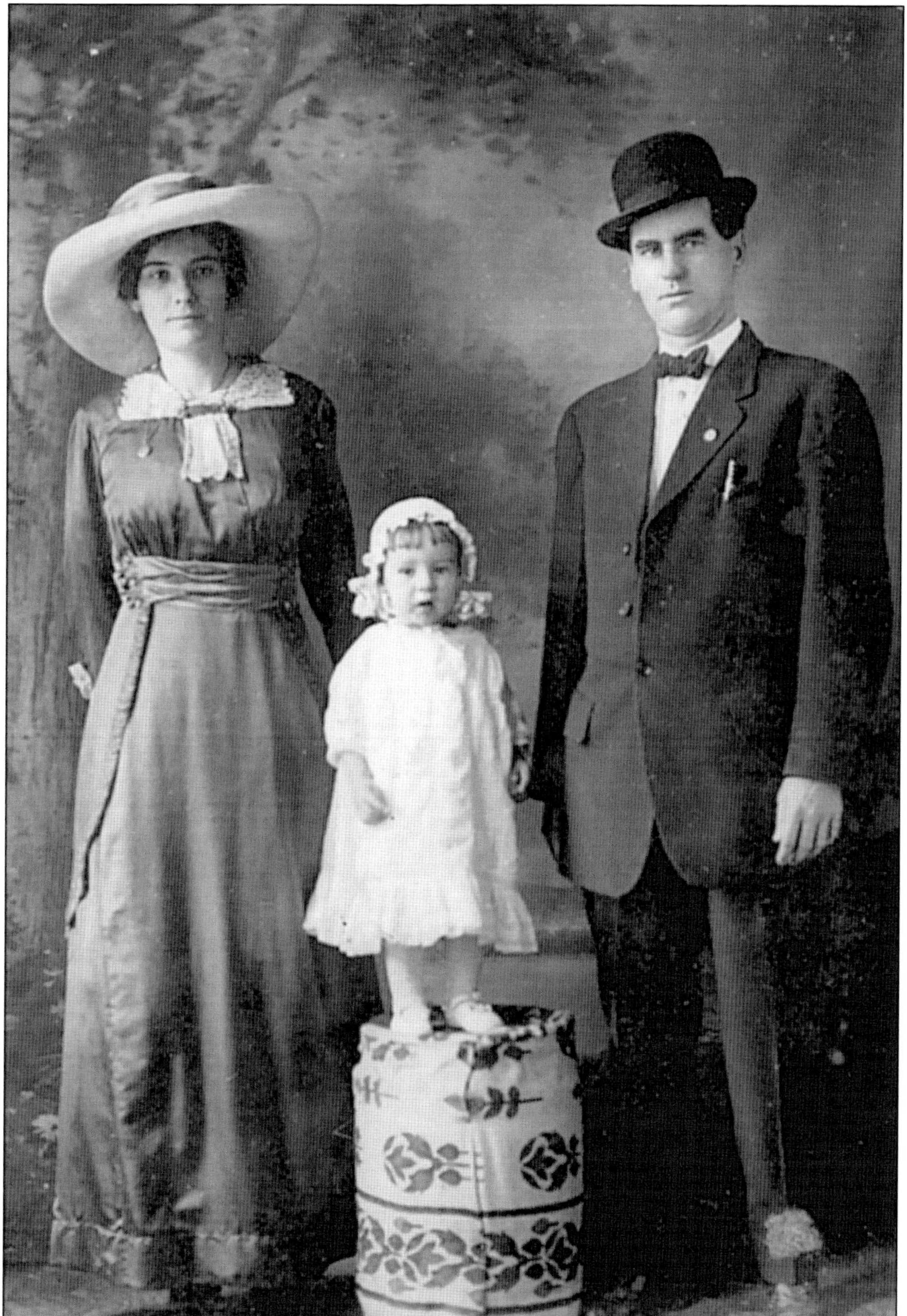

The Snow family lived at Mount Airy, later known as Chinsegut Hill. Pictured in 1868 from left to right are Charlotte Edrington Snow, Carolina Edrington, and James Russell Snow.

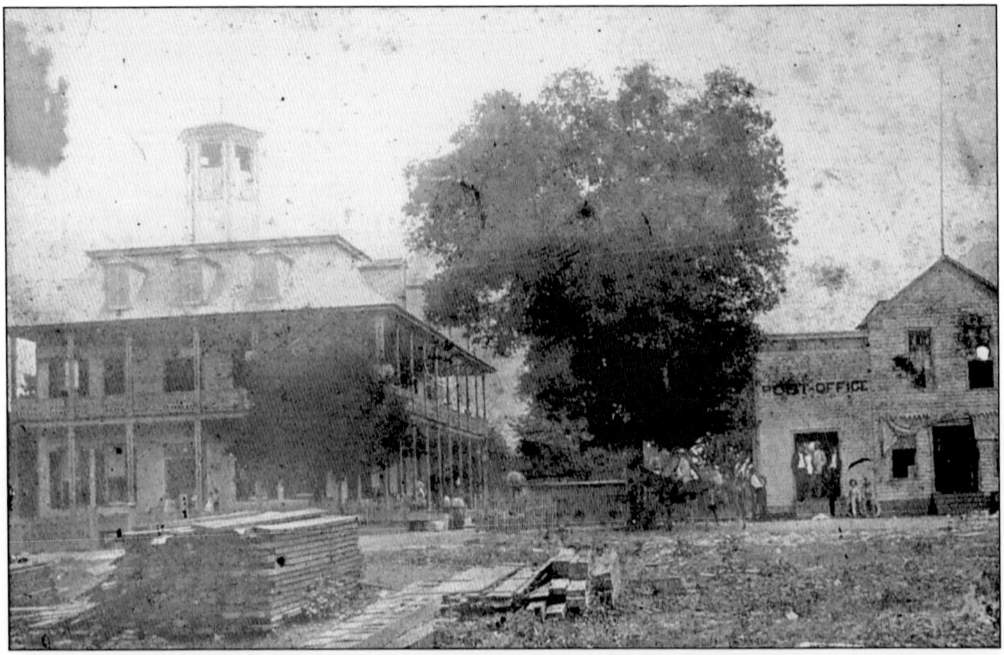

Pictured is downtown Brooksville in 1875. This is North Main Street where it now intersects Ft. Dade Avenue. The building on the left is the Hernando Hotel and the post office is on the right. Ft. Dade Avenue did not exist back then.

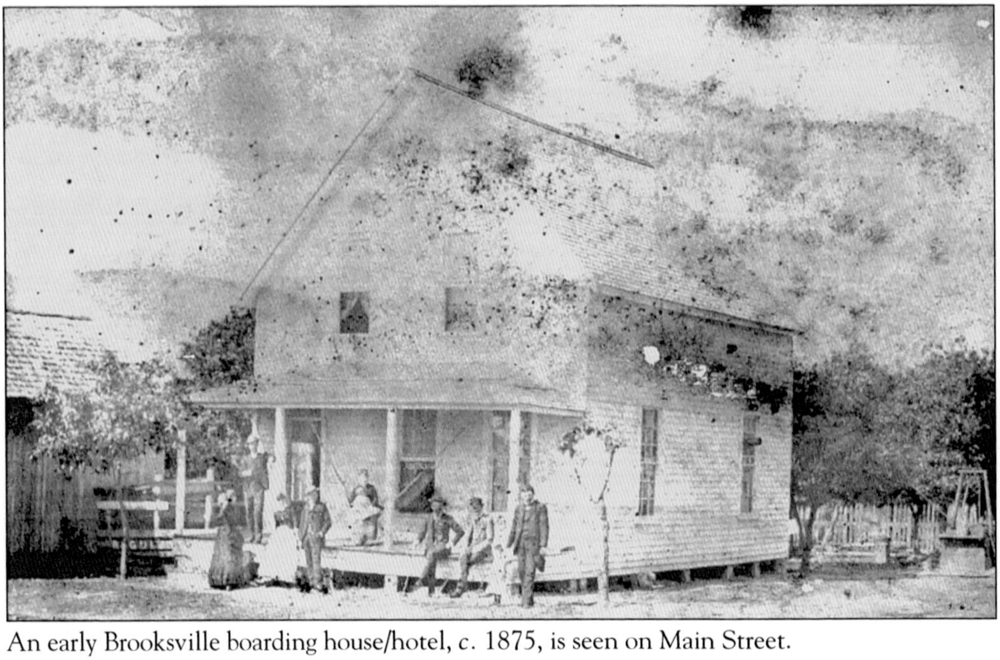

An early Brooksville boarding house/hotel, *c.* 1875, is seen on Main Street.

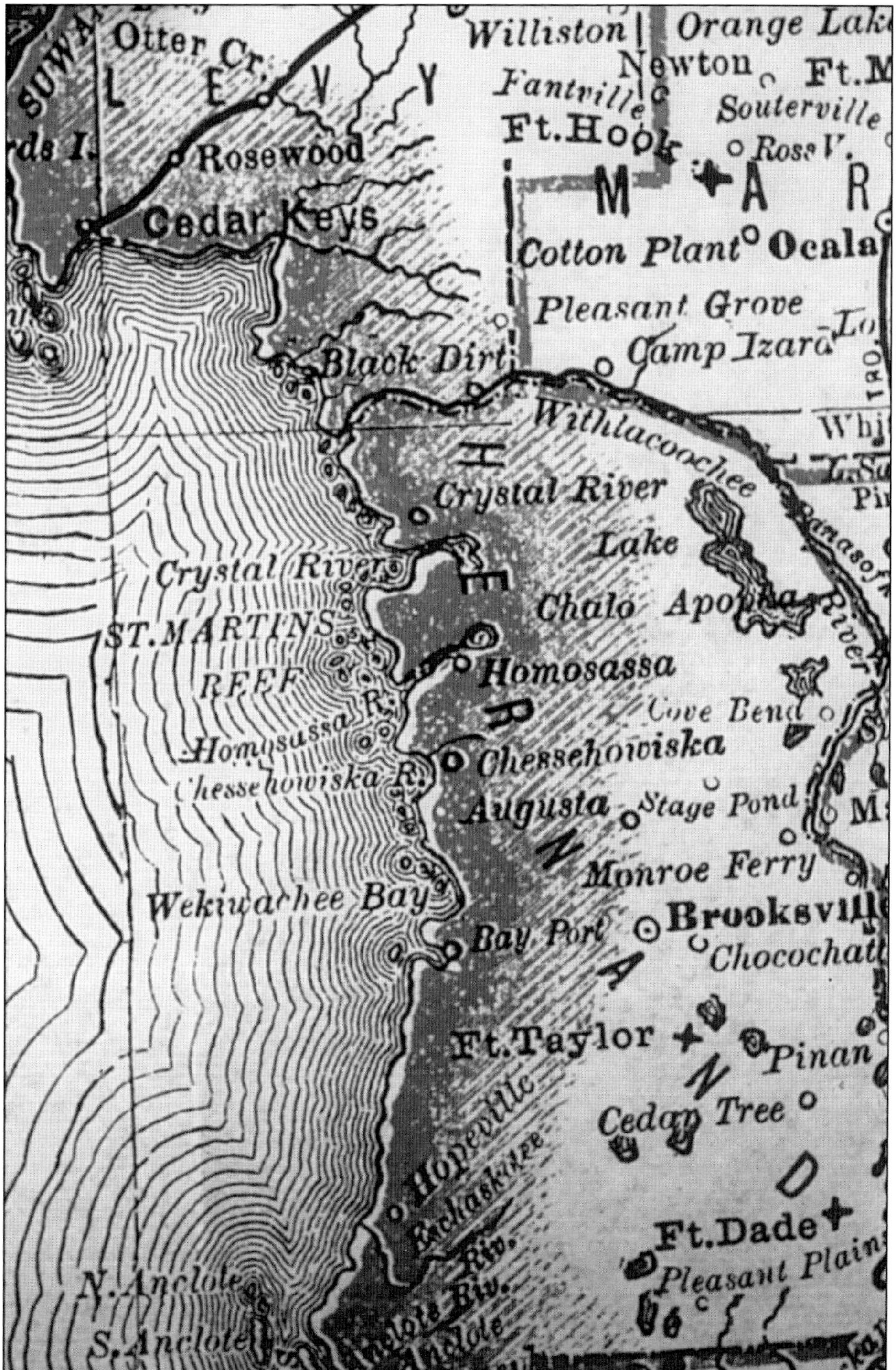

This 1885 map shows the Brooksville area. Before 1887, Hernando County included what is now Citrus County to the north and Pasco County to the south. The population of the county in 1885 was around 5,000.

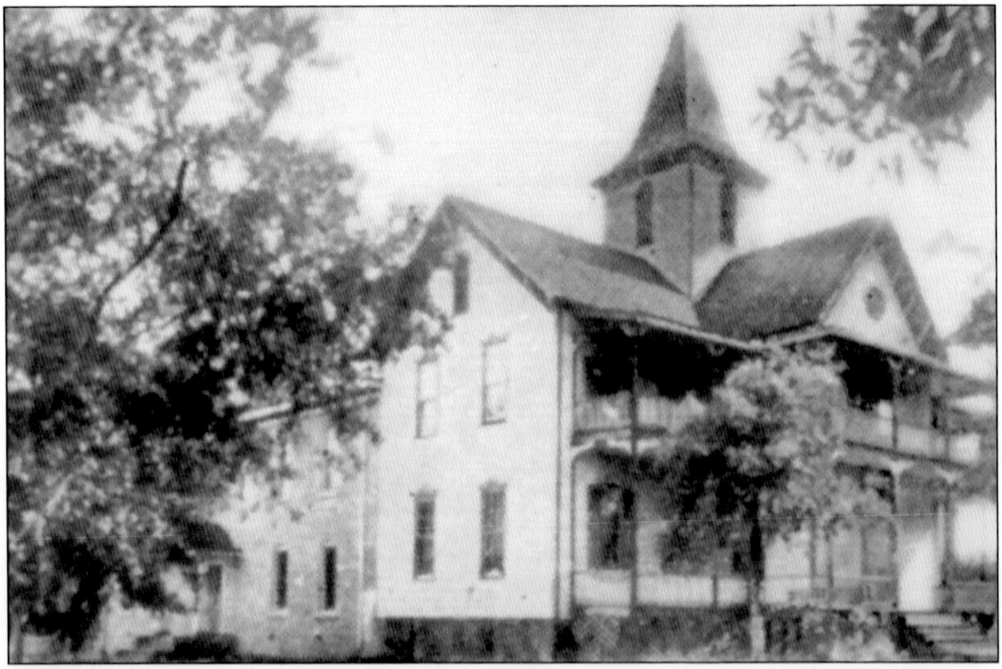

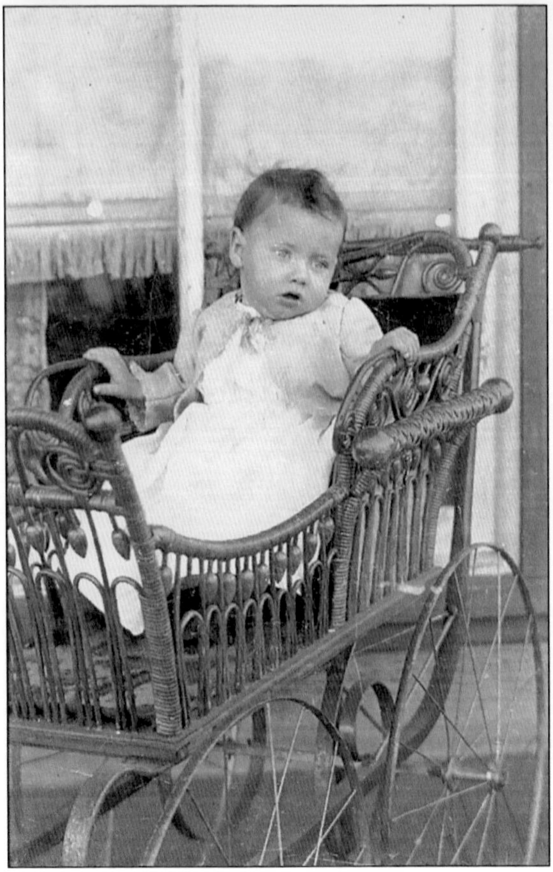

The brand new and first Hernando High School, built in 1889, was about half a mile southwest of the courthouse near what is now Martin Luther King Boulevard. It was considered obsolete by 1910 and was replaced with a new brick structure.

Pictured is Clarence Russell, a Brooksville lad, in 1894. He was the son of A.M.C. Russell, one of Brooksville's first newspaper publishers. Clarence would later work for his dad as a linotype operator.

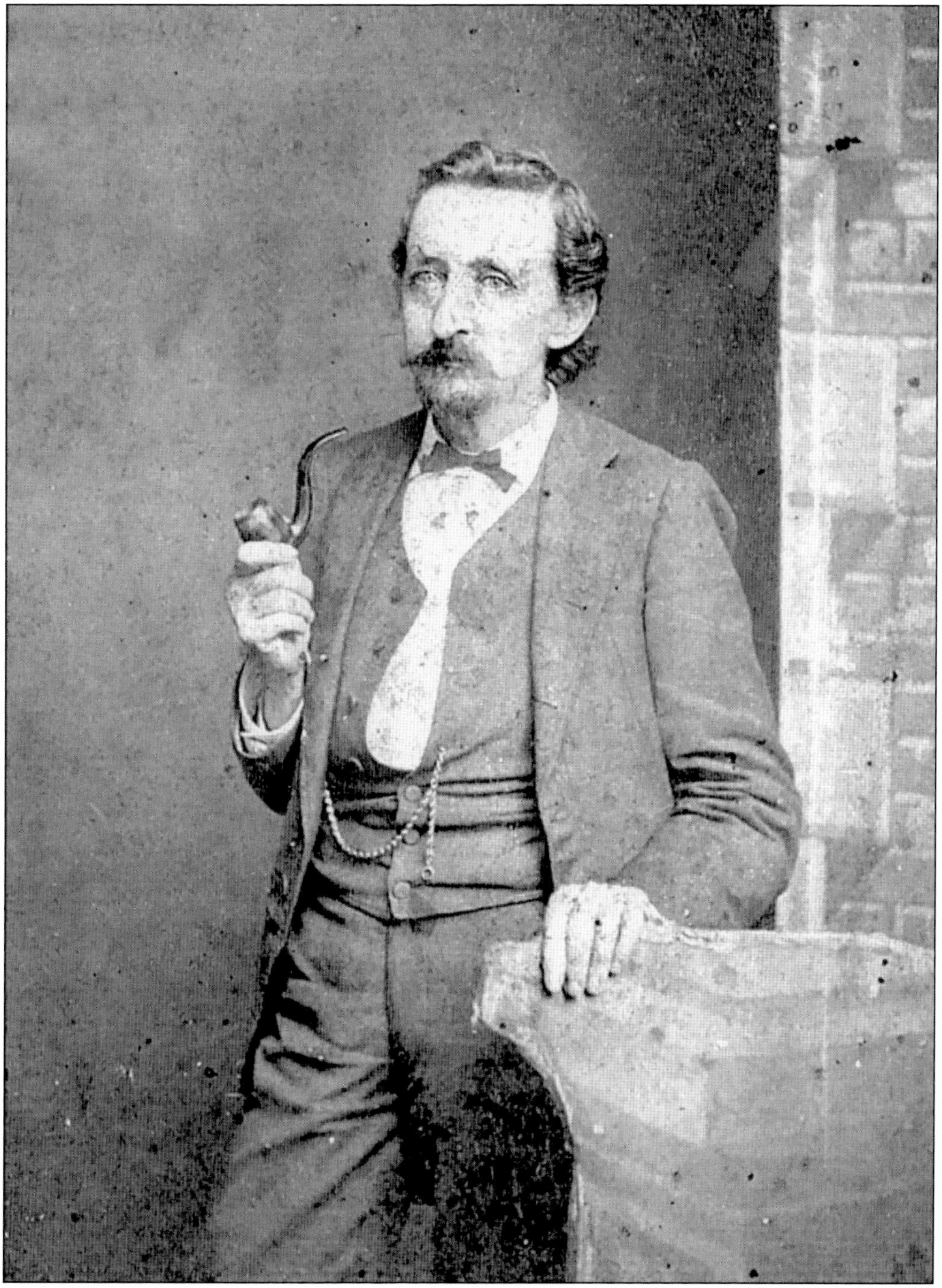

The king of the city in 1887, Frank Saxon was perhaps Brooksville's most popular citizen during the 19th century. After serving heroically for the South in the Civil War, he was the city's first elected marshall in 1880, the clerk of circuit court between 1887 and 1909, tax assessor (1891–1893), and he served in the state legislature from 1887 to 1889. He was also active in the development of many area churches and schools. From 1867 to 1872, he lived in the house that is now the Heritage Museum in Brooksville.

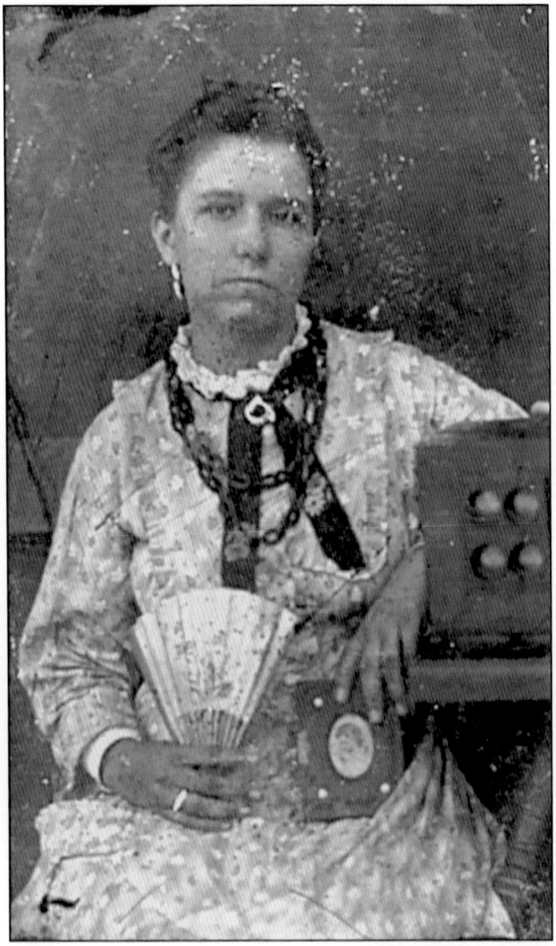

Jincey Baker, seen in 1886, was born in Brooksville in 1869 and married by 1885. Baker was named after her father's first wife, Jincey, who Mr. Baker fatally poisoned in 1866 when he accidentally picked up a bottle of poison instead of the medicine she had asked for. Mr. Baker married Pathenia Weaver the following year and, showing great remorse, named his new baby girl Jincey in her honor.

Children do a circle dance at Twin Lakes School in 1892, an African-American school south of Brooksville.

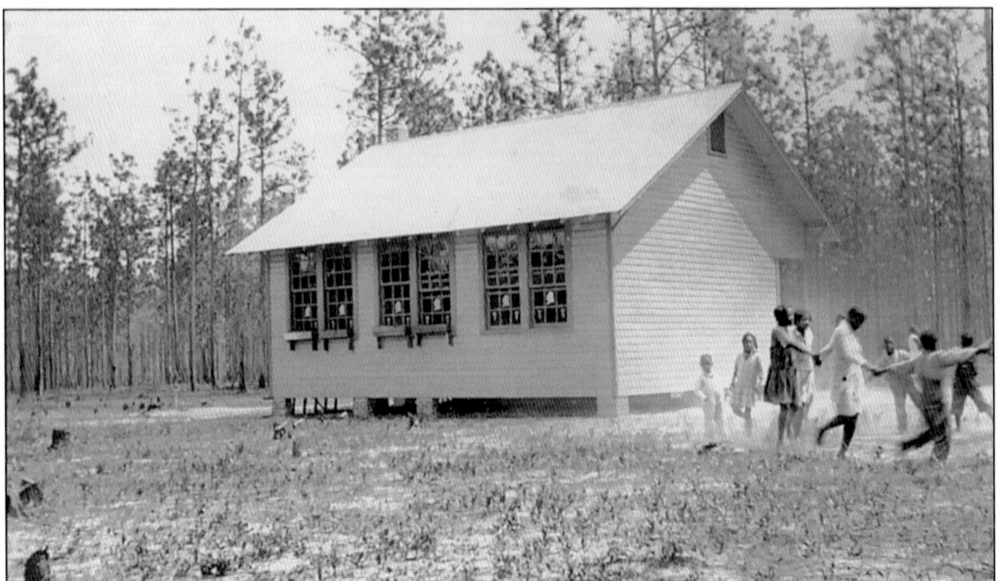

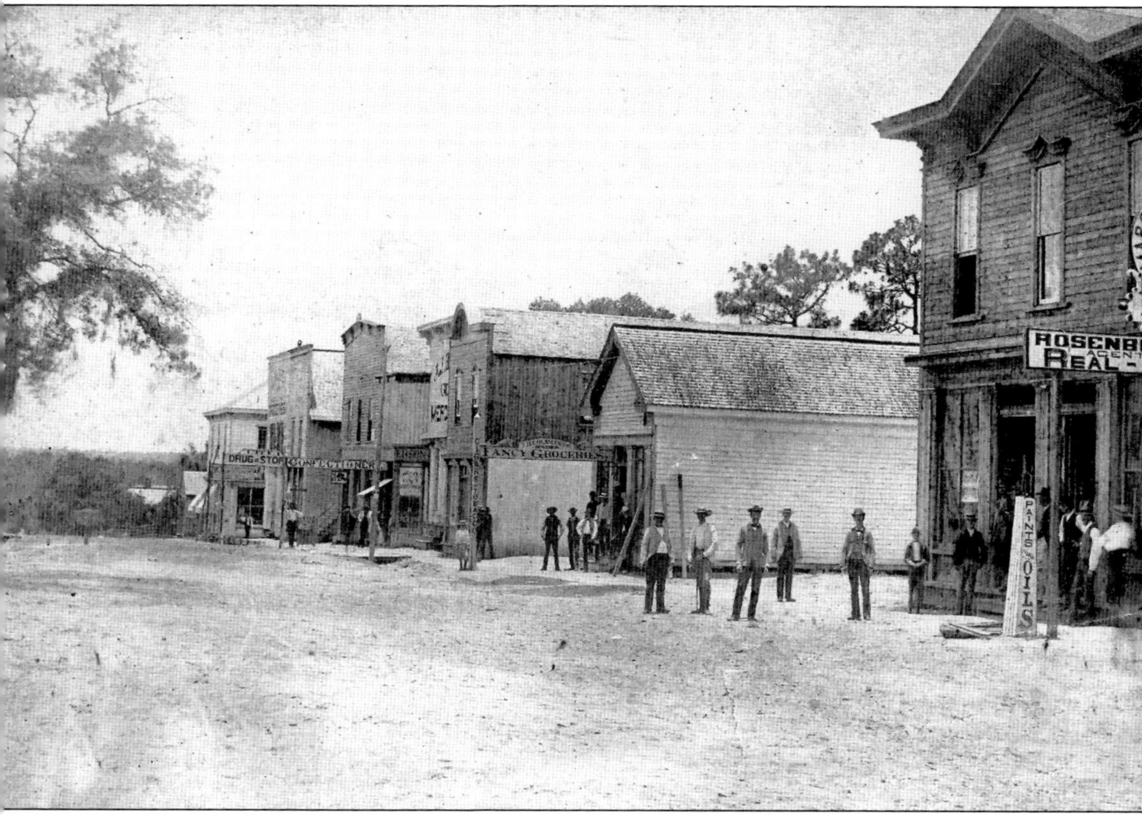

Shown here is downtown Brooksville's Main Street about 1890.

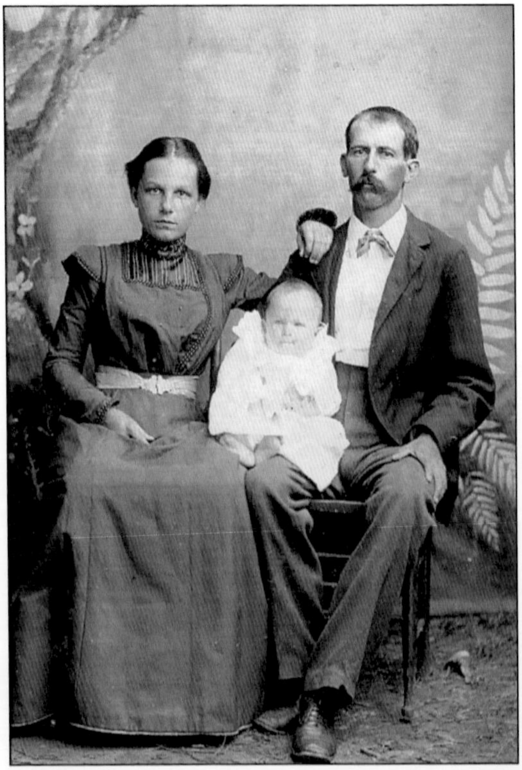

Here is a young Brooksville family in 1888. They lived just north of the city.

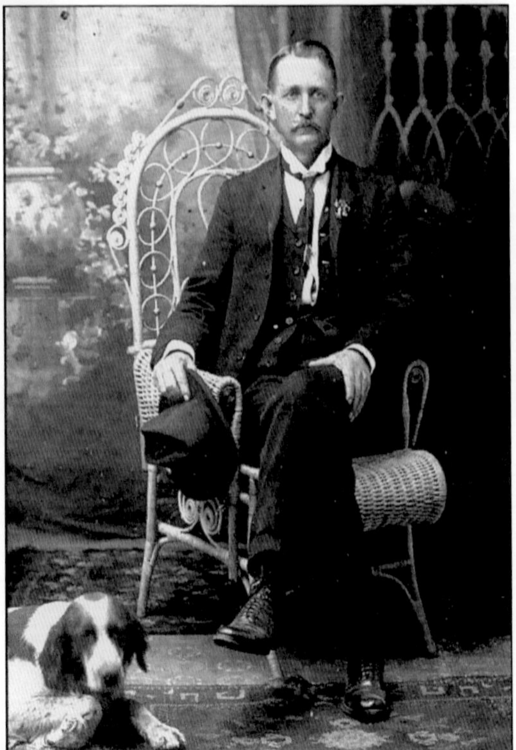

Ben Saxon, seen in 1875, served as Hernando County sheriff from 1871 until 1876. His brother Frank was a political star and his father Dr. Benjamin Saxon was famous throughout the state. Ben was also the county surveyor. Soon after his stretch as sheriff in 1877, some missing hogs turned up in his yard. The next morning, he was found hanging from a large oak tree about three miles north of Brooksville.

Leroy McKeown Jr., seen in 1894, lived north of Brooksville near Lake Lindsey.

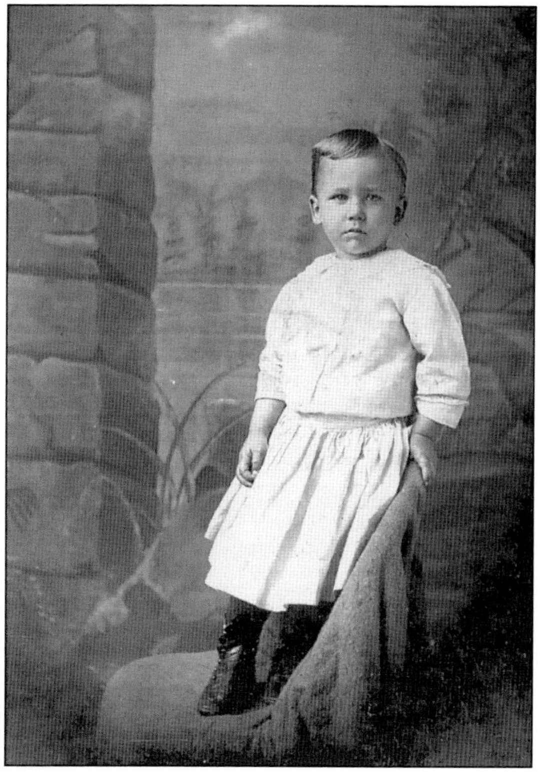

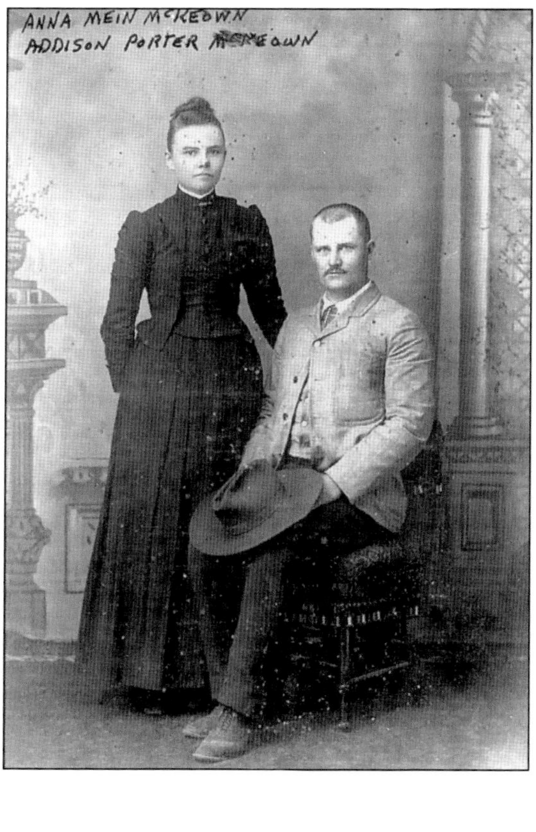

Anna Mein McKeown and Addison McKeown are pictured in 1888. McKeown was postmaster of Add, just north of Brooksville. He also ran the general store and was one of the area's first really successful and astute businessmen.

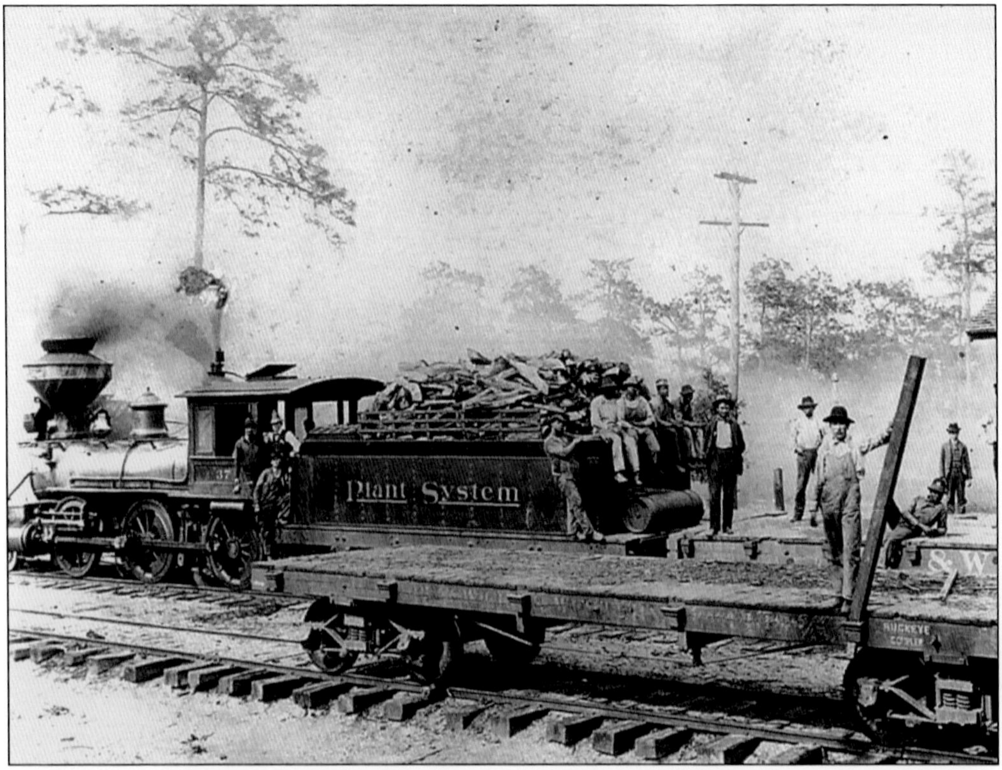

By 1885, Brooksville was connected with the railroad for both freight and passenger travel. Here a train rolls into Brooksville about 1895.

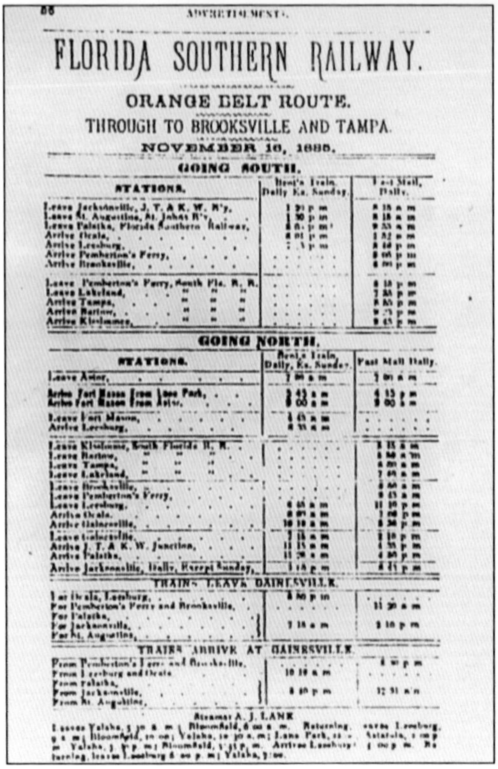

ADVERTISEMENTS.

FLORIDA SOUTHERN RAILWAY.

ORANGE BELT ROUTE.

THROUGH TO BROOKSVILLE AND TAMPA.

NOVEMBER 10, 1885.

GOING SOUTH.

GOING NORTH.

According to this 1885 Brooksville railroad schedule, the train connected Brooksville east to Croom, which connected to the Plant Railroad system south to Tampa and north to Jacksonville.

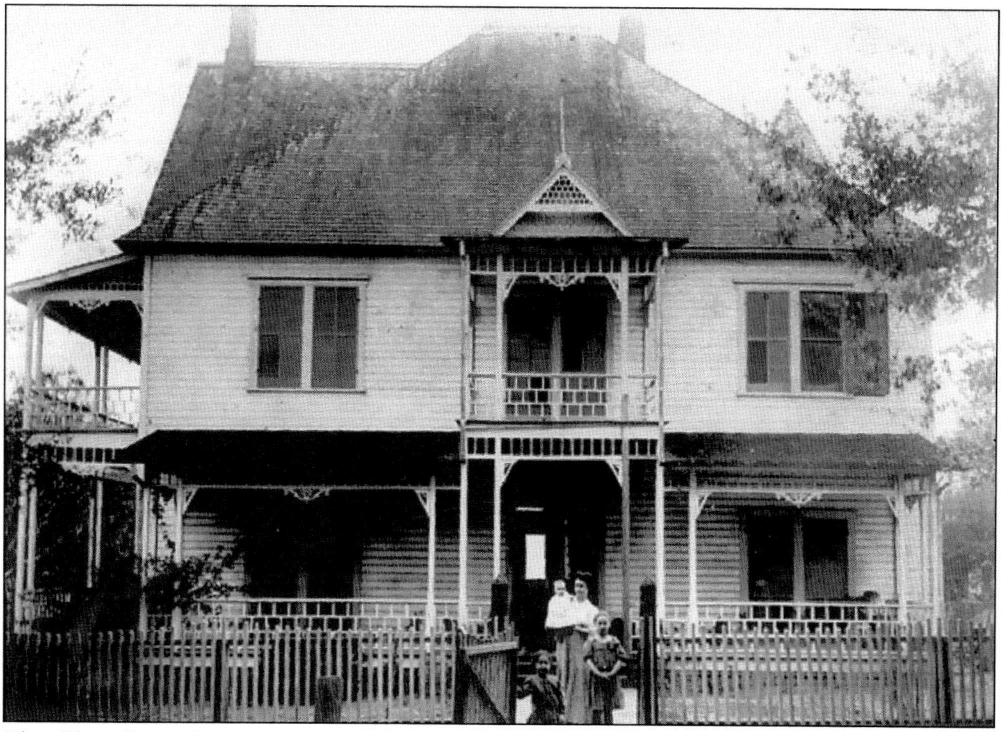

The Olive Street home of soon-to-be governor William S. Jennings is shown in 1899, with Mrs. Mae Mann Jennings and their three children. The home is now owned by Margaret Rogers Ghiotto, owner of Rogers' Christmas House. Mr. Jennings would become governor of Florida in 1900.

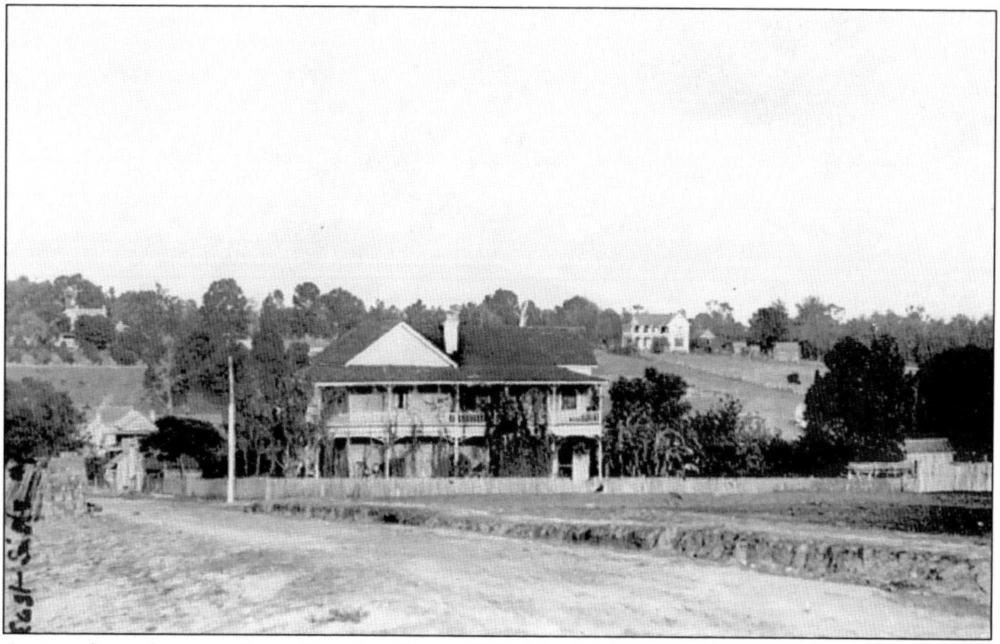

A view from the west shows Brooksville in 1893. The building on the far right in the distance is the Saxon house.

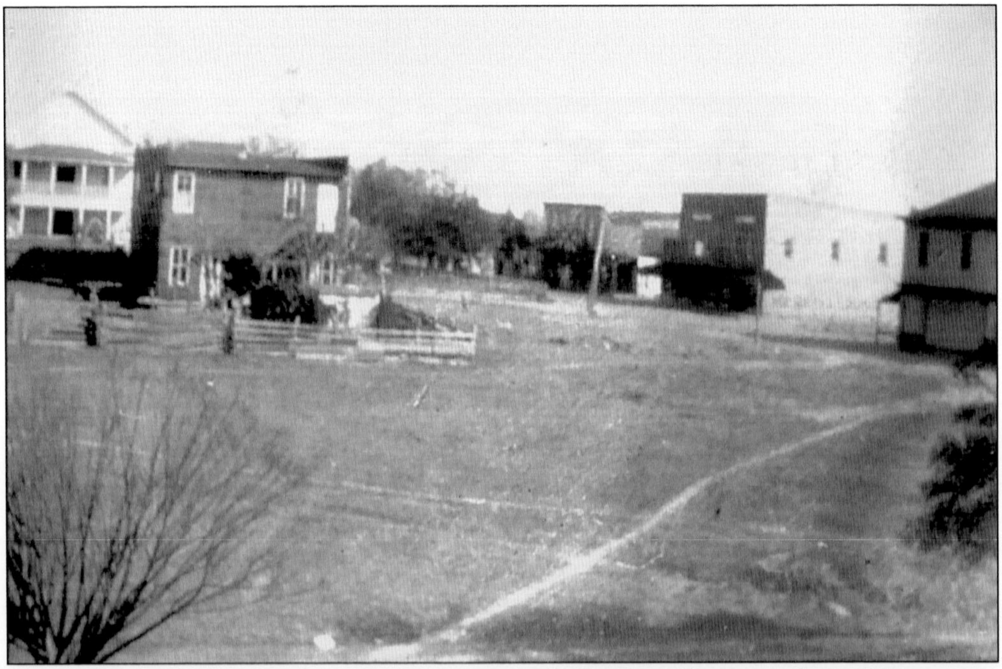

Brooksville during the 1890s is seen as one approached it from the west. The building on the far left is the old courthouse, which was built in 1877 and torn down in 1913. The right row of buildings runs along what is now U.S. Highway 41 (Broad Street).

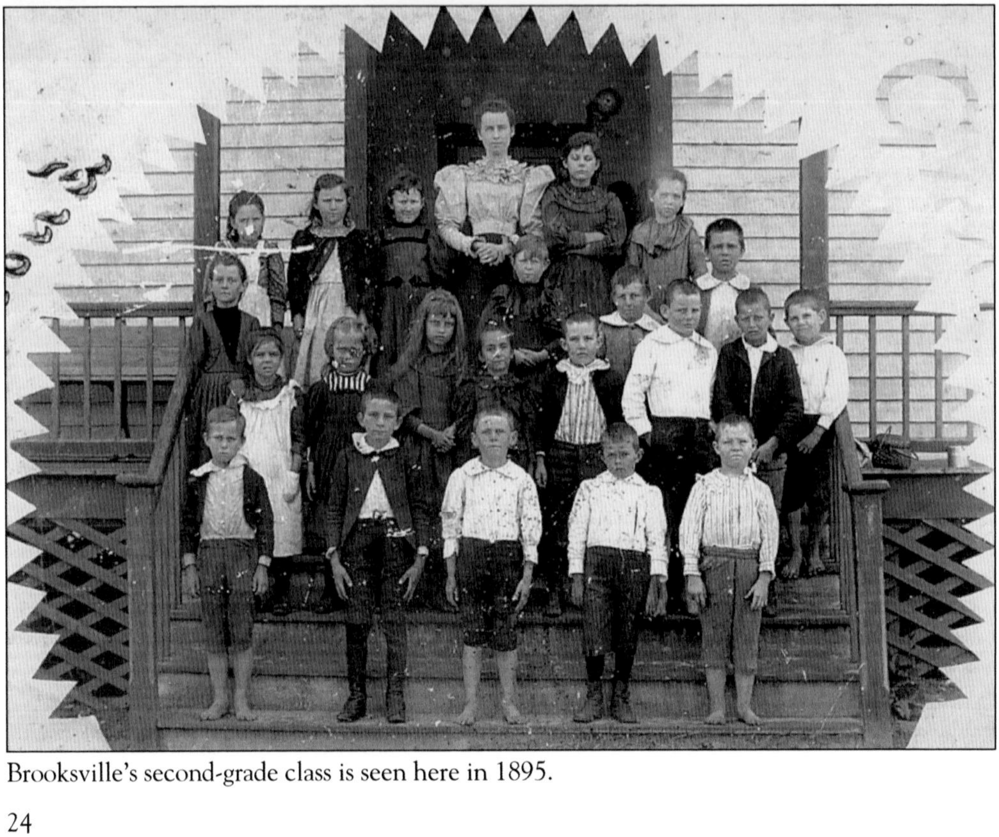

Brooksville's second-grade class is seen here in 1895.

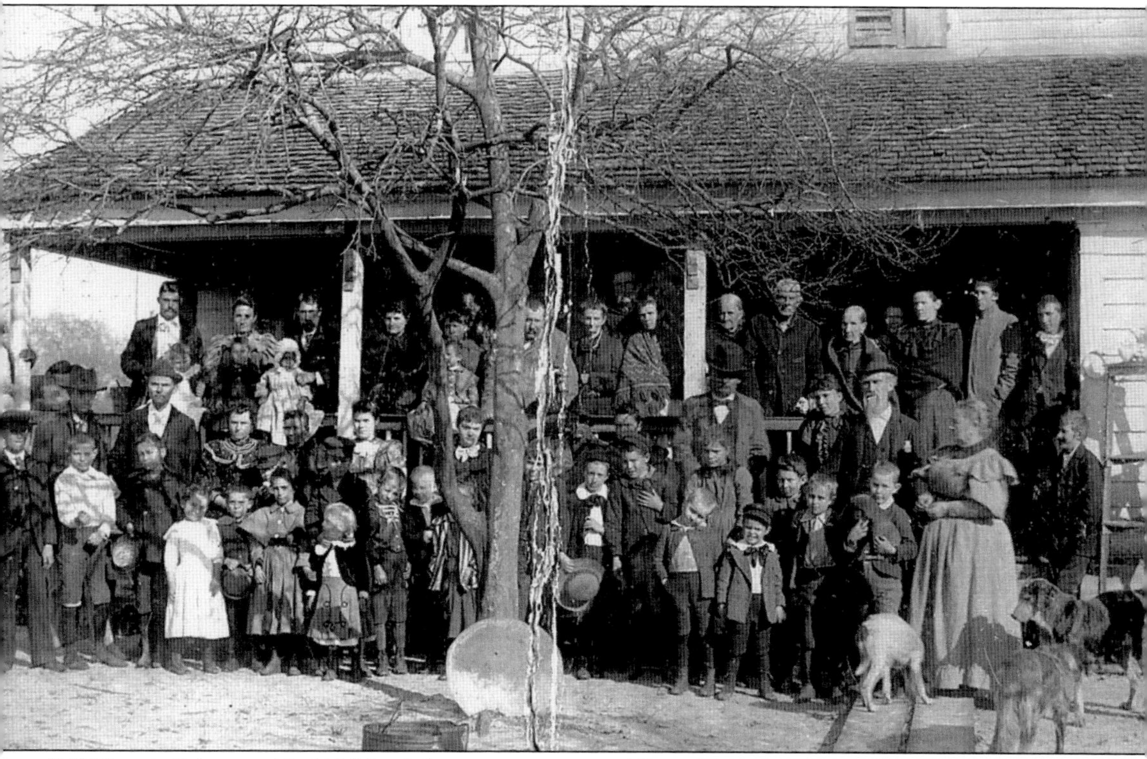

Bill Hope's February 10, 1895 birthday party is pictured here. Hope was one of the first settlers in Brooksville, first coming to the area in 1835. The night before this photo was taken, a giant freeze wiped out his entire citrus crop.

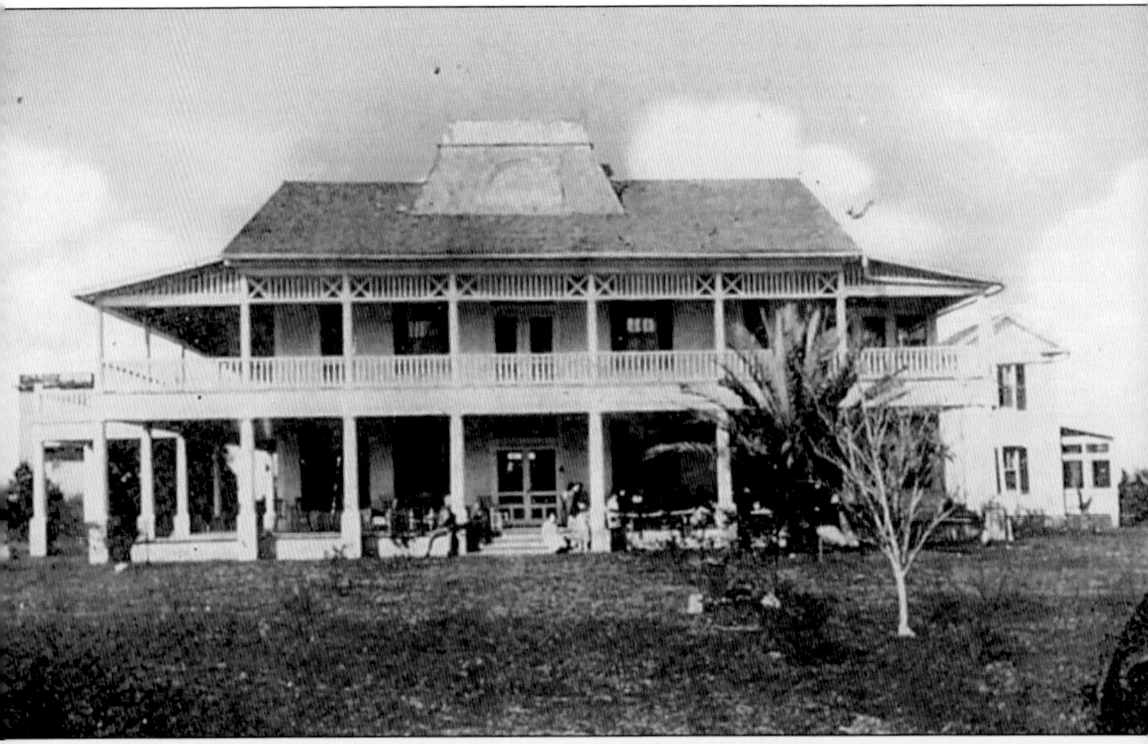

Mount Airy, also known as Chinsegut Hill, provides a breathtaking view of pristine beauty at 225 feet above sea level, making it one of Florida's highest points. The hilltop home was built in 1849 by Colonel Pearson. In 1852, Francis Edrington, from South Carolina, settled his family on the property and enlarged the house to its pictured size. During the late 1860s it was occupied by the Snow family.

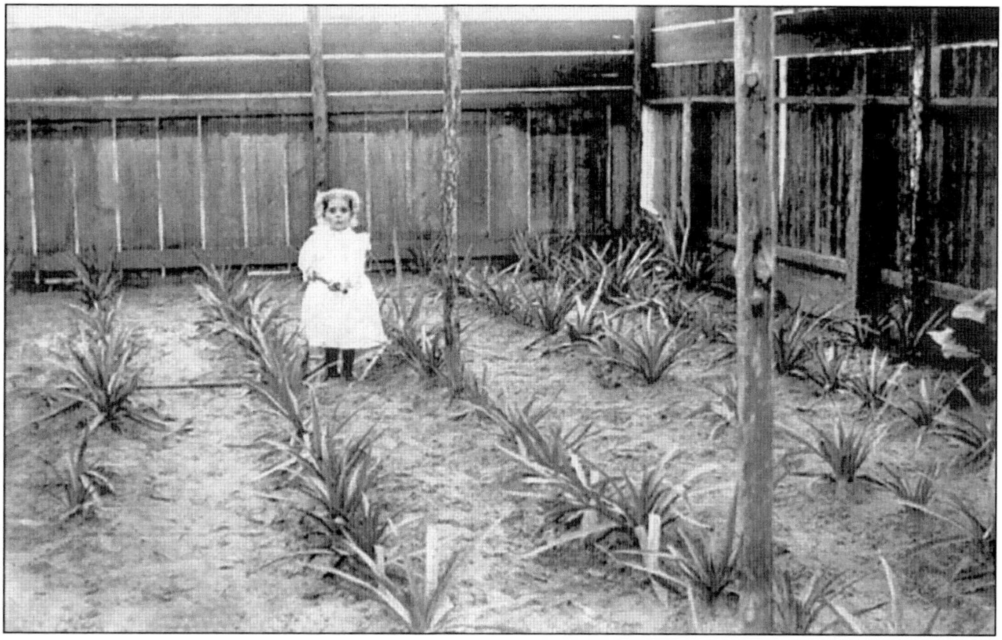

Baby Grace Burwell stands in her mom and dad's pineapple patch next to their Olive Street home in 1899. Mr. Burwell was a successful newspaper publisher, and his home was said to be the first with electricity and running water.

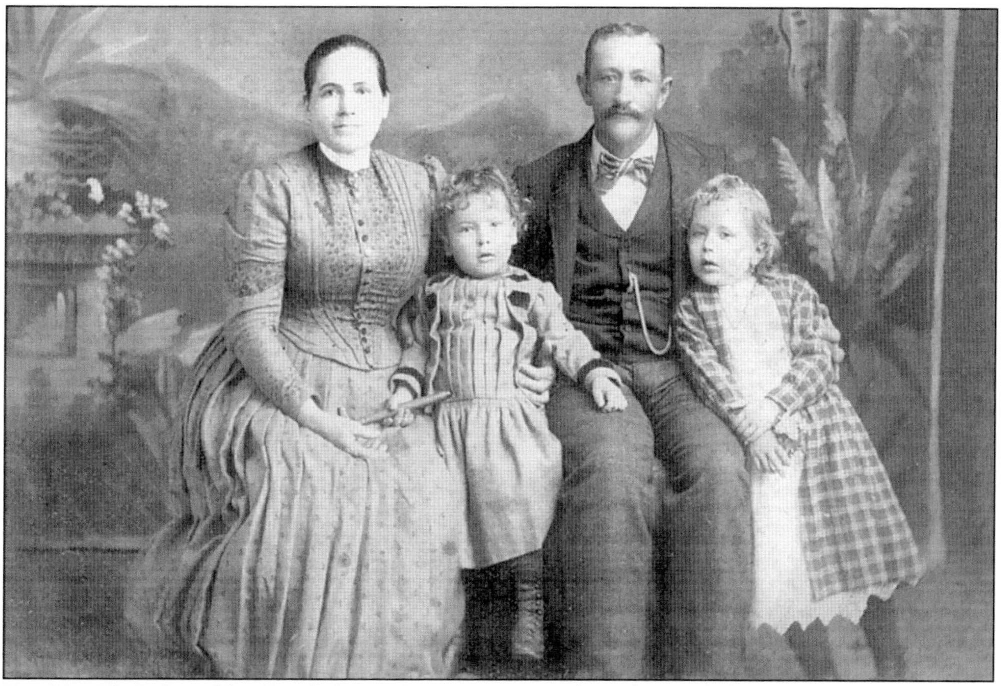

Franklin Hedick and his family have their portrait made in front of a backdrop of Lake Lindsey in 1884. They are, from left to right, Smithie M. Sanders Hedick, Lizzie, Franklin Hedick, and Sarah.

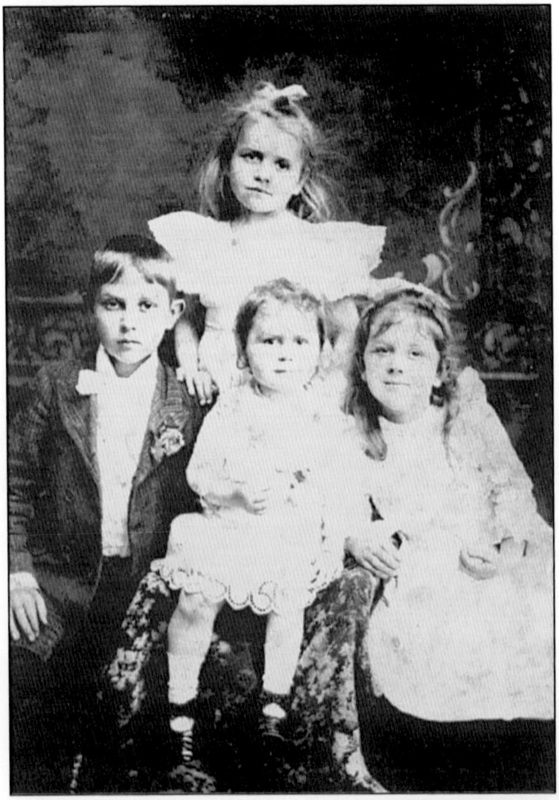

The MacKenzie children of Brooksville are seen in 1899. They came from a family tradition of lawyers, judges, and real estate dealers.

After the 1895 freeze, the citrus industry in Brooksville and Hernando County was almost wiped out. It eventually recovered its lofty heights.

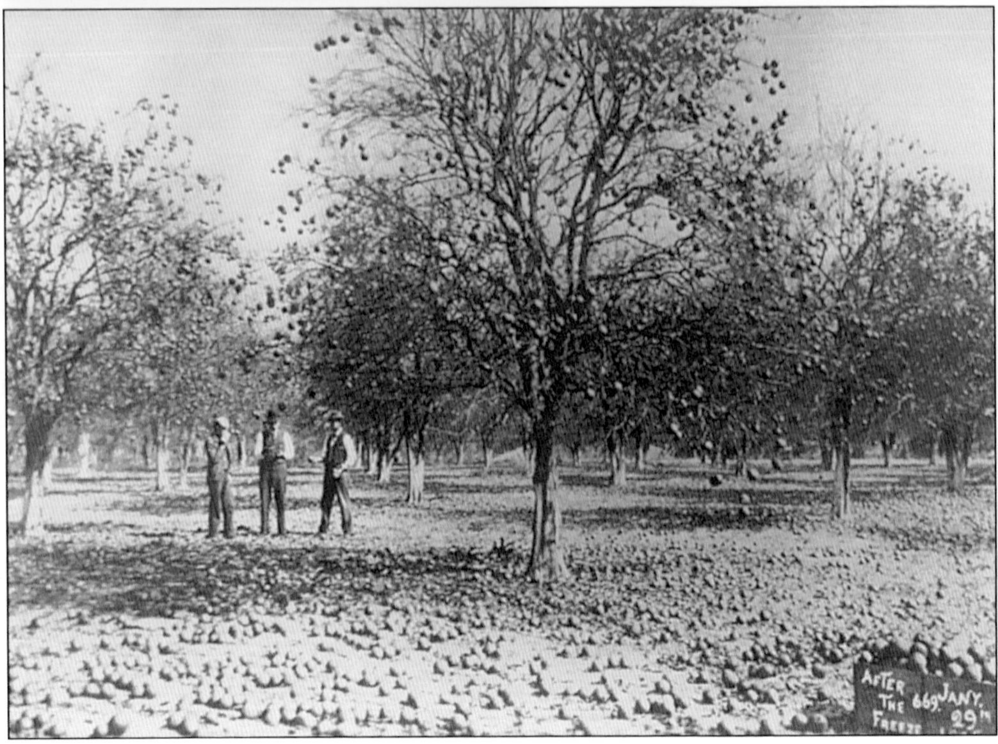

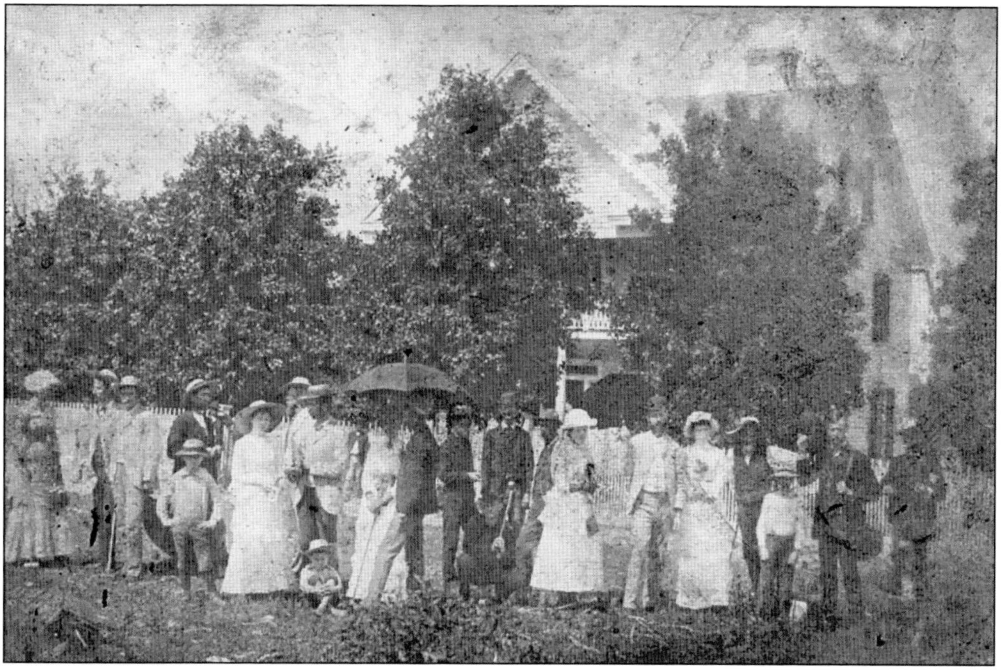

Shown is a Brooksville Sunday outing on Main Street in 1875. The building behind them is the Hernando Hotel.

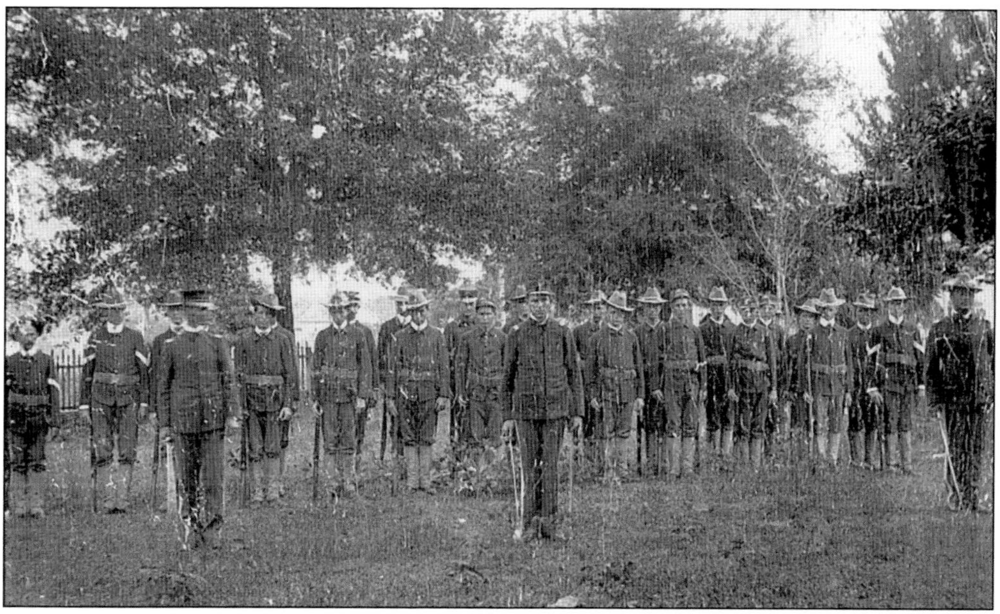

Brooksville soldiers in 1898 tune up for the Spanish-American War in front of the courthouse. They shipped out to Cuba from Tampa.

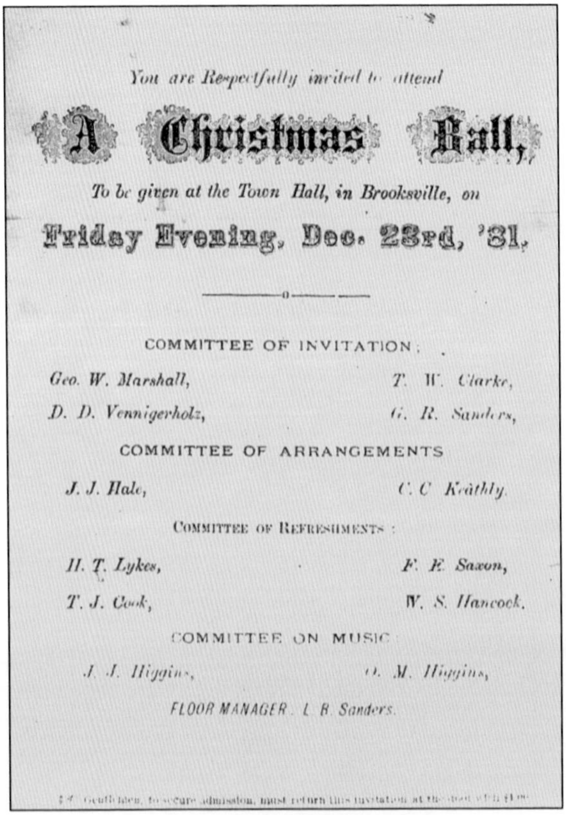

You are Respectfully invited to attend

A Christmas Ball,

To be given at the Town Hall, in Brooksville, on

Friday Evening, Dec. 23rd, '81,

COMMITTEE OF INVITATION:

Geo. W. Marshall, *T. W. Clarke,*

D. D. Vennigerholz, *G. R. Sanders,*

COMMITTEE OF ARRANGEMENTS

J. J. Hale, *C. C. Keathly.*

COMMITTEE OF REFRESHMENTS:

H. T. Lykes, *F. E. Saxon,*

T. J. Cook, *W. S. Hancock.*

COMMITTEE ON MUSIC

J. J. Higgins, *O. M. Higgins,*

FLOOR MANAGER. L. B. Sanders.

An 1881 invitation to the Brooksville Christmas Ball is shown. The ball was held downtown and its committee featured some of Brooksville's oldest names: J.J. Hale, C.C. Keathley, Frank Saxon, Howell Tyson Lykes, and W.S. Hancock, to name a few.

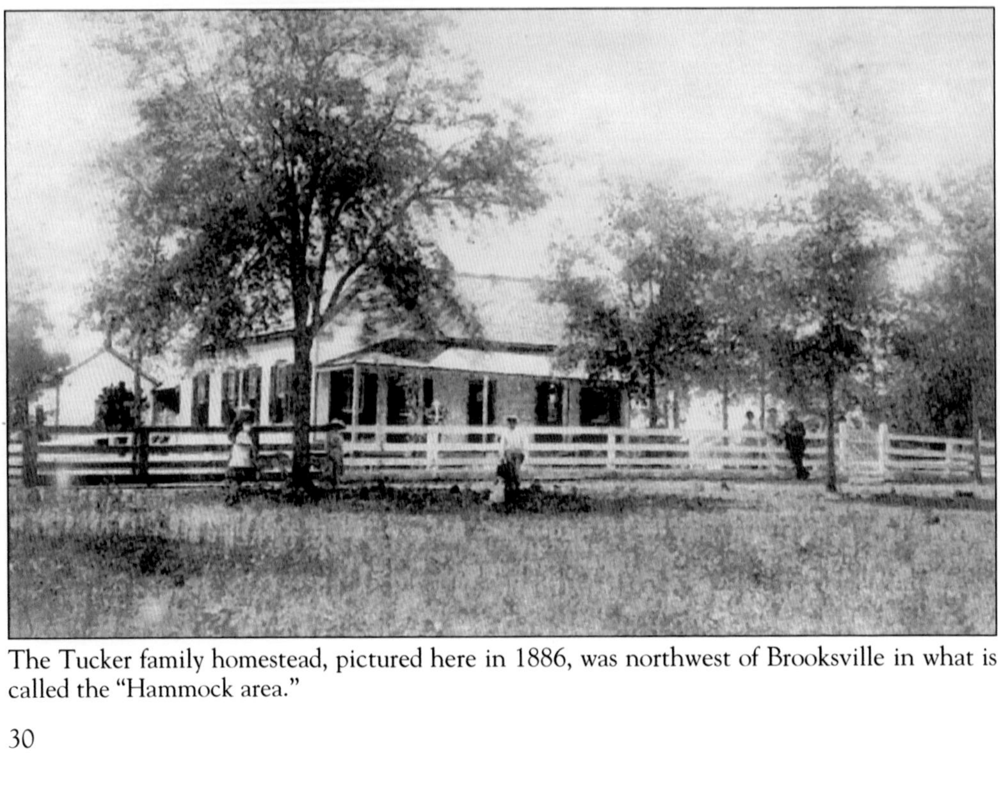

The Tucker family homestead, pictured here in 1886, was northwest of Brooksville in what is called the "Hammock area."

Anna McKeown of the Lake Lindsey area north of Brooksville is seen in 1888. She was the wife of A.P. McKeown, who owned the general store/post office in Add, north of Brooksville. She would later be this area's first historian, writing news articles well into the 1950s.

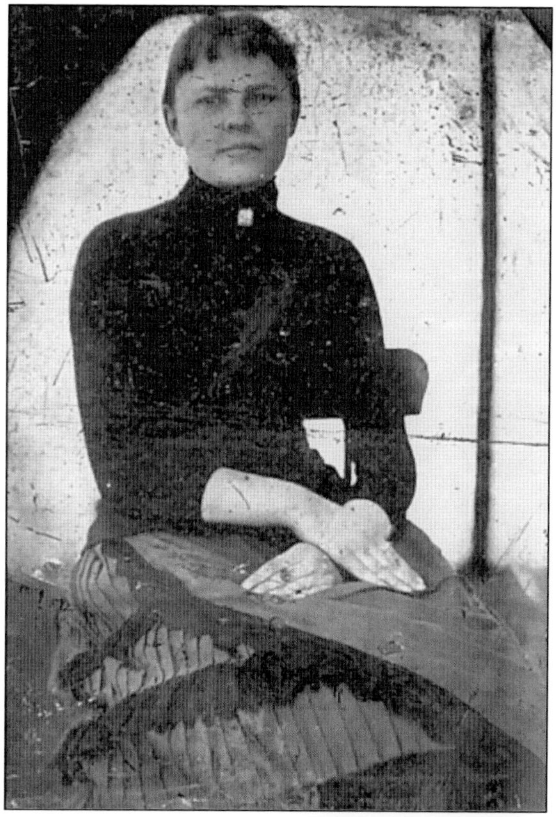

The Lykes Home, west of Brooksville in the village of Spring Hill, was originally built in 1850, making it one of the oldest homes in the county.

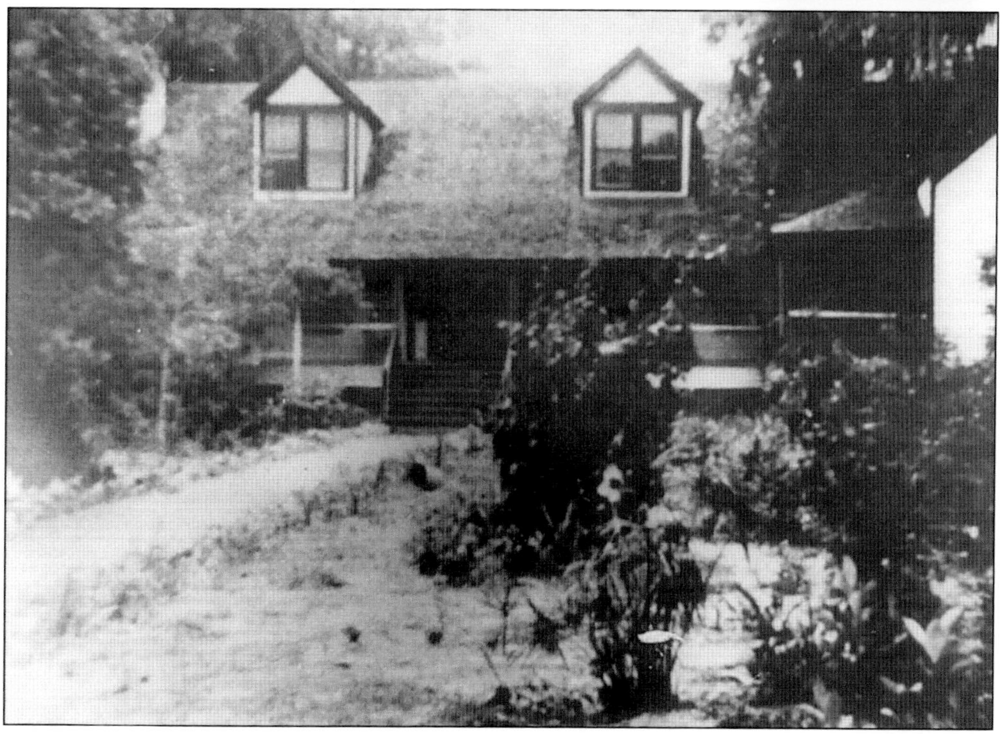

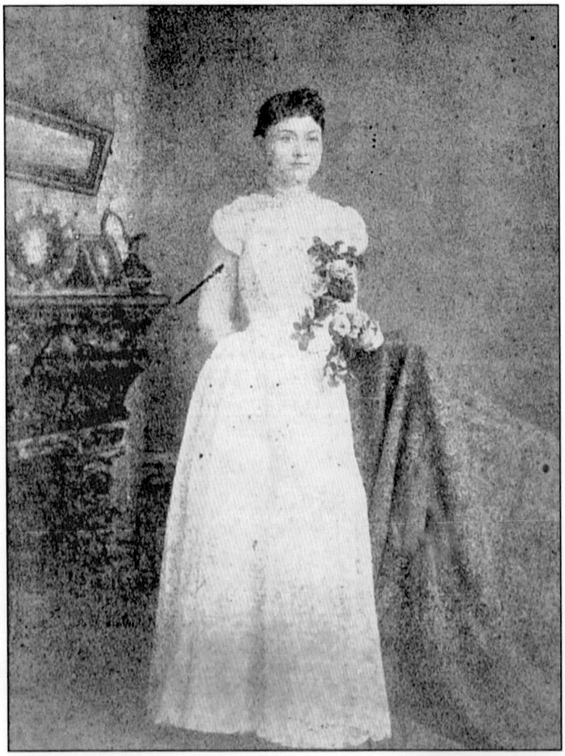

Miss B. Wilson of Brooksville is pictured in June 1891 on her wedding day.

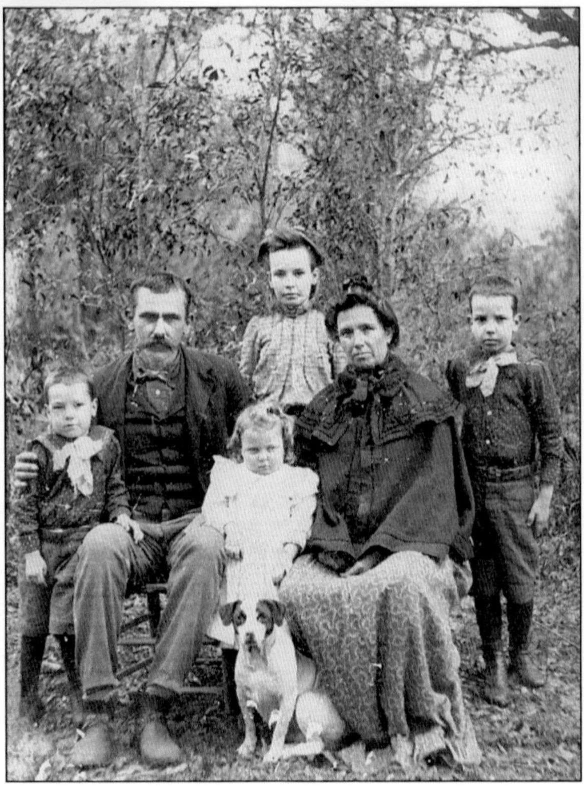

The Mein family—from left to right, Claude, Wm. H. Mein, Thelma, Jessie (standing back), Nannie K., and Clarence—is pictured here in 1900. They lived north of Brooksville in Lake Lindsey.

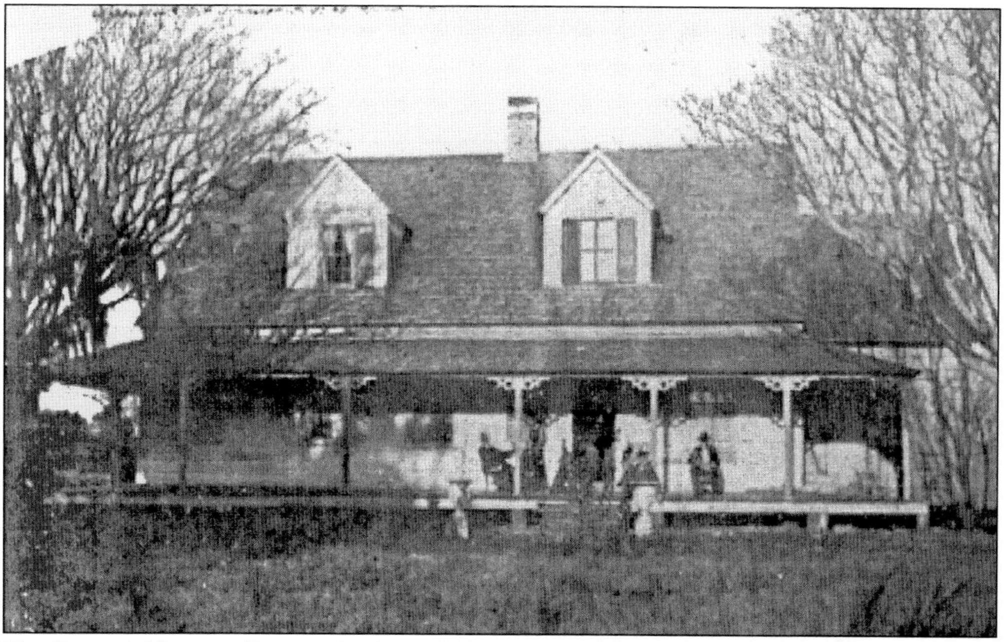

The Parson's House in Bayport, built in 1842, was one of the county's first homes.

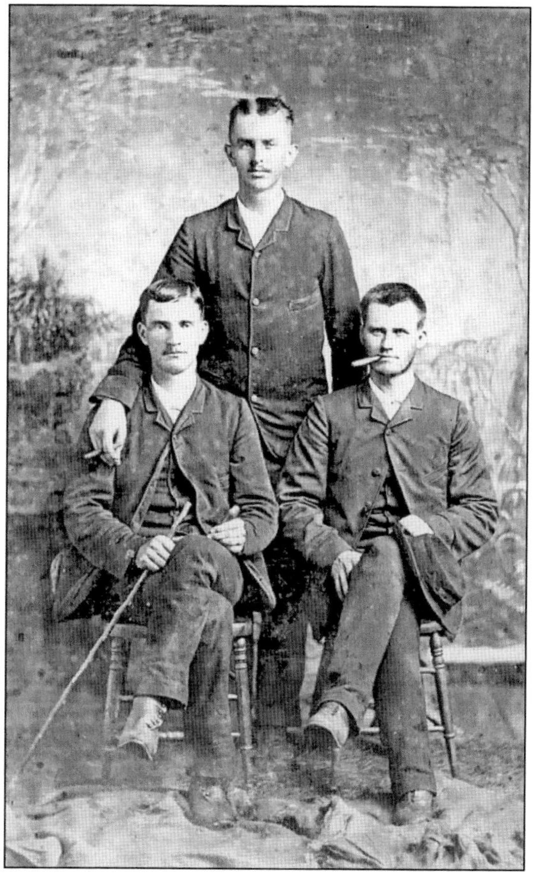

Lake Lindsey gentlemen in 1887 are, from left to right, John McKeown, Billy Kelly, and A.P. McKeown.

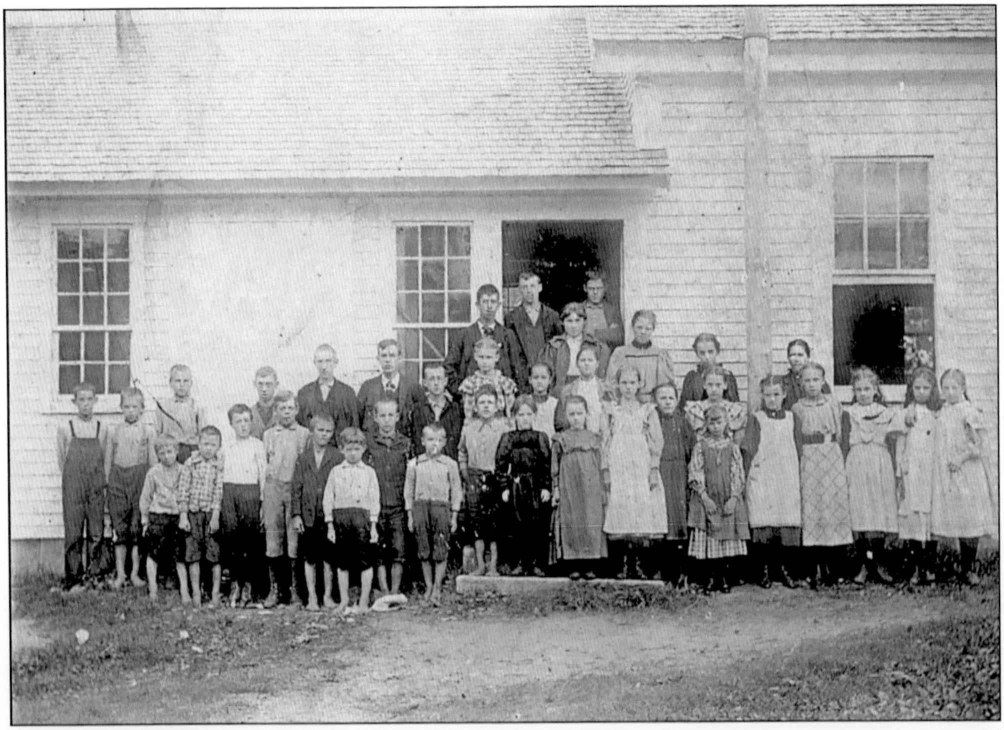

This rural schoolhouse in Brooksville is shown about 1898. In those days, one classroom would hold grades one through eight.

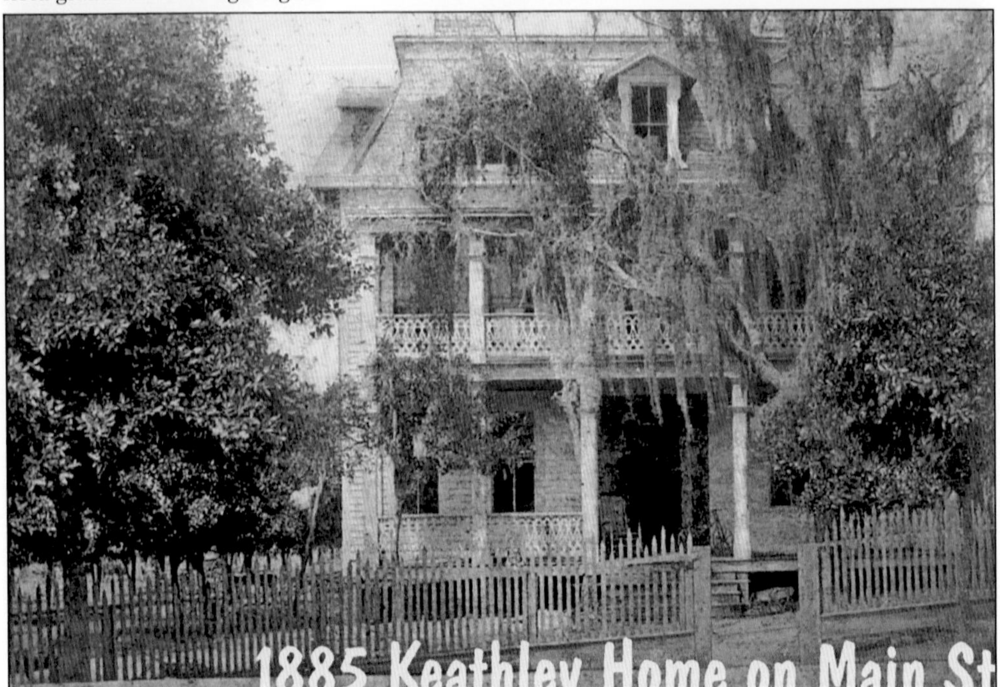

Brooksville's Keathley Home on South Main Street is shown in 1885. This was the home of C.C. Keathley, who served as clerk of circuit court from 1870 to 1875.

Two

1900–1920

Brooksville welcomed the 20th century, but, like most of Middle America, there was still very much a Victorian lifestyle. Citrus ruled, but a new industry also arose with rock mining. The timber and lumber industry gave birth to its own community west of Brooksville called Centralia. The automobile began to emerge, slowly taking over from the horse and buggy, but the decades of 1900–1920 still practiced a way of life very similar to the last century in its rigidity and its restraint.

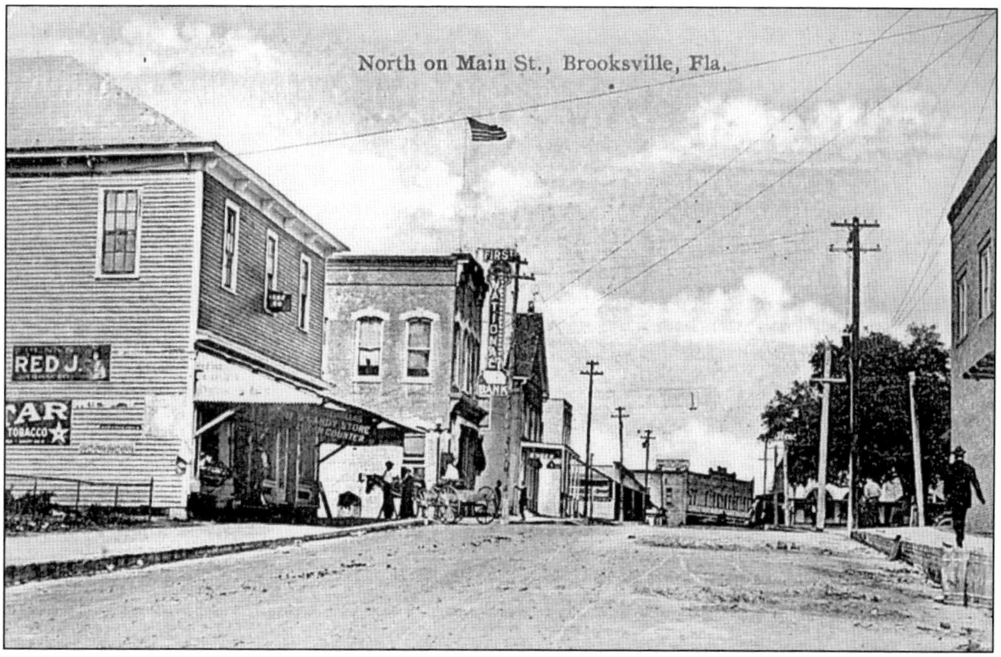

Looking north on Main Street in 1910, the slanted building down the street is the old Brooksville Hardware, located where City Hall is today, at the corner where Main becomes Howell Avenue.

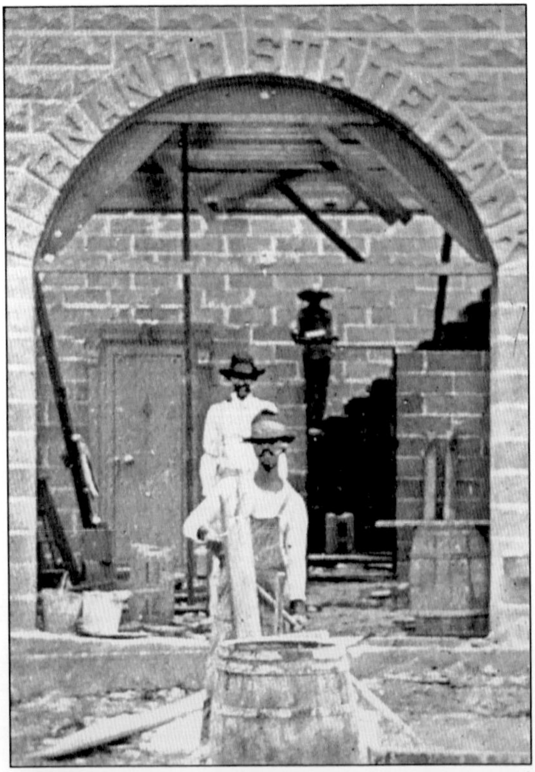

Workers at the construction site of the new Hernando State Bank are pictured in 1905 at the corner of Jefferson and Main.

The Democratic Convention in Jacksonville in June 1900 nominates Brooksville's own William S. Jennings as candidate for governor of Florida.

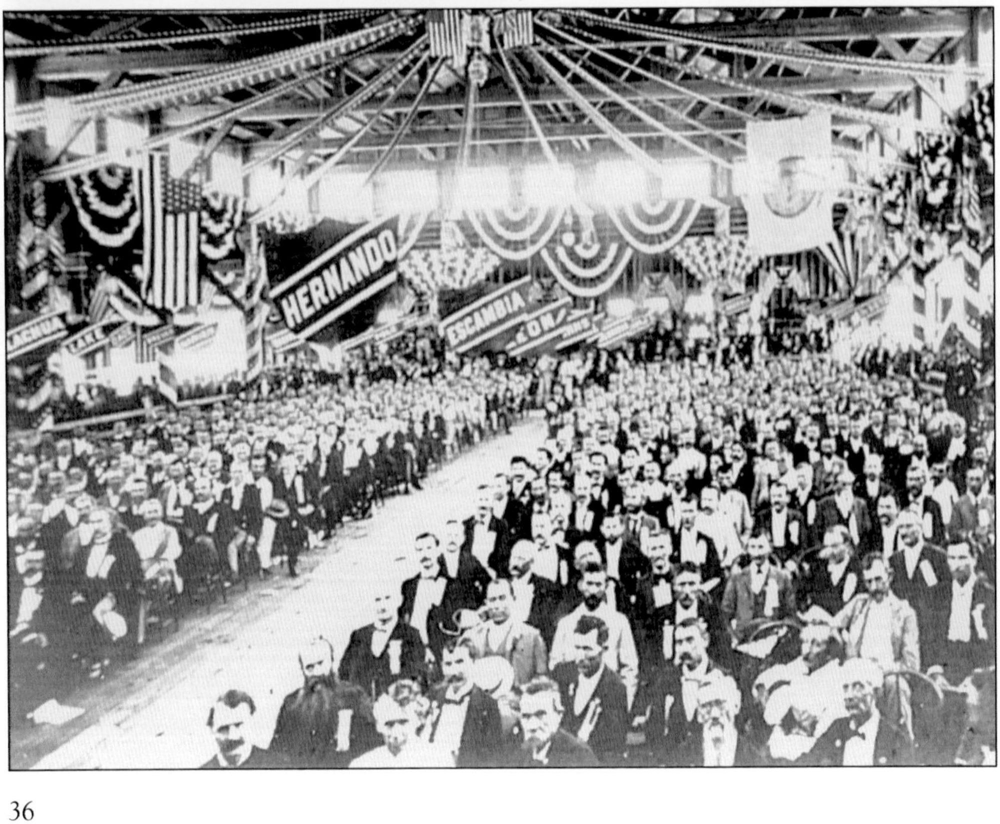

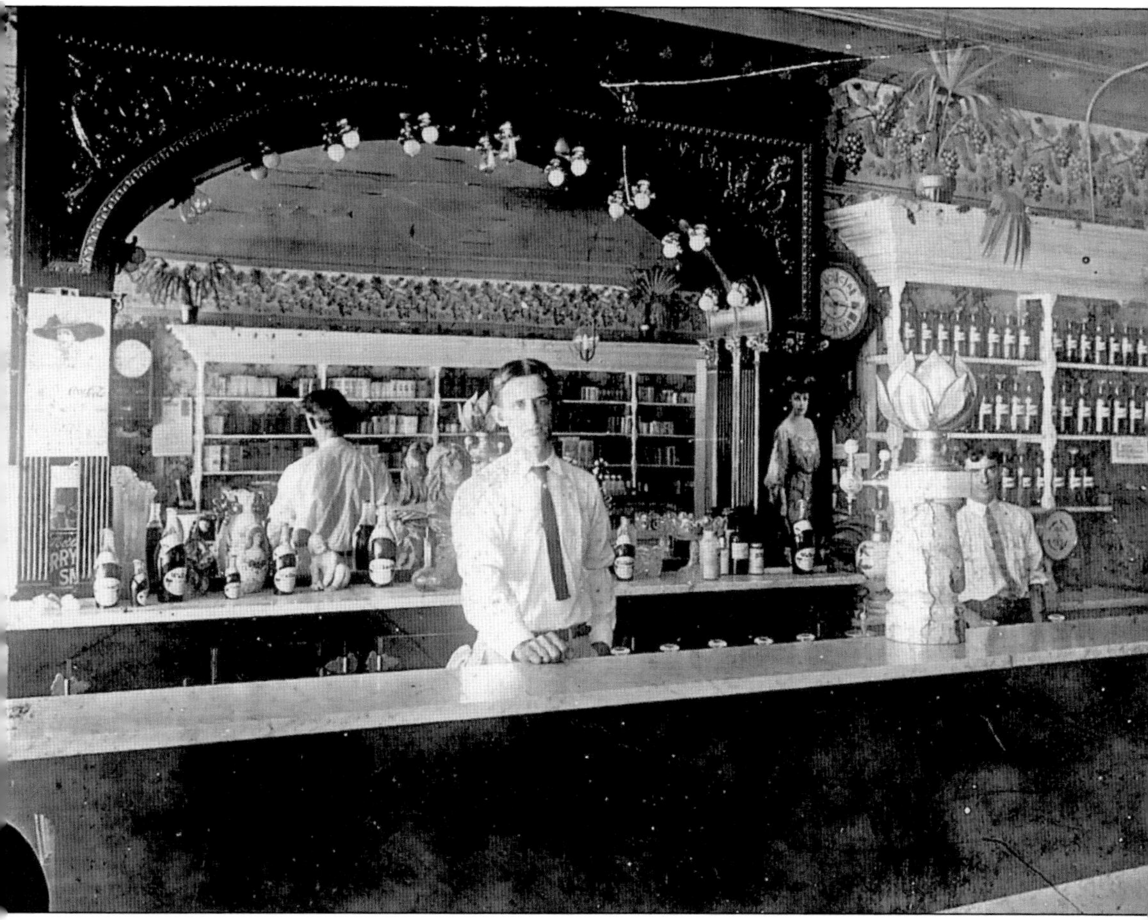

R.N. Chelf's Drug Store, pictured in May 1910, located in the old Jennings Building on Broad Street in Brooksville, was the fanciest drug store of its day, complete with a first-class soda fountain.

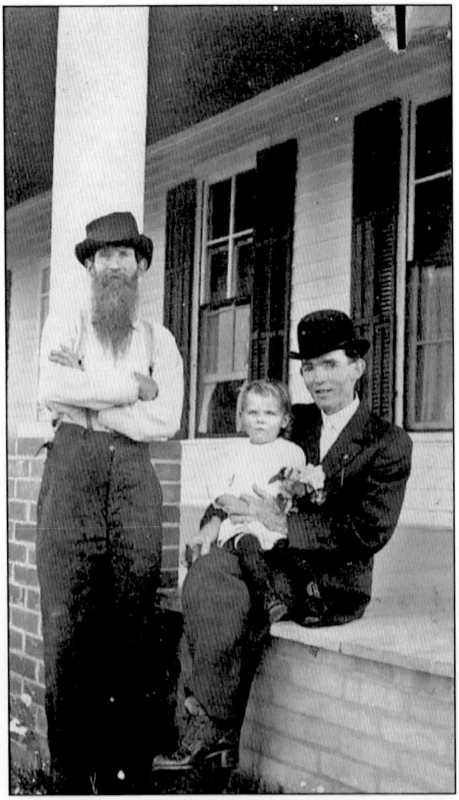

Three generations of the Morton family of Brooksville are shown in 1911. They lived just north of the city and were farmers.

Twelve picnickers share one car in 1913. Young family members find an ideal spot for a spring picnic just north of Brooksville. Pictured are, from left to right, (seated) Nathan Smith, Lucious Harris, Ridgeway Higgenbotham, Birdie Smith, Cora McKeown, Grace Paterson, Joella Higgenbotham, Lenora Smith, Antoinette Higgenbotham, Ida Peterson, Arthur McKeown, and LeRoy McKeown; (standing front) Mitchell Langford.

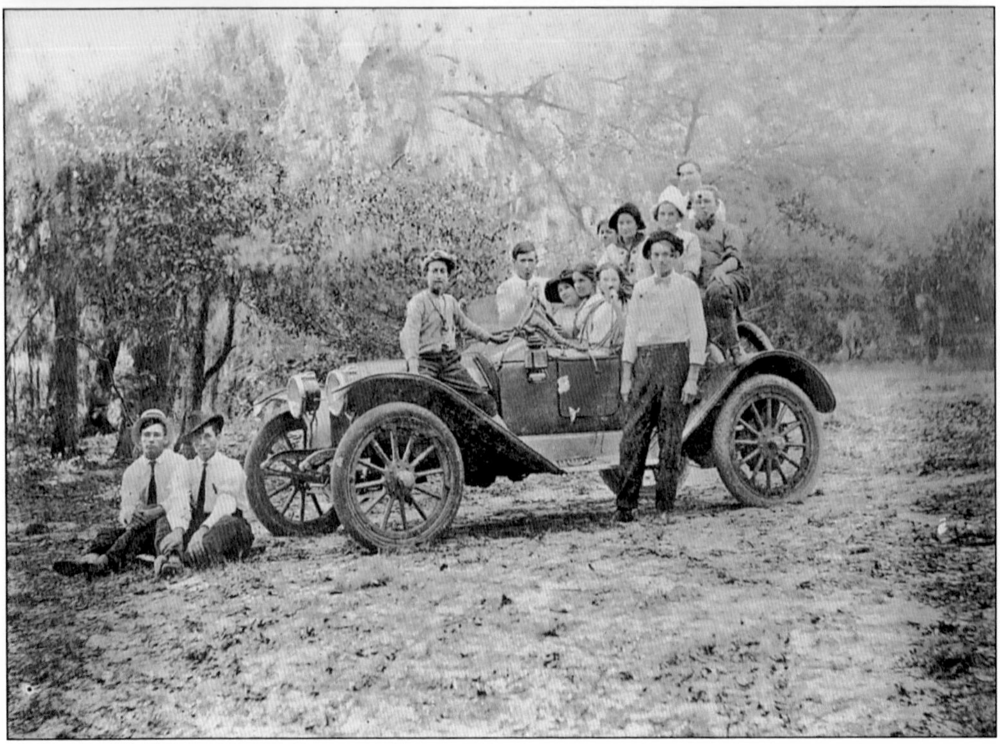

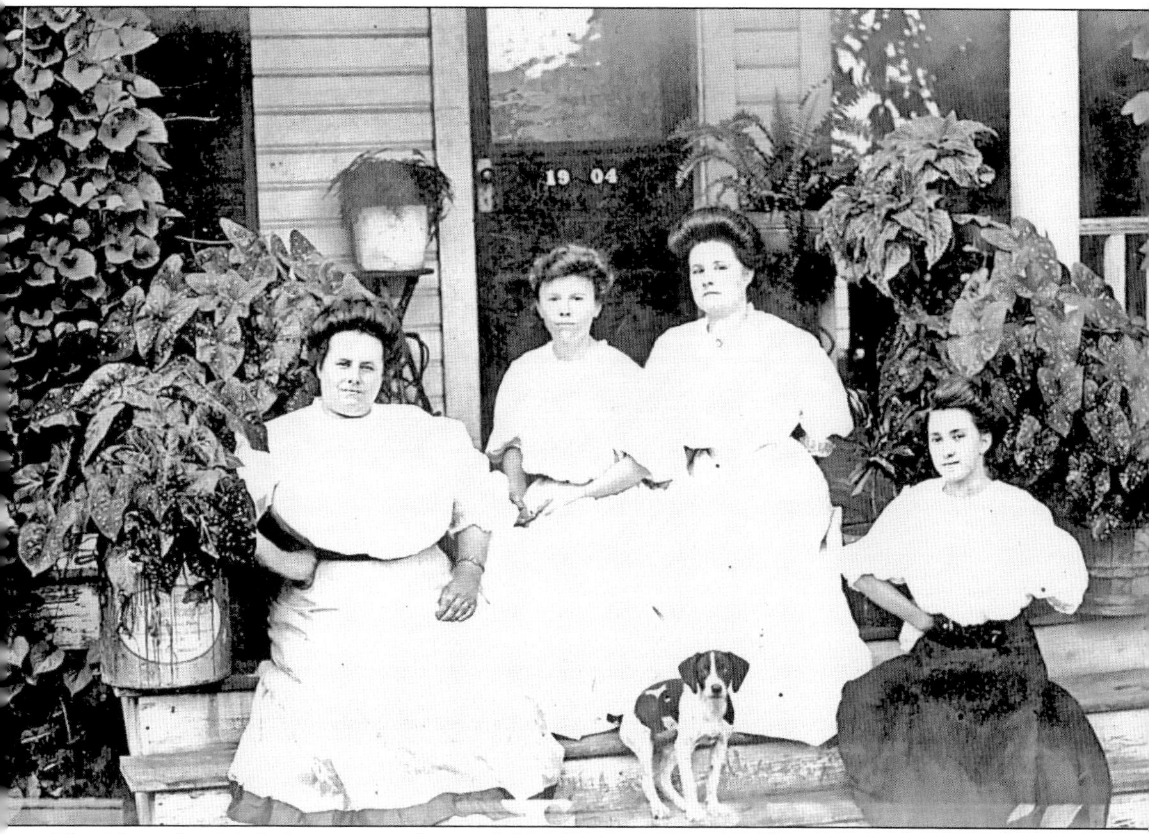

The Hope family's ladies pose in front of their home on Brooksville Avenue in 1904. Their roots are among those of the first settlers to this area, dating as far back as 1835.

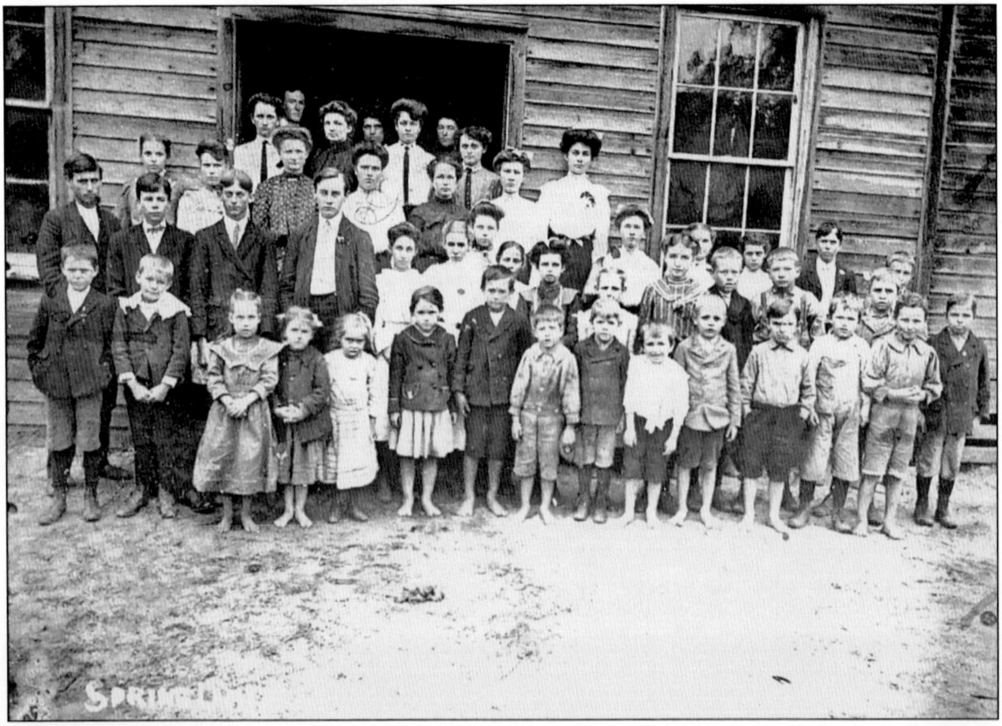

This 1905 image shows the Spring Lake School. Spring Lake is a charming and quaint little hamlet about seven miles east-southeast of Brooksville and at one time had a good portion of the county's citrus groves.

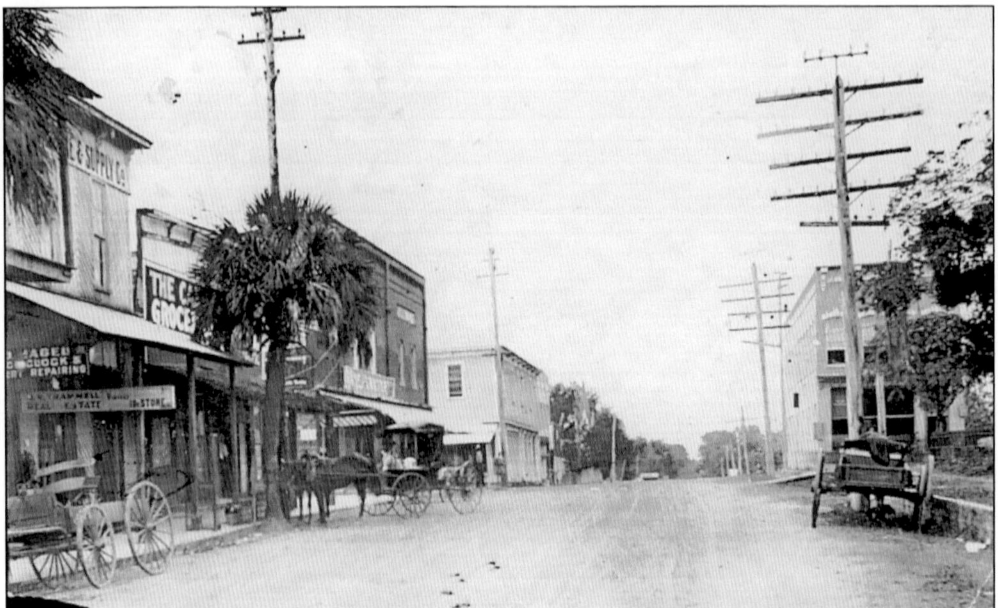

Broad Street, pictured about 1911, still depended greatly on the horse and carriage.

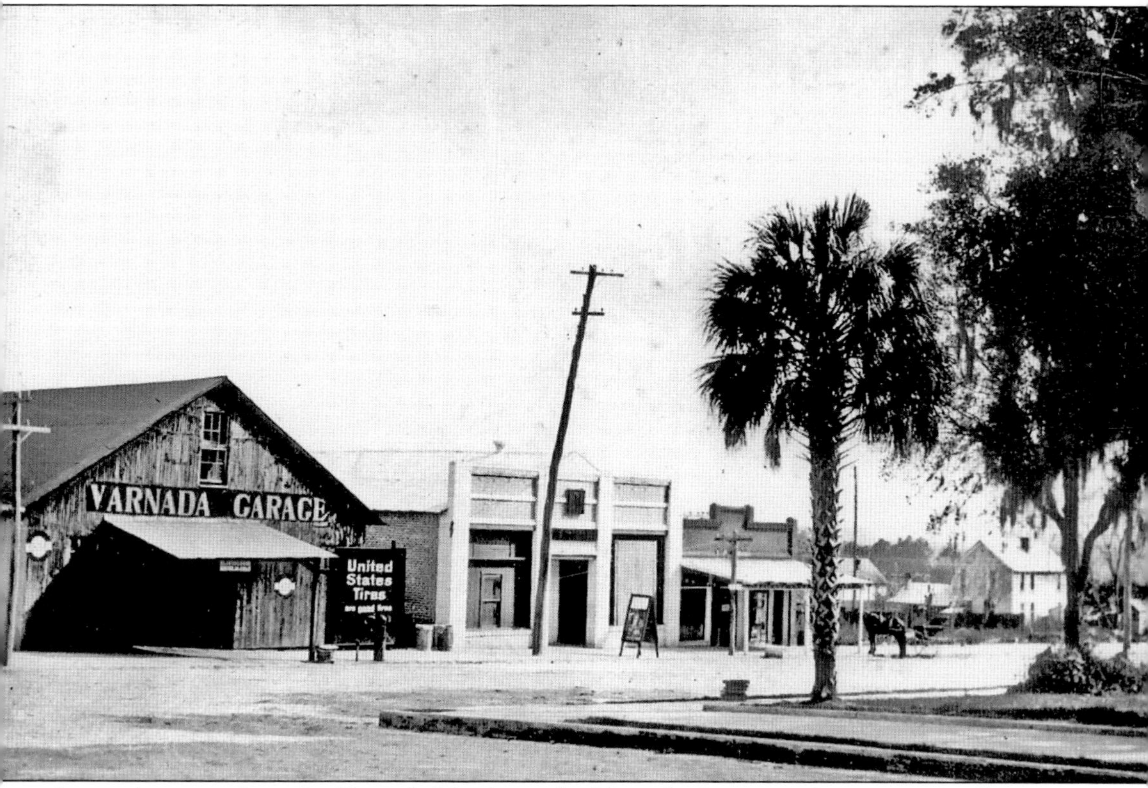

Across the street from the Varnada Hotel was the Varnada Garage at the corner of Jefferson and Brooksville Avenue, pictured in 1912.

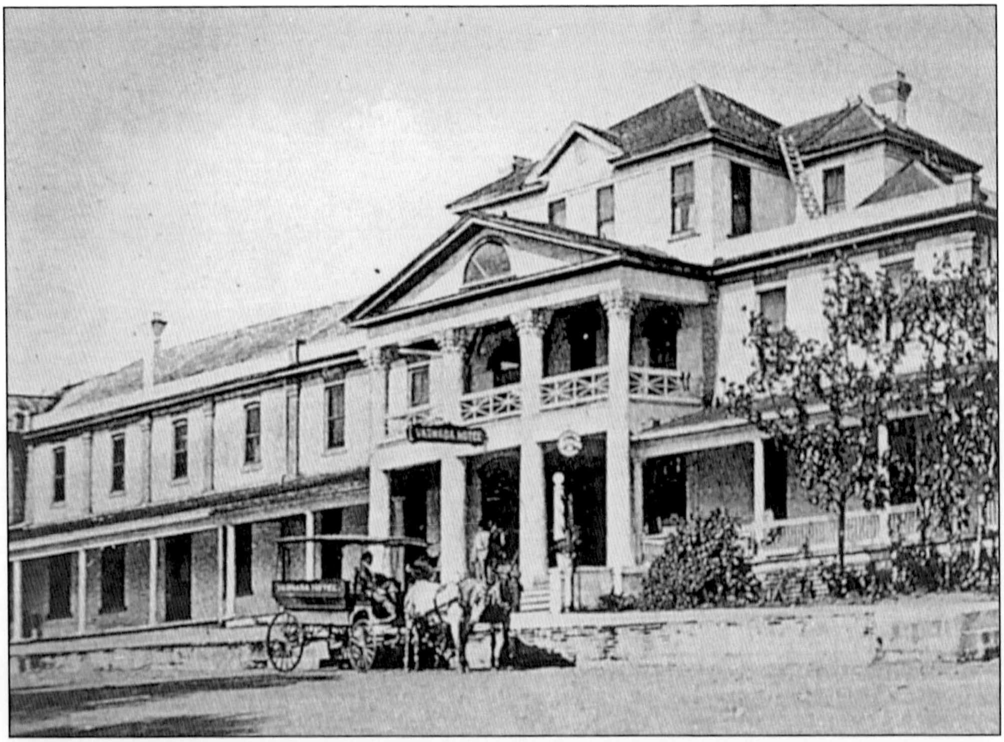

The Varnada Hotel on Jefferson Street is pictured in 1905. The grand hotel was a first-class tourist destination. It served sumptuous meals and provided its guests newspapers, barbers, and fine cigars. Built by a Mr. Varn around 1900, it burned to the ground in 1918.

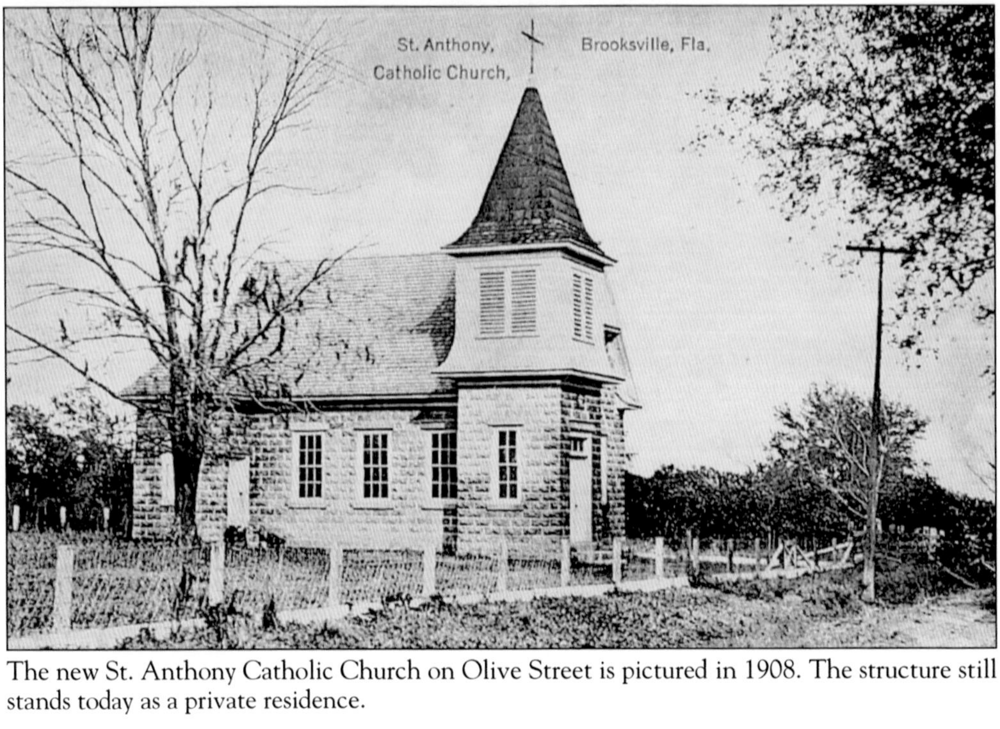

The new St. Anthony Catholic Church on Olive Street is pictured in 1908. The structure still stands today as a private residence.

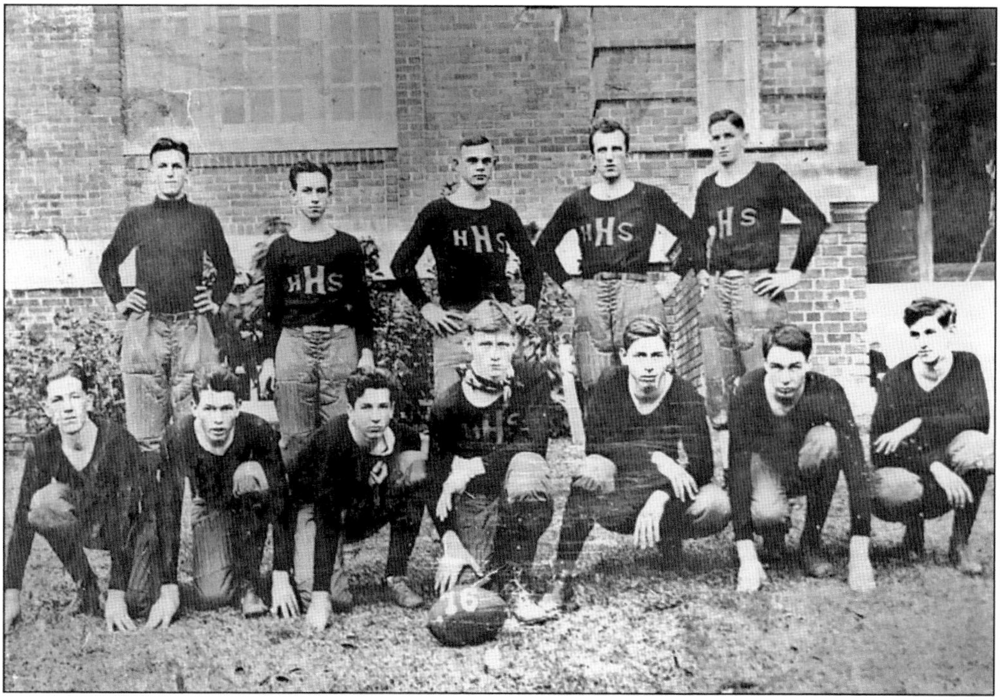

The first Hernando High School football team is pictured in 1916. Go Leopards!

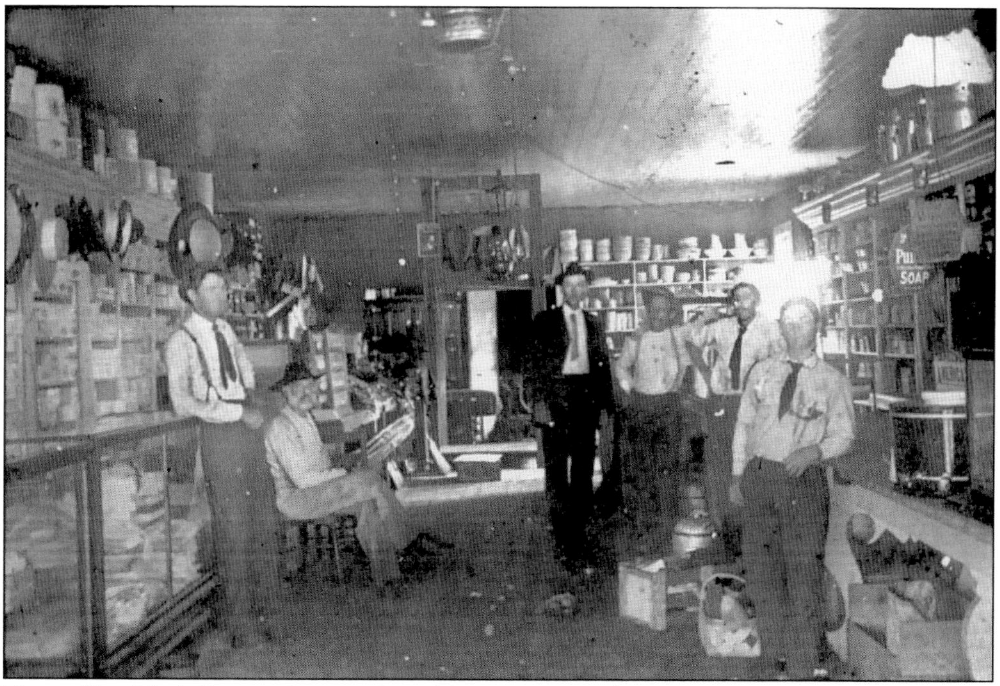

Norton Keathley's Grocery Store on Broad Street is pictured in 1910. The old bearded gentleman sitting to the left is one-time sheriff "Hopp" Smith, who served from 1868 to 1871.

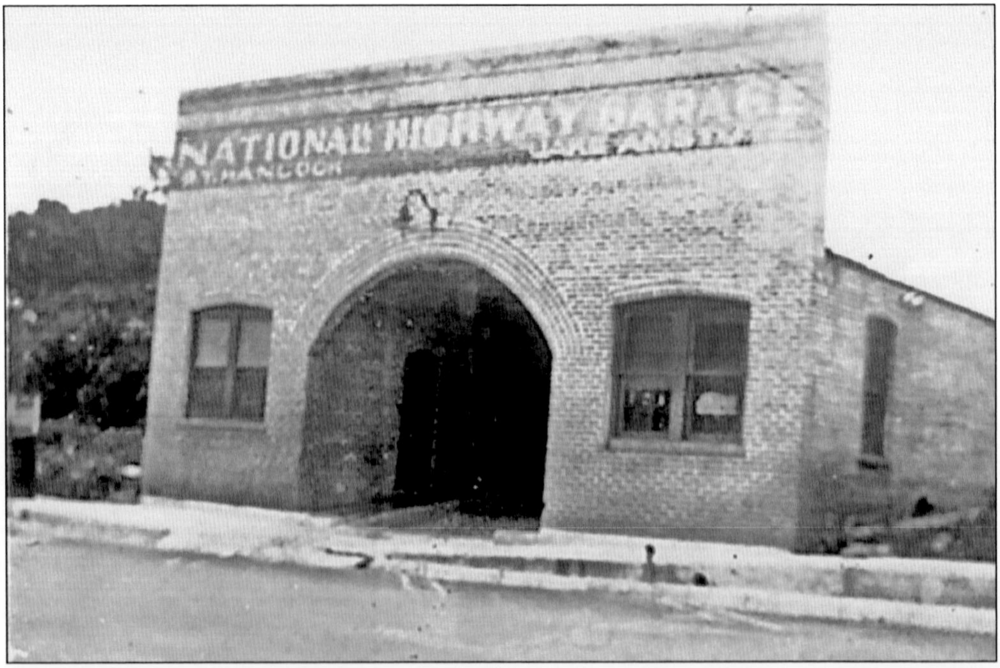

Hancock/Amstutz auto dealership and garage is seen in 1912. This was the second Ford dealership in the state of Florida. The facility was located on Broad Street and is now a law firm. The Ford dealership moved during the mid-1920s to the old site of the Varnada Garage and would operate as a Ford dealership from that location until 1974.

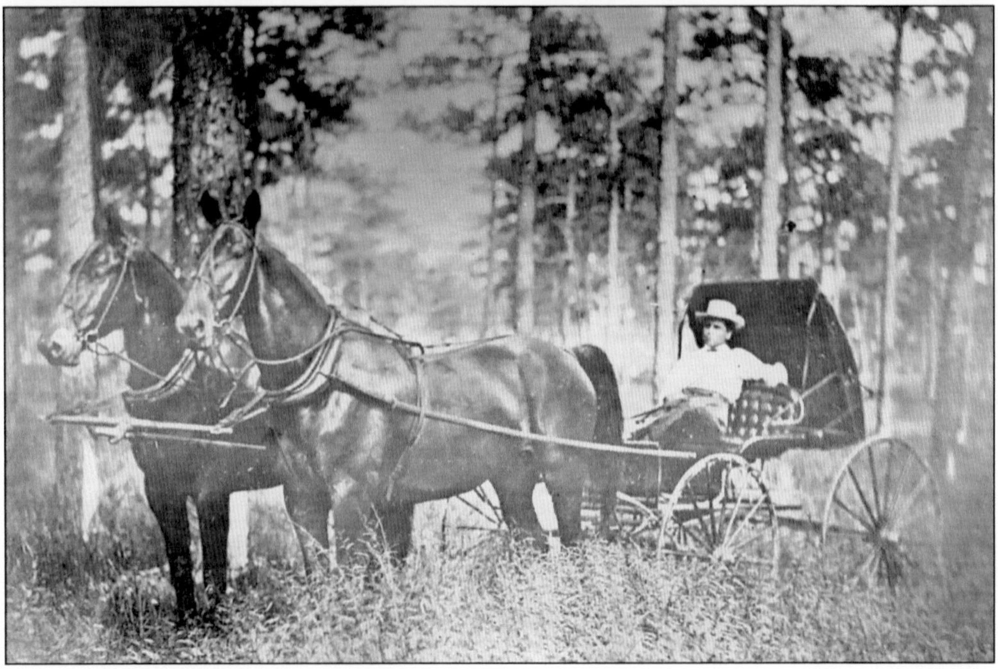

Lewis Petteway goes to town in 1910. Petteway operated one of the area's largest turpentine ventures. Turpentine was a major industry during the early 20th century in Brooksville. Petteway also operated Petteway Farms.

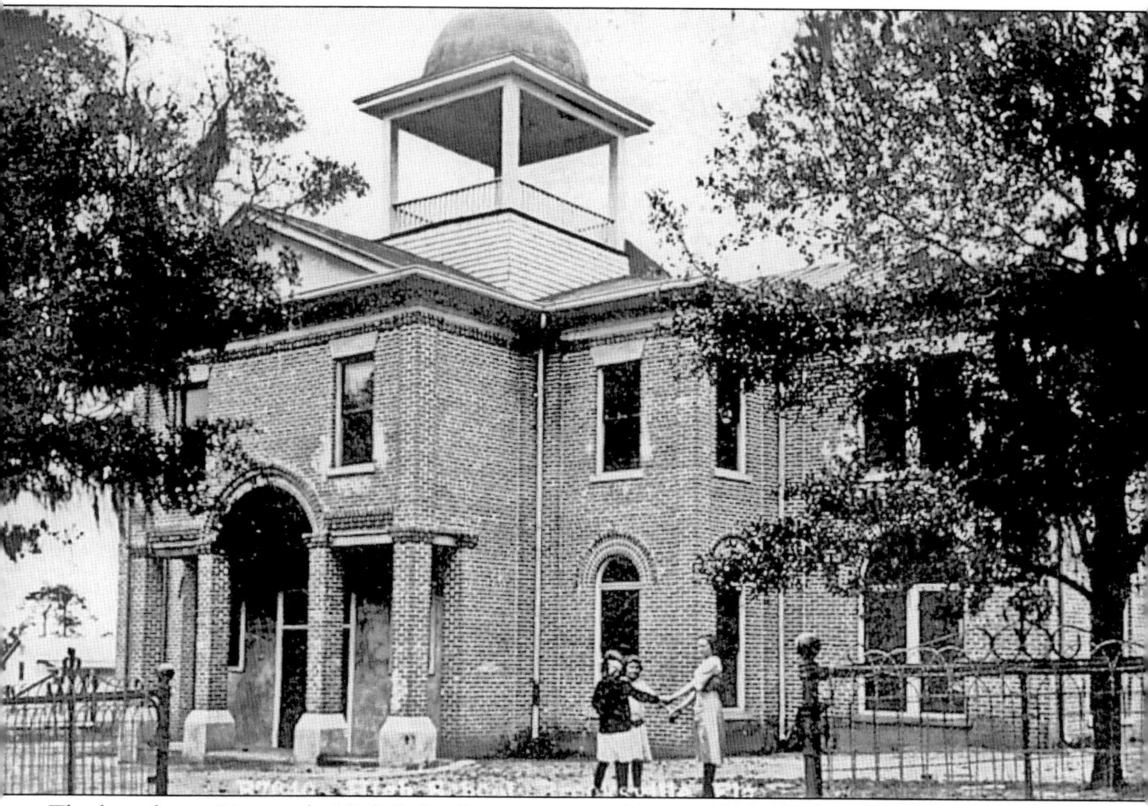

The brand-new Hernando High School was a *cause celebre* in 1910. The impressive new brick structure was built in the Brooksville area of Saxon Heights southwest of the courthouse. By 1914 it was already overcrowded, and in 1918 it burned down.

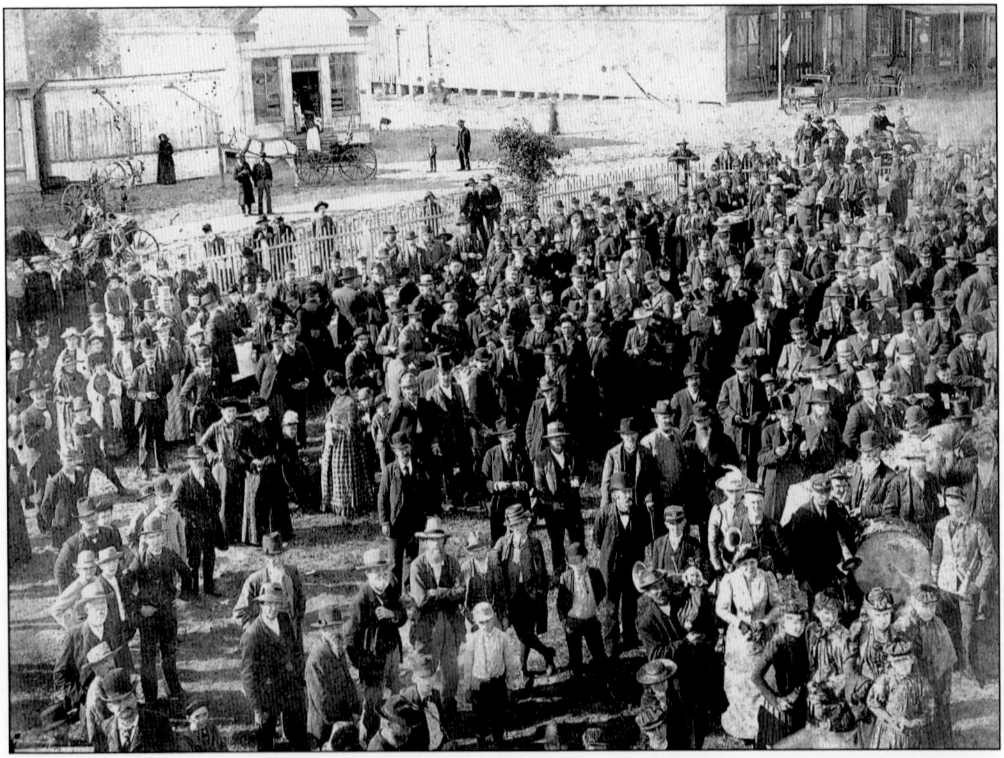

It was a big day in downtown Brooksville in 1900 when a large crowd complete with marching bands, entertainers, and vendors surrounded the courthouse to welcome Brooksville's own William S. Jennings as governor of Florida. The street behind the crowd is Main Street.

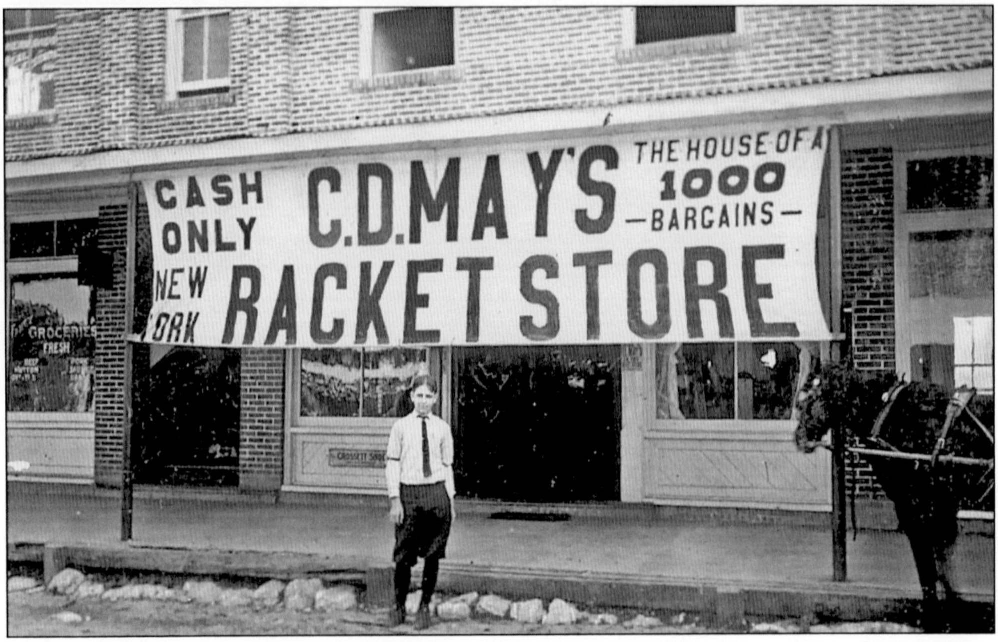

Brooksville Department Store on North Main Street is seen in 1908. It was then called the New York Racket Store and in 1912 became Rogers's Department Store.

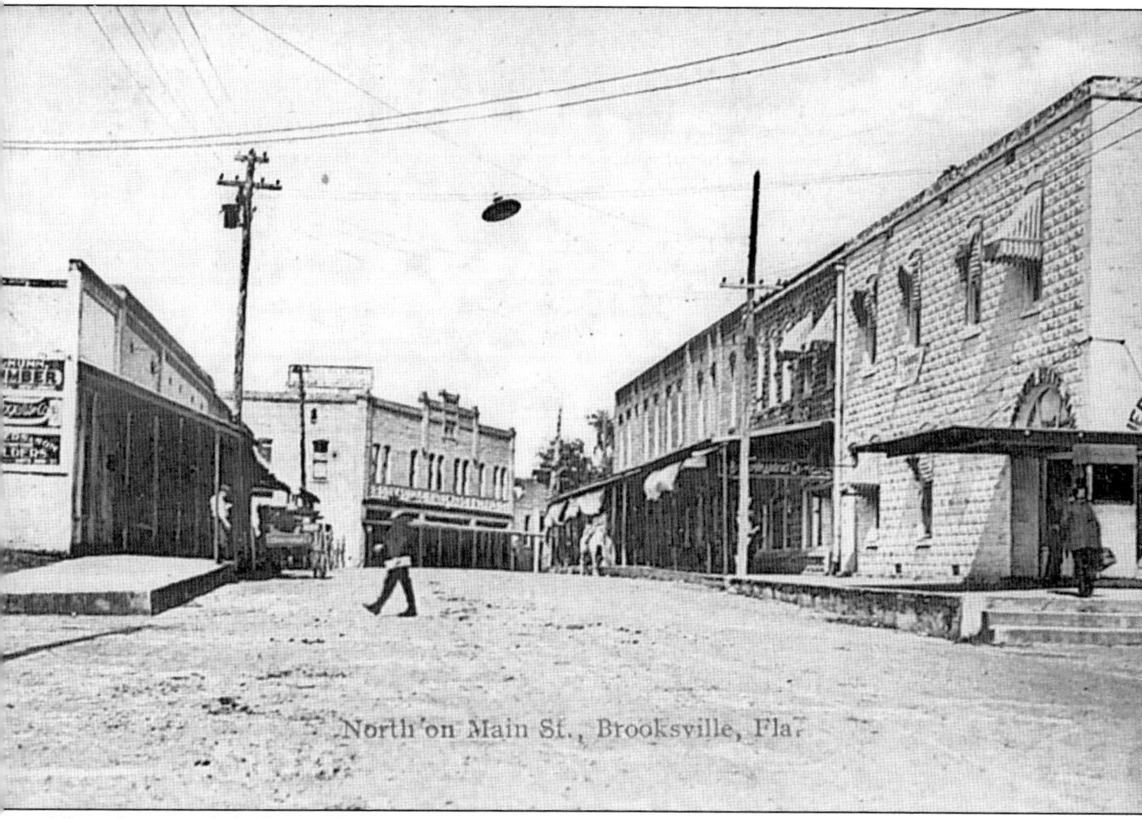

This photograph looks north on Main Street from Jefferson in 1909. The strange object in the sky is not a UFO but the earliest form of a traffic light.

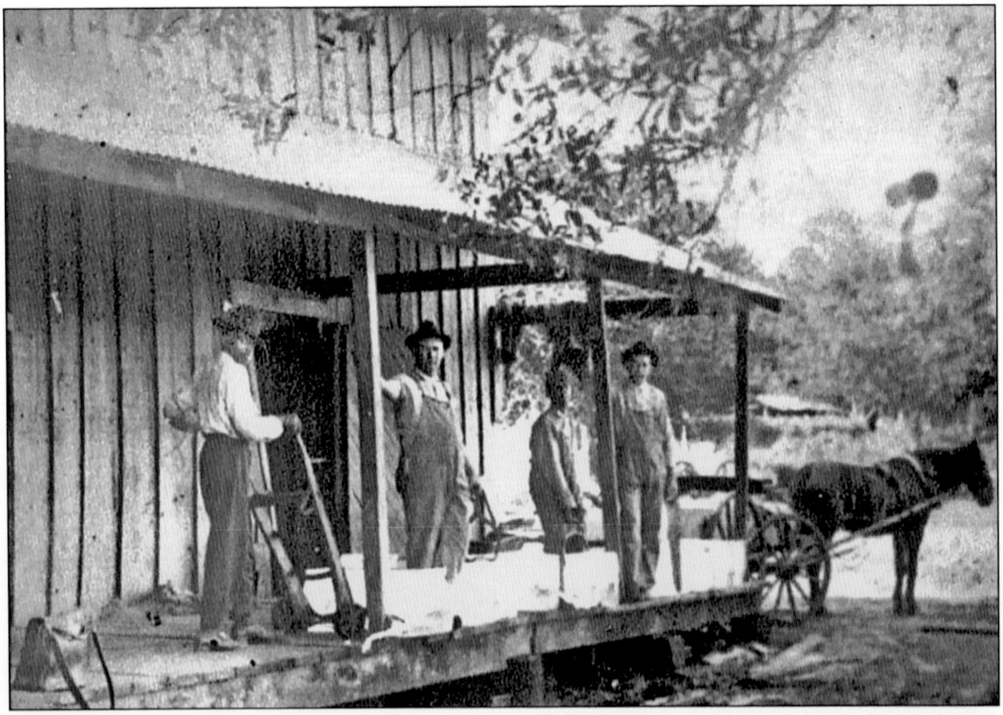

Brooksville Ice Plant, pictured in 1906, was operated by Lester Varn and was located near downtown Brooksville on Broad Street.

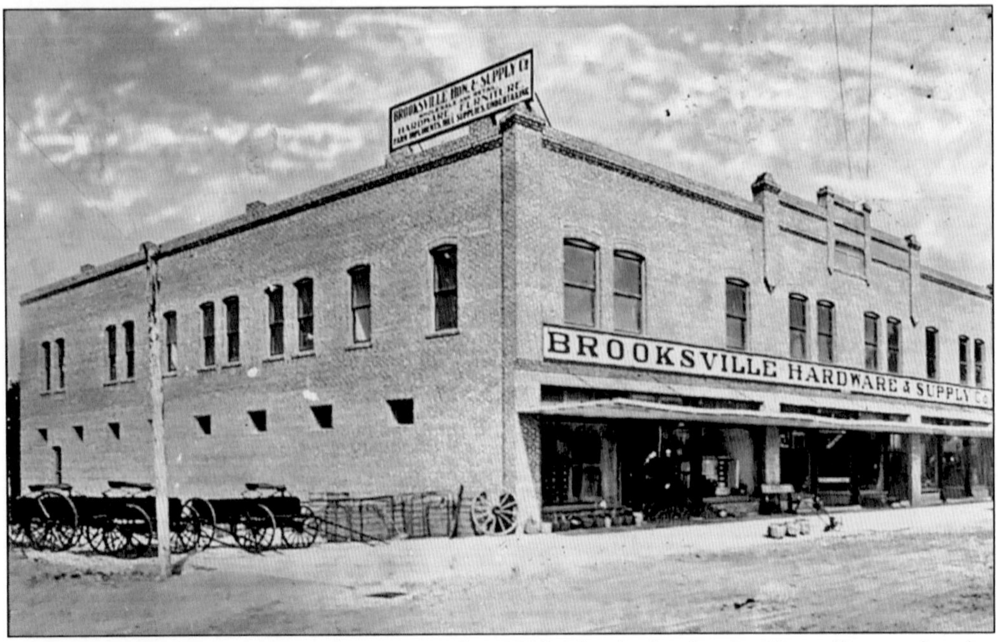

Brooksville Hardware and Supply is pictured in 1905. This had to be the Home Depot of its day from its sheer size. Built during the 1890s, it burned down around 1914. It was located where Brooksville City Hall is today at the corner of Howell Avenue and Ft. Dade Avenue.

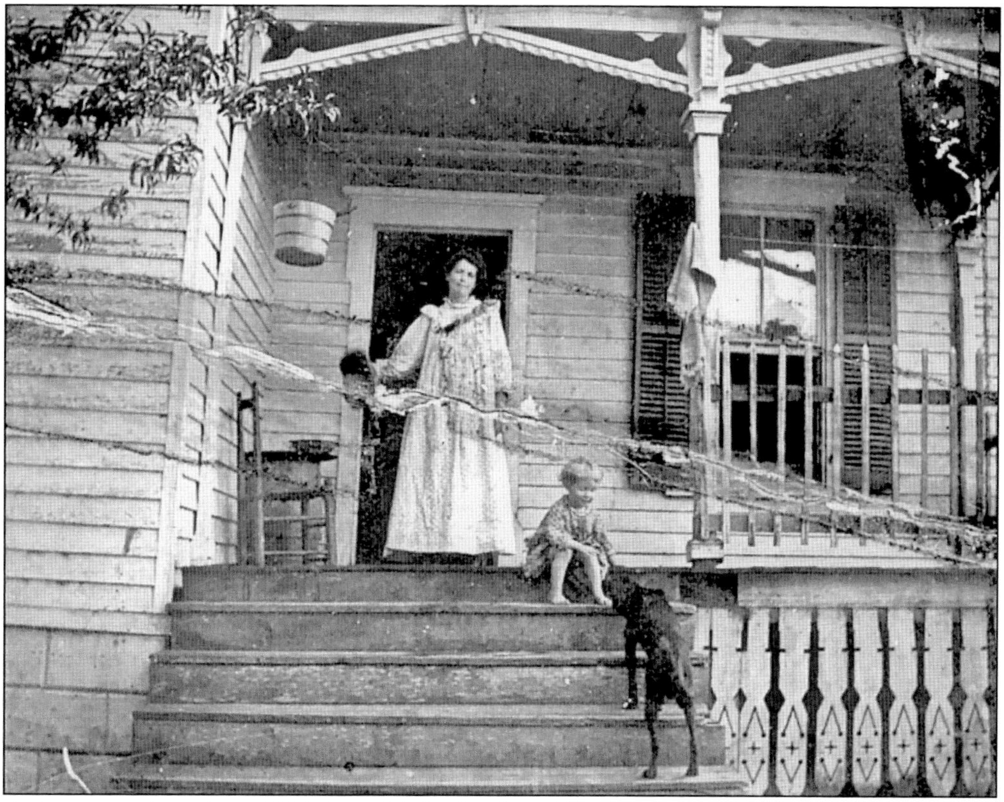

A charming photo from 1902 shows Molly Arick and her son A.W. and his dog. The home still stands on Howell Avenue.

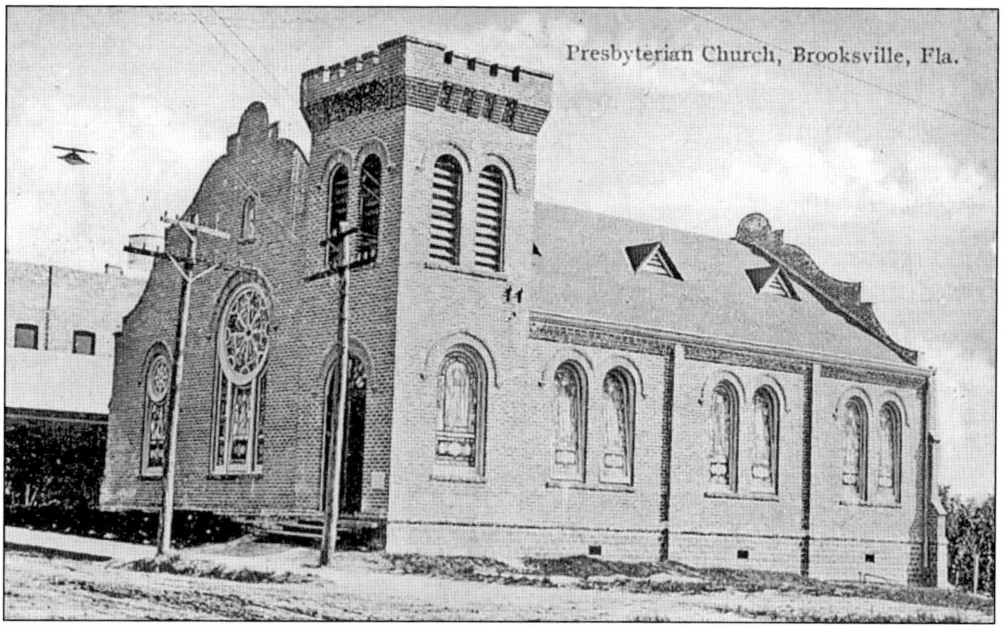

The new Brooksville Presbyterian Church on Broad Street was one of the city's most impressive structures in 1914.

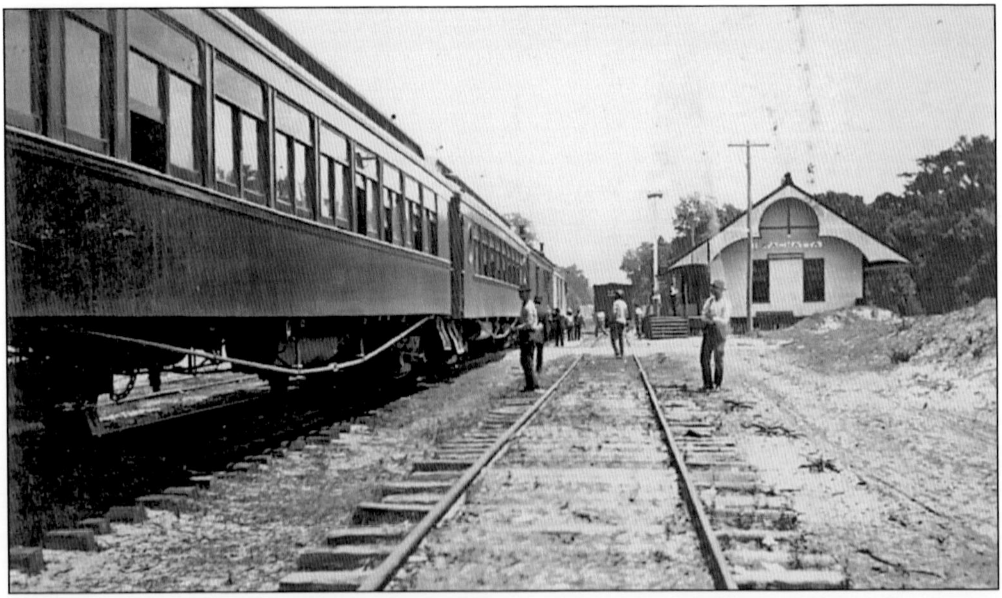

Istachatta Train Station is seen in 1911. Before our love affair with the automobile came to fruition, passenger rail travel was quite common and was considered a quicker and cleaner alternative to the horse and carriage. This train was headed to Tampa.

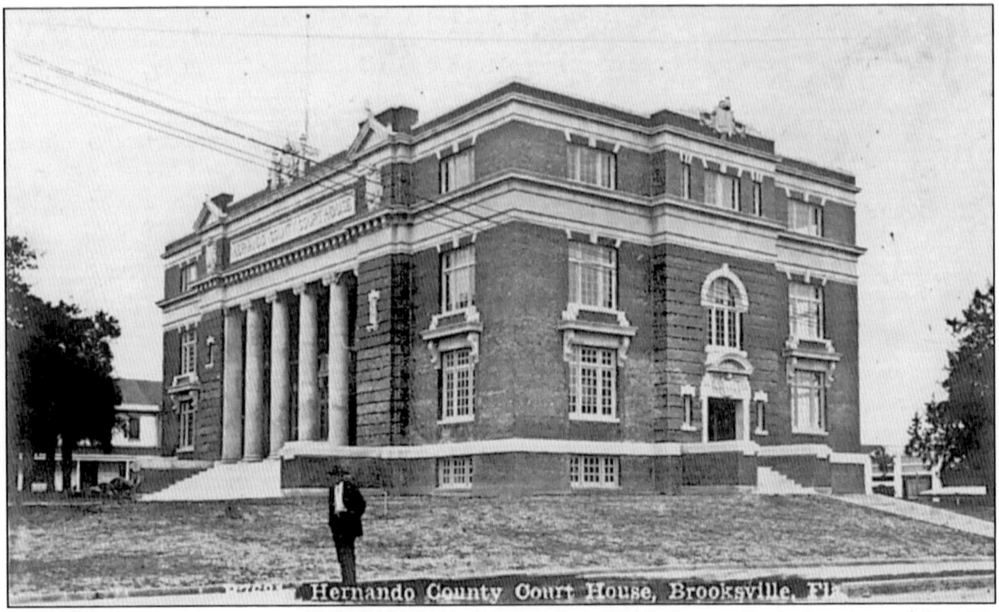

The all new Hernando County Court House opened in 1913. It was built for about $50,000. Today, the courthouse is surrounded by huge oaks and palm trees, but in 1913, it was pretty plain and bare.

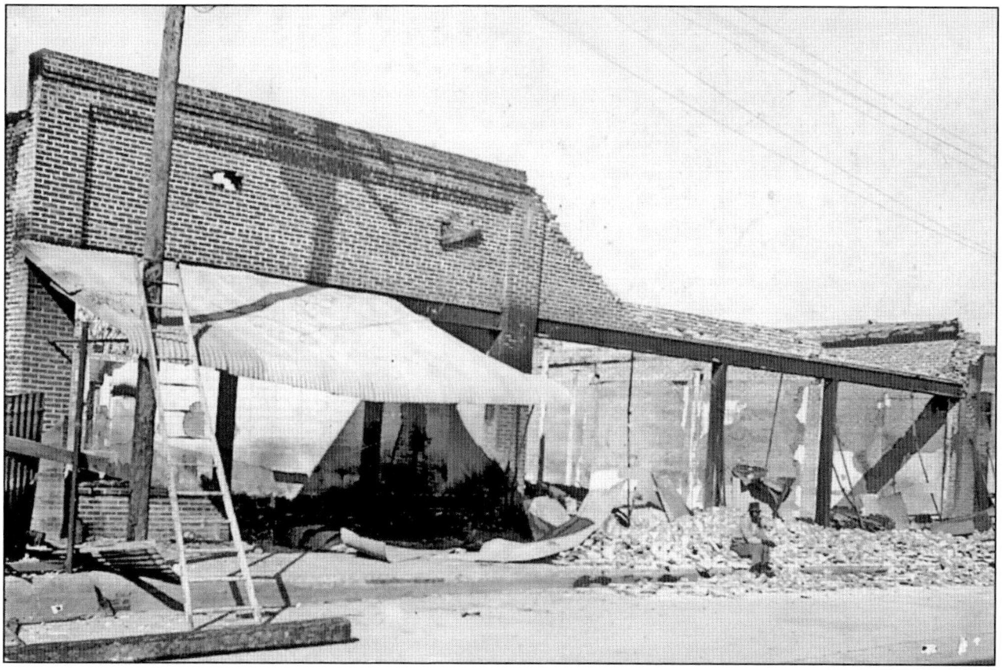

The 1914 Brooksville Fire destroyed all the shops along the west side of Main Street. Fires were so common during the early 20th century that insurance companies labeled Brooksville "a hot town." After Brooksville got its own water system in 1918, the fires subsided, but before that virtually every building at one time or another burned to the ground. Some were rebuilt, like the Jennings Building in 1915; some were forgotten, like the Varnada Hotel and Brooksville Hardware.

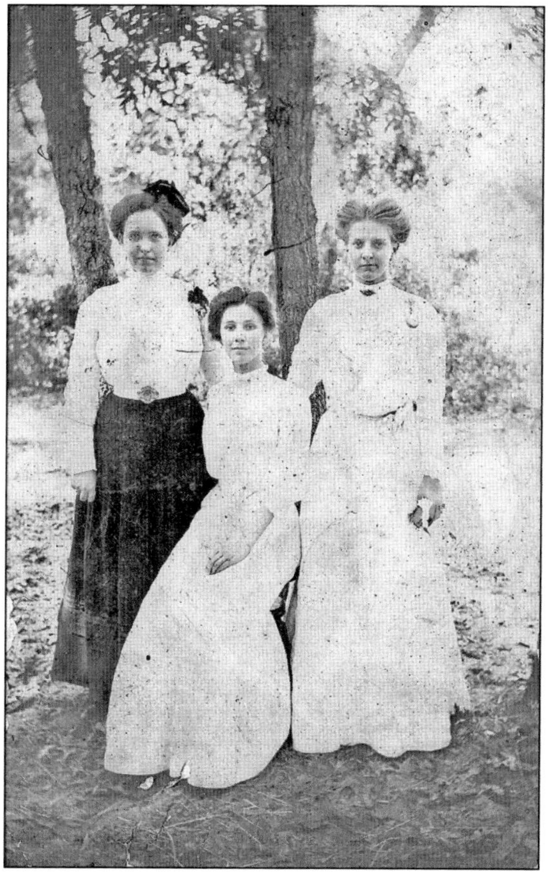

Three pretty ladies from the Lake Lindsey area, north of Brooksville, are pictured in 1912.

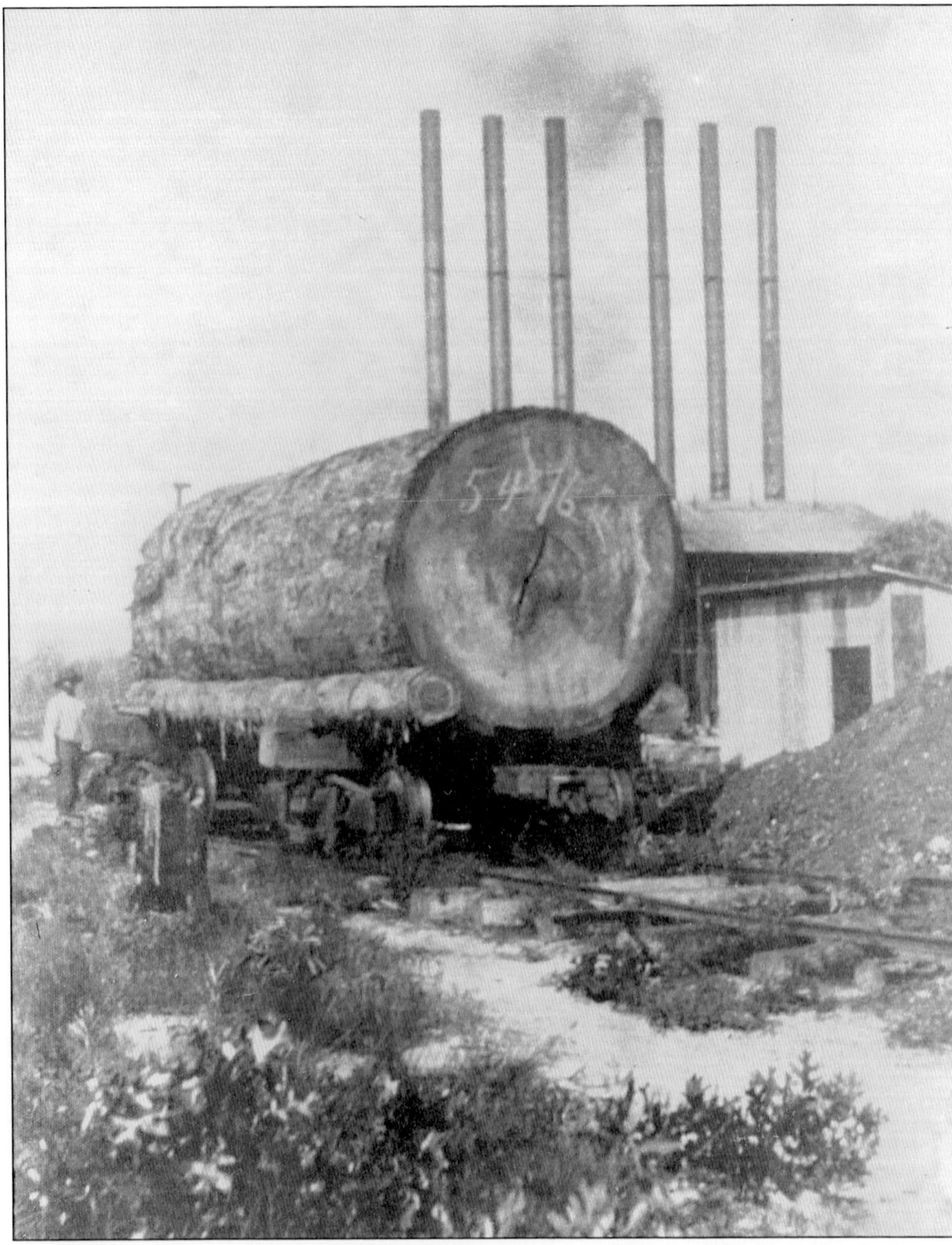

The logging community of Centralia once boasted a population of nearly 2,000. It thrived from 1910 until about 1917, and was a ghost town by 1922. This cypress tree cut down in 1912 was the largest in the world. It measured 20 feet in width and sawed out 5,476 board feet of lumber. Centralia was about 15 miles northwest of Brooksville and about 5 miles north of Weeki Wachee.

Ernest and Hattie Cappleman from Brooksville are seen on their 1903 wedding day.

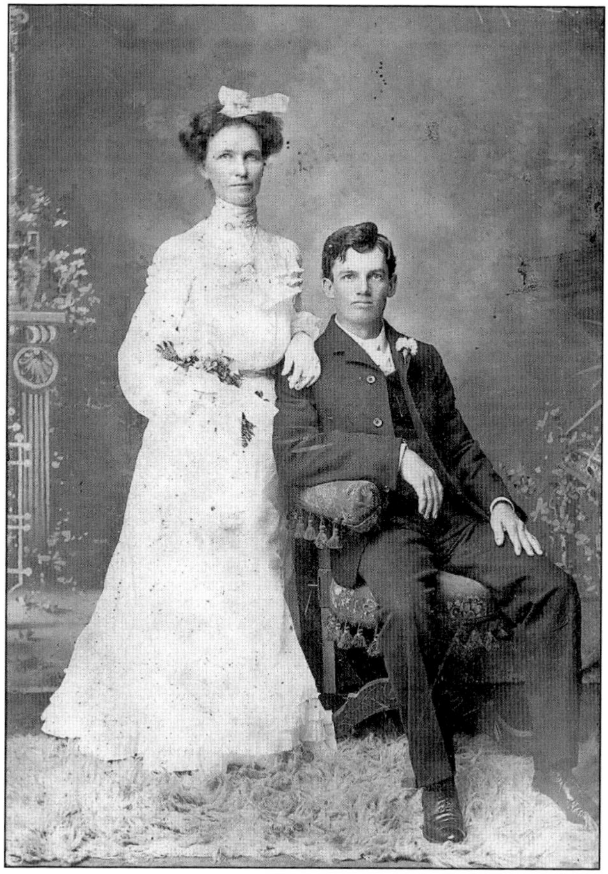

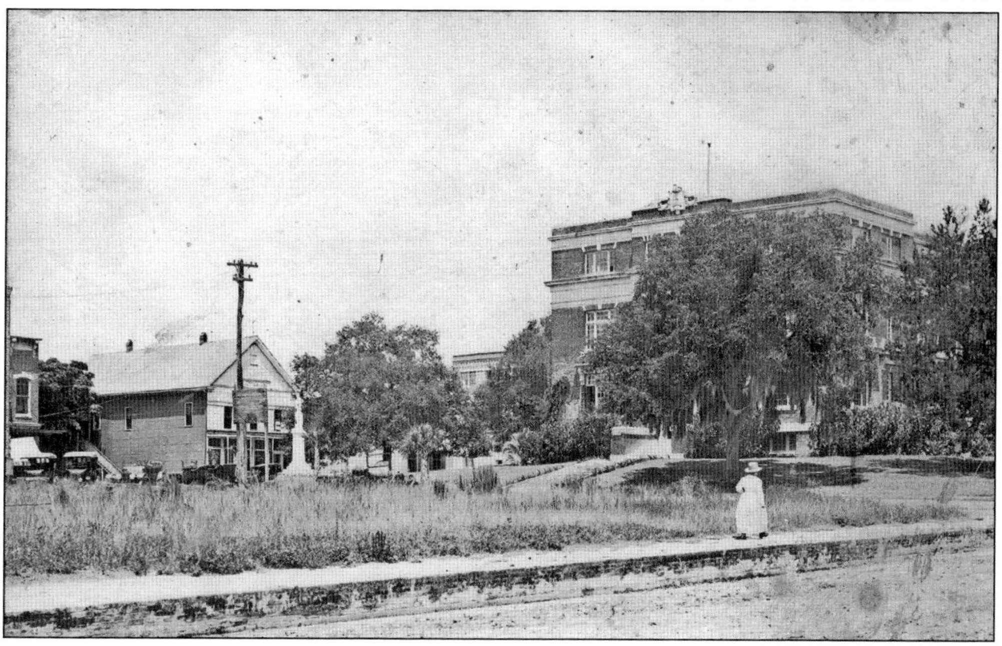

A Brooksville citizen walks to the courthouse square in 1917. This view is from the southeast.

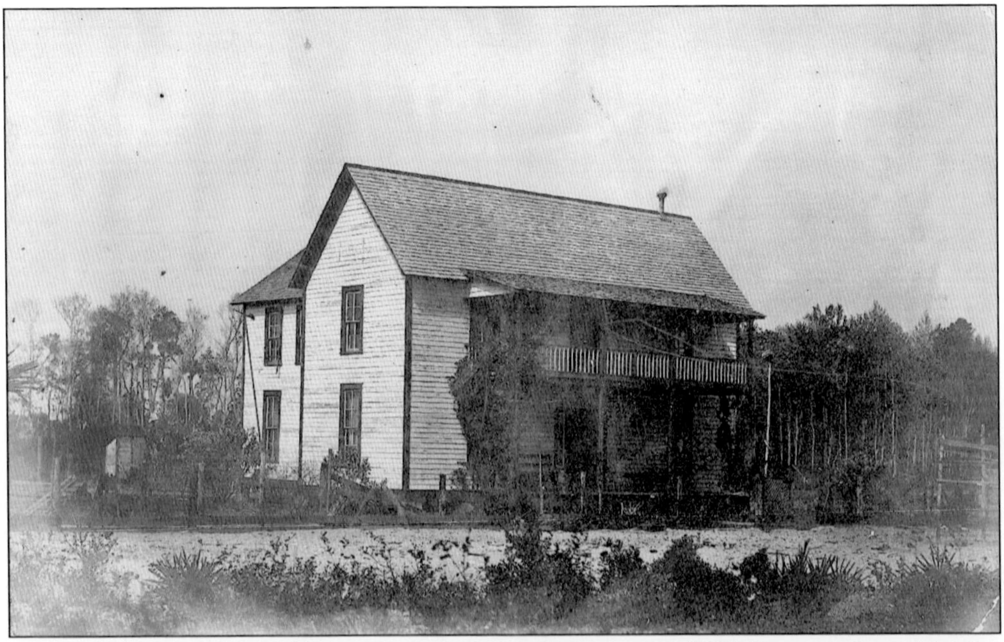

This early home in the Gulf coastal town of Aripeka is seen in 1902. Located about 15 miles southwest of Brooksville, Aripeka was a fishing community on the Gulf and attracted tourists like Babe Ruth, legendary Yankee slugger, for fishing trips during the 1920s.

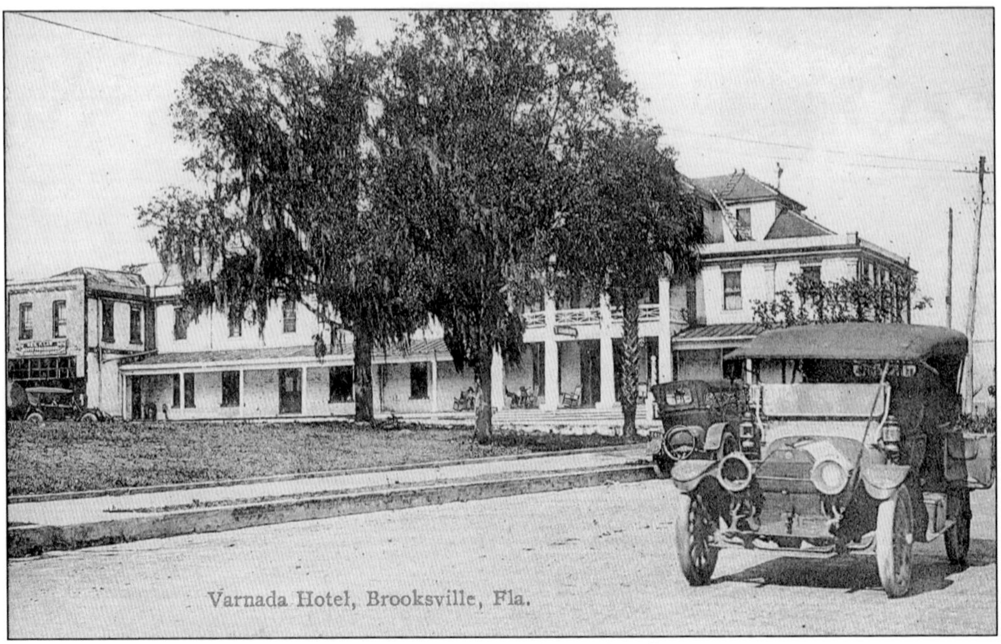

Here is another view of the Varnada Hotel from old Brooksville Avenue in 1914.

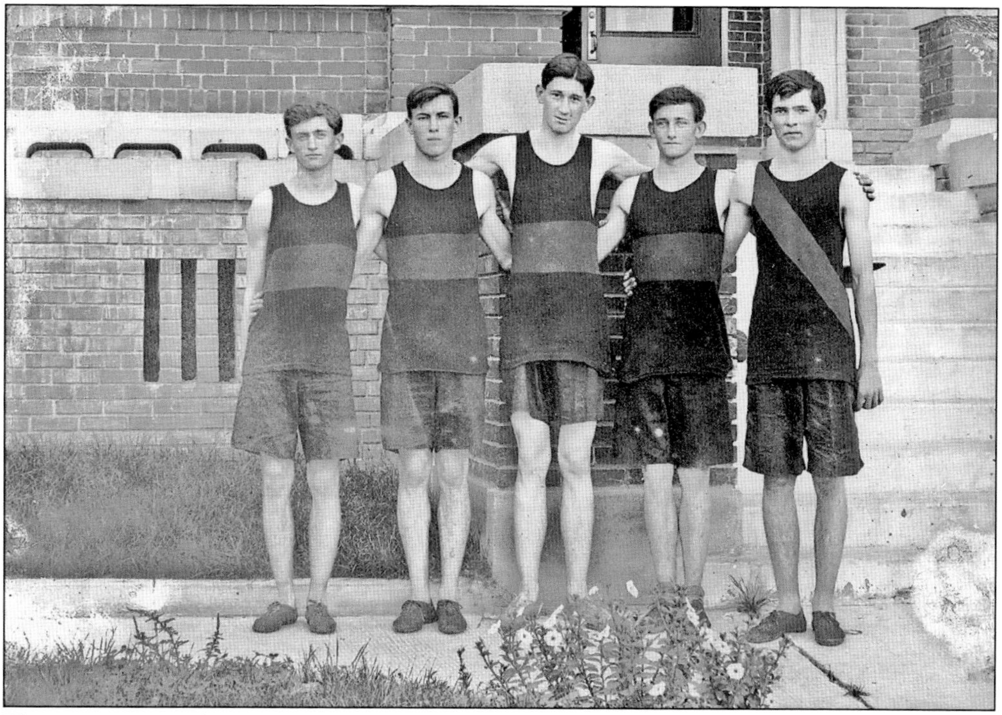

The 1914 Hernando High Track Team is, from left to right, Jessie Smith, Raymond Pearson, Clarence Law, Frank Grozier, and Ernest Rutledge.

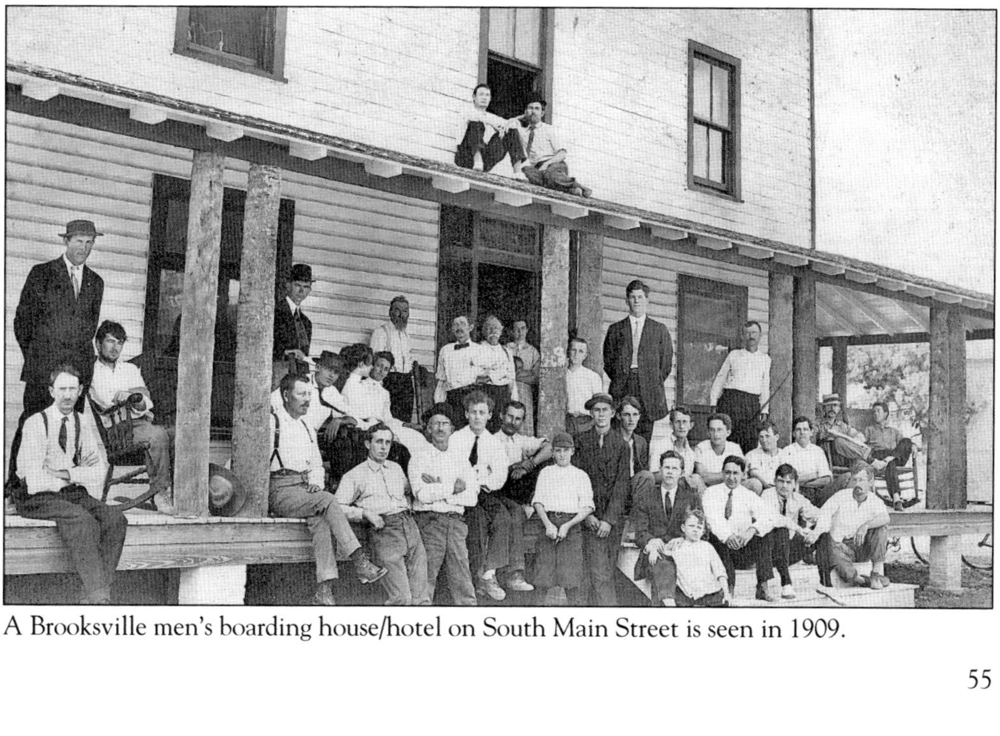

A Brooksville men's boarding house/hotel on South Main Street is seen in 1909.

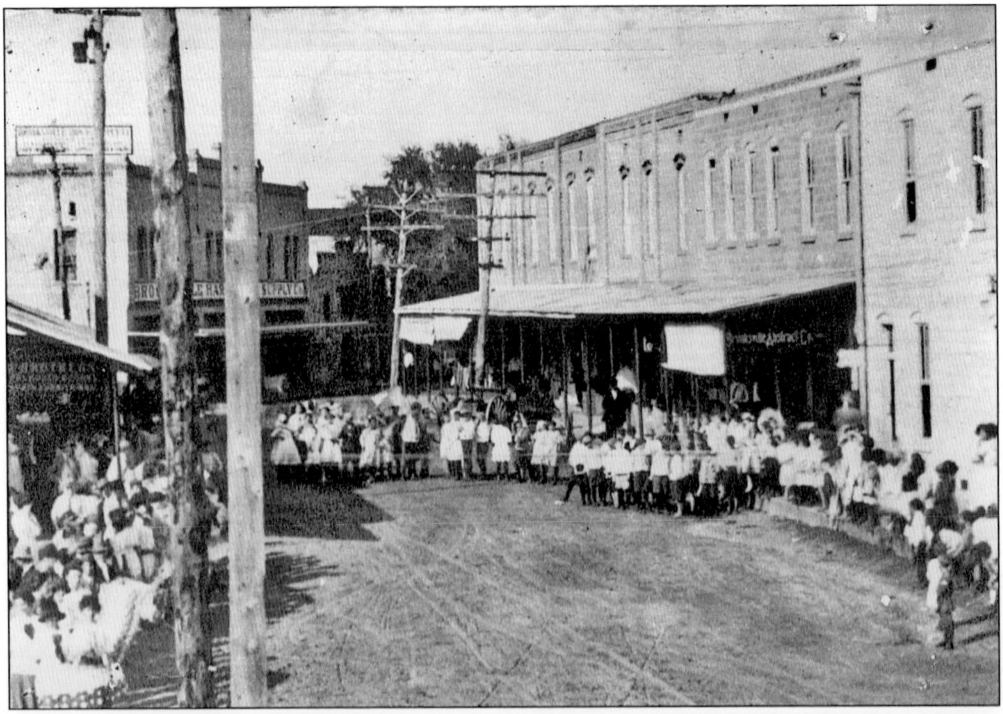

This Brooksville street celebration took place in 1905. This is North Main Street, most likely during a July 4 celebration, featuring a race of some sort.

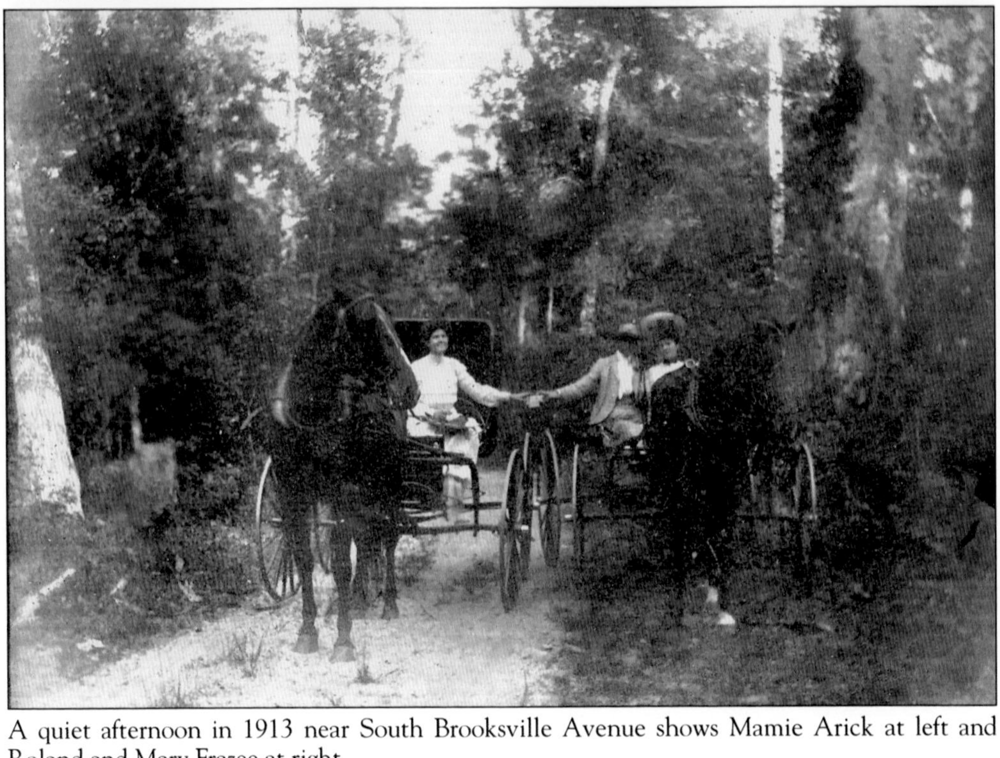

A quiet afternoon in 1913 near South Brooksville Avenue shows Mamie Arick at left and Roland and Mary Frazee at right.

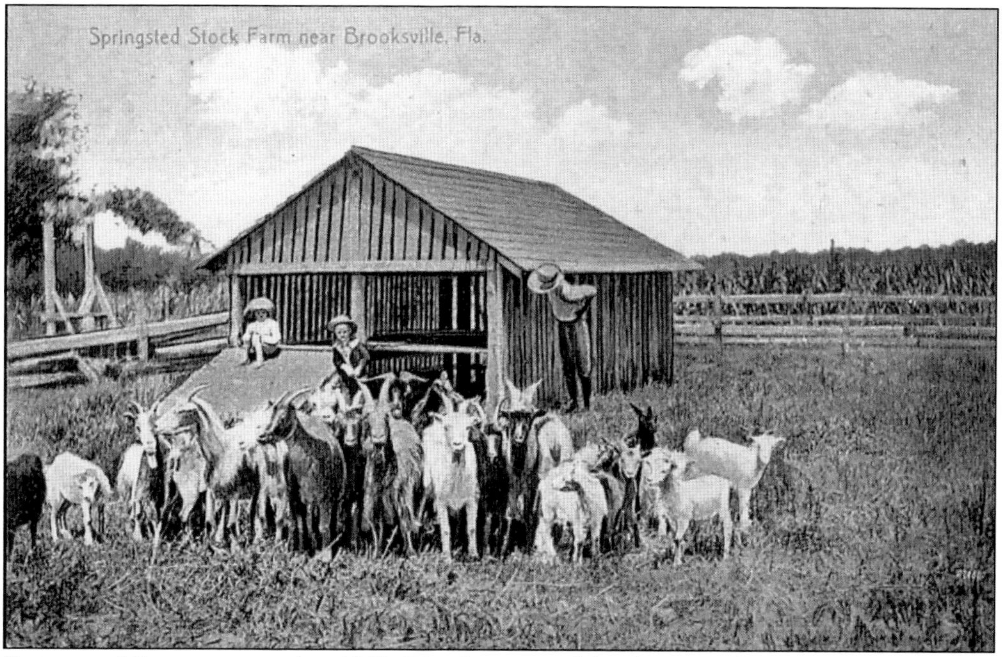

Springstead Farm is pictured in 1909. The Springstead family originally came from Wisconsin during the 1880s and were successful dairy farmers and merchants.

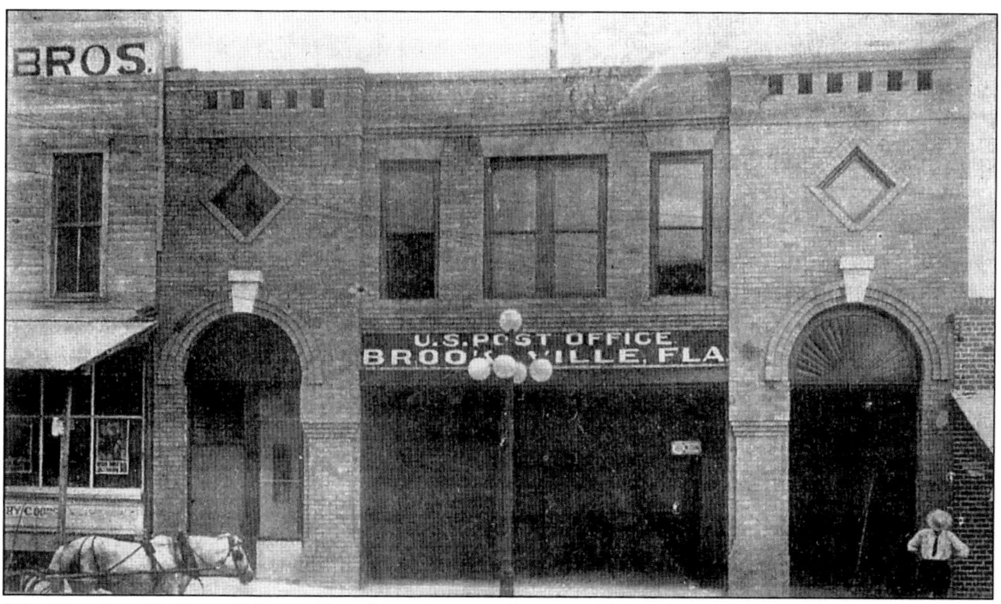

The Brooksville Post Office offered a unique architectural style in 1914. At the time, the post office was on South Main Street between Broad and Liberty Streets.

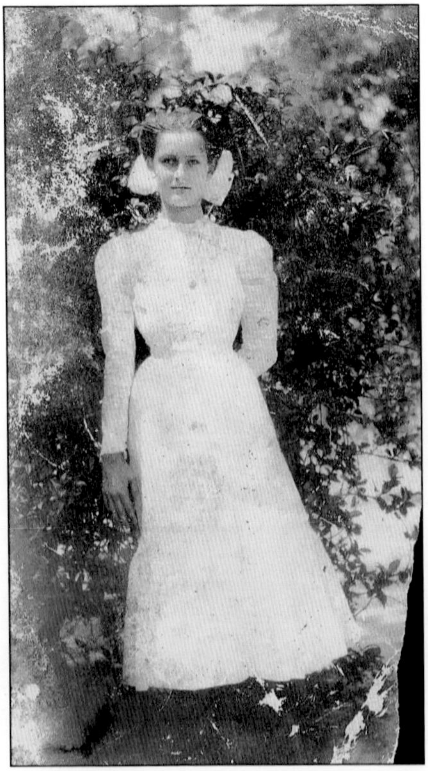

This 1910 photograph shows Labelle Bean, a beauty from Lake Lindsey.

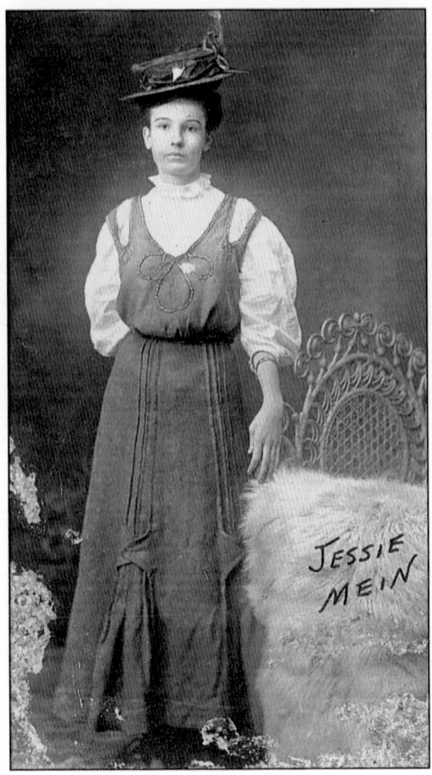

Jessie Mein, from north of Brooksville near the Chinsegut Hill area, is seen in 1907. The Mein family were one of the earliest settlers to the area, with roots going back to the 1850s.

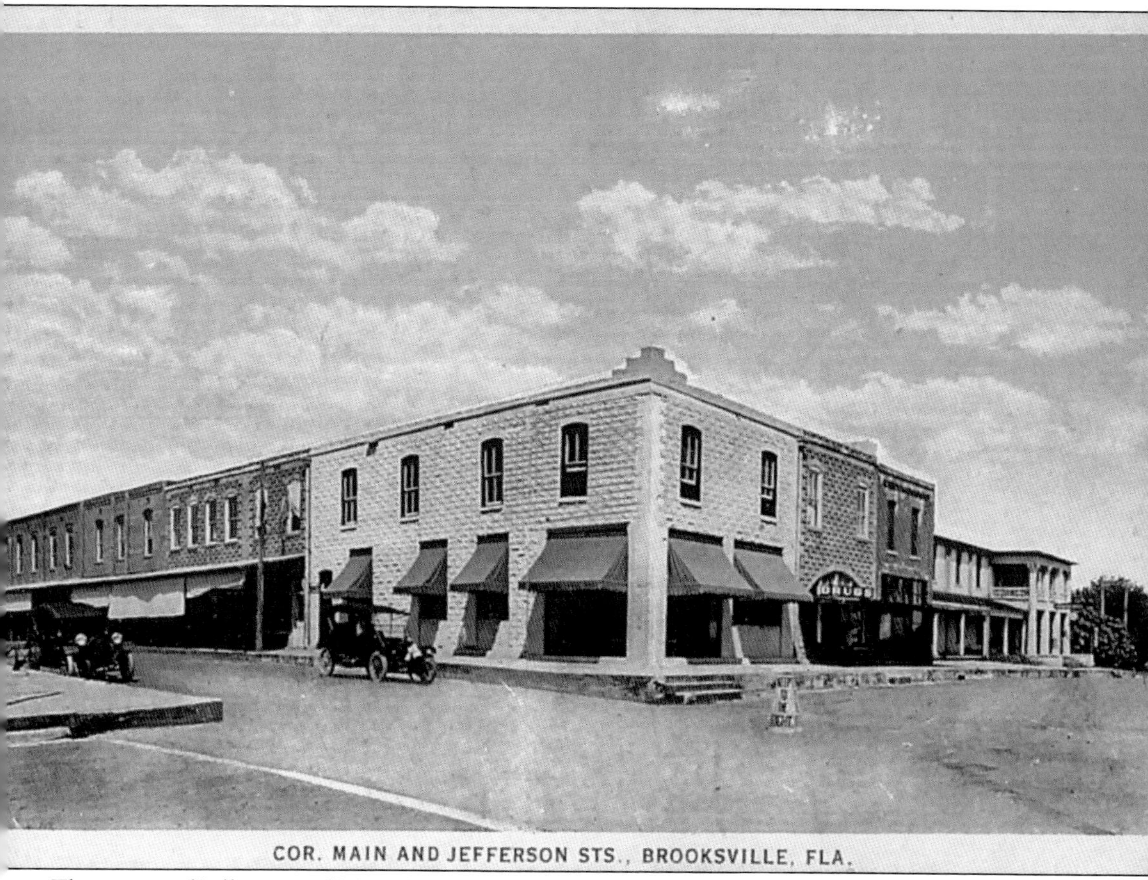

The corner of Jefferson and Main Streets is seen in 1913. The building in the center is Hernando State Bank, which began in 1905. To the right is Coogler's Drug Store, originally started in the 1880s, and to the far right is the grand Varnada Hotel, which burned down in 1918. Streets were paved when the new courthouse was built in 1913. The automobile was becoming more and more common. Note the cone in the street reading "Keep To The Right."

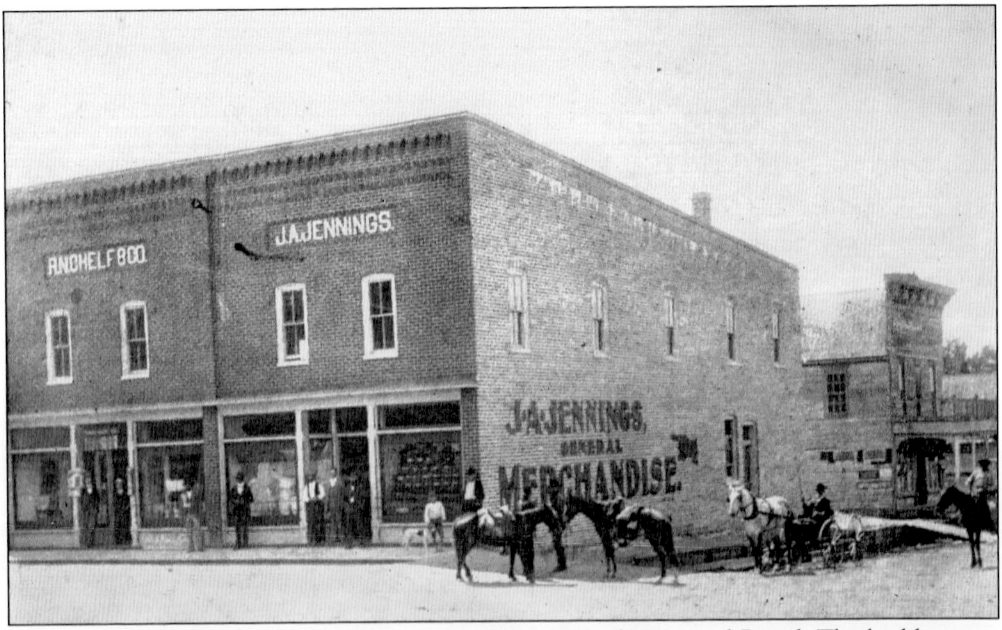

The Jennings Building, seen in 1905, was at the corner of Main and Broad. The building was originally owned by James Jennings around 1900. Jennings, an astute Brooksville businessman who served as sheriff from 1885 to 1888, was also first president of Hernando State Bank in 1905. The entire Jennings Building and block burned down in a large downtown fire in 1914, but it was rebuilt by the following year. The building still stands with the date 1915 on it.

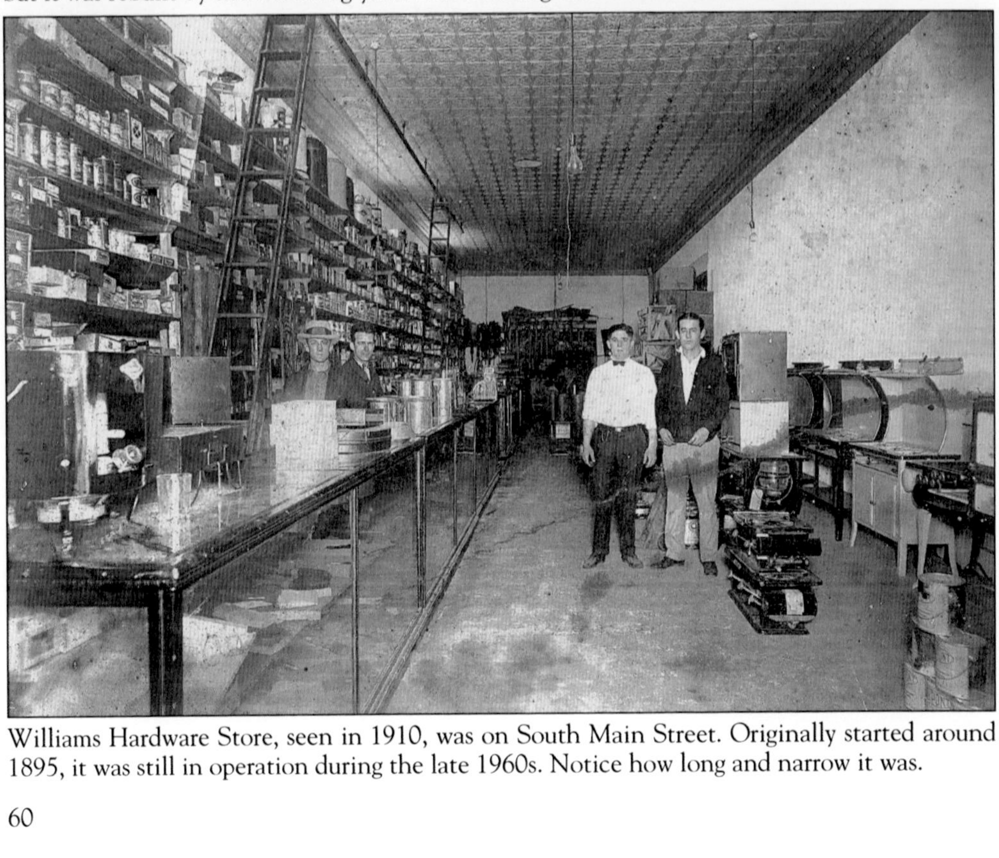
Williams Hardware Store, seen in 1910, was on South Main Street. Originally started around 1895, it was still in operation during the late 1960s. Notice how long and narrow it was.

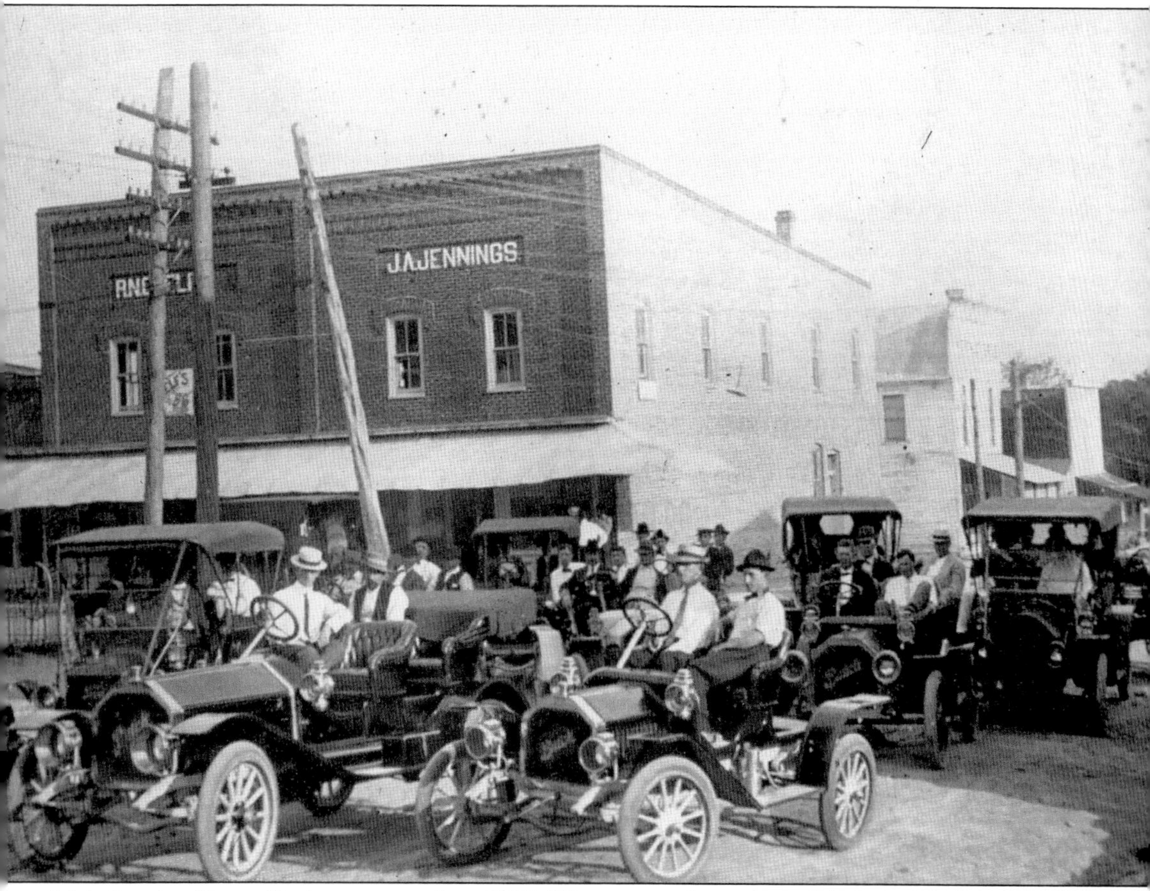

This Brooksville traffic jam occurred in 1913. This was perhaps the celebration of the brand new courthouse in 1913; for this many cars to be seen on the newly paved streets during this period had to be a very special event. There was also an early auto race held about that time through the streets of Brooksville.

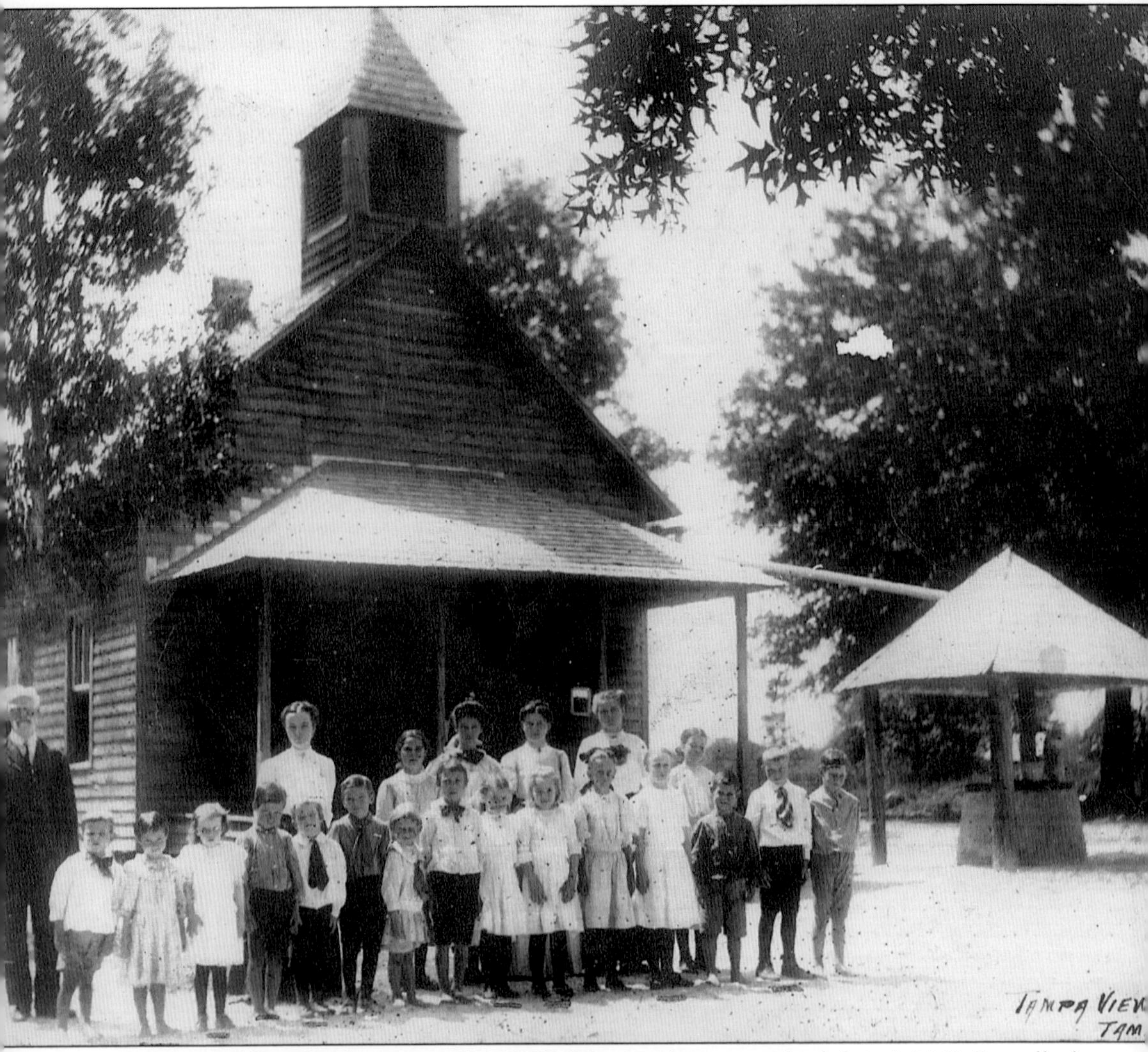

This Brooksville school is pictured in 1907. The gentleman on the left is A.M.C. Russell, the superintendent of schools and one of the earliest newspaper publishers.

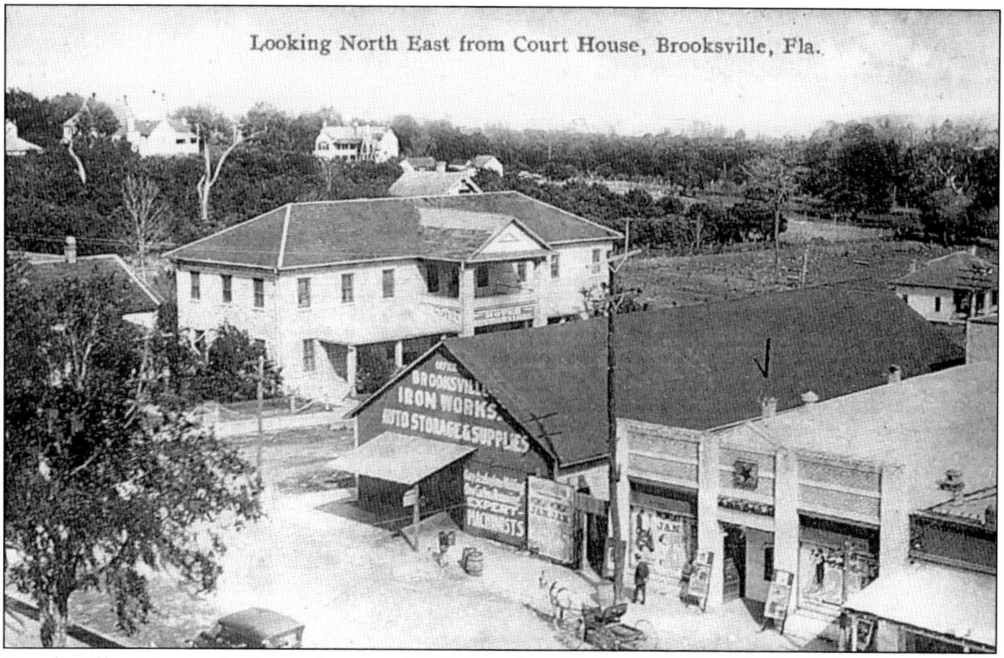

Brooksville Avenue is shown here in 1915. Brooksville Iron Works stands where the Varnada Garage used to be. On the right is one of Brooksville's earliest movie theatres, the Star; note the star on the building and the ad posters. The big building behind the garage is the Brooksville Hotel, which burned down around 1923.

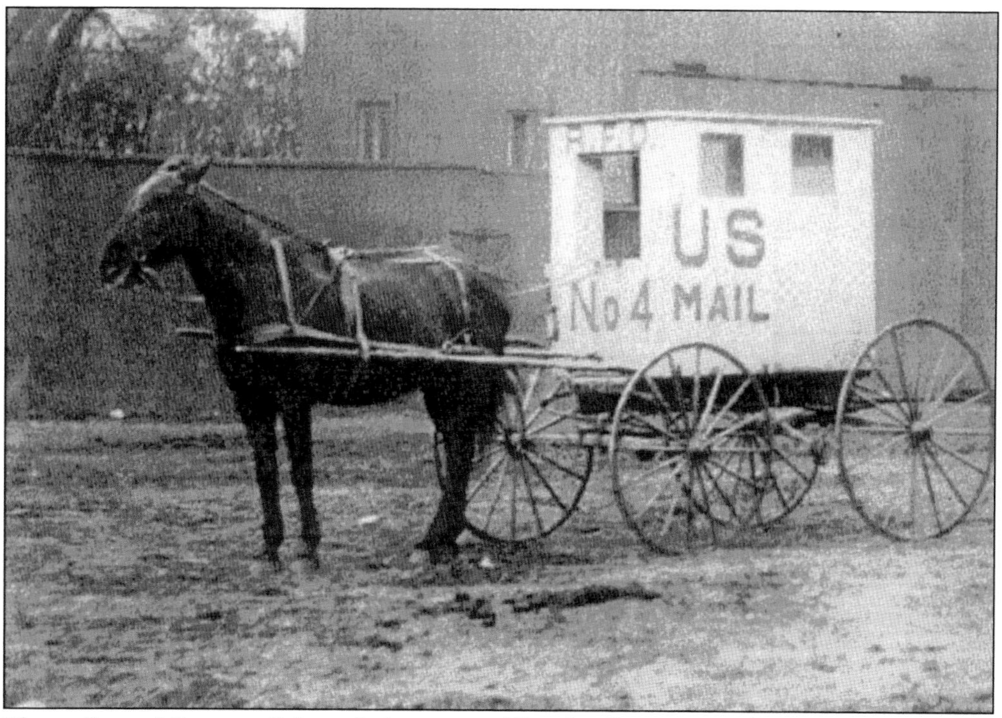

The mailman delivers mail through the streets of Brooksville in 1900. This is along Main Street near the old post office. Notice that Main Street back then was a dirt road.

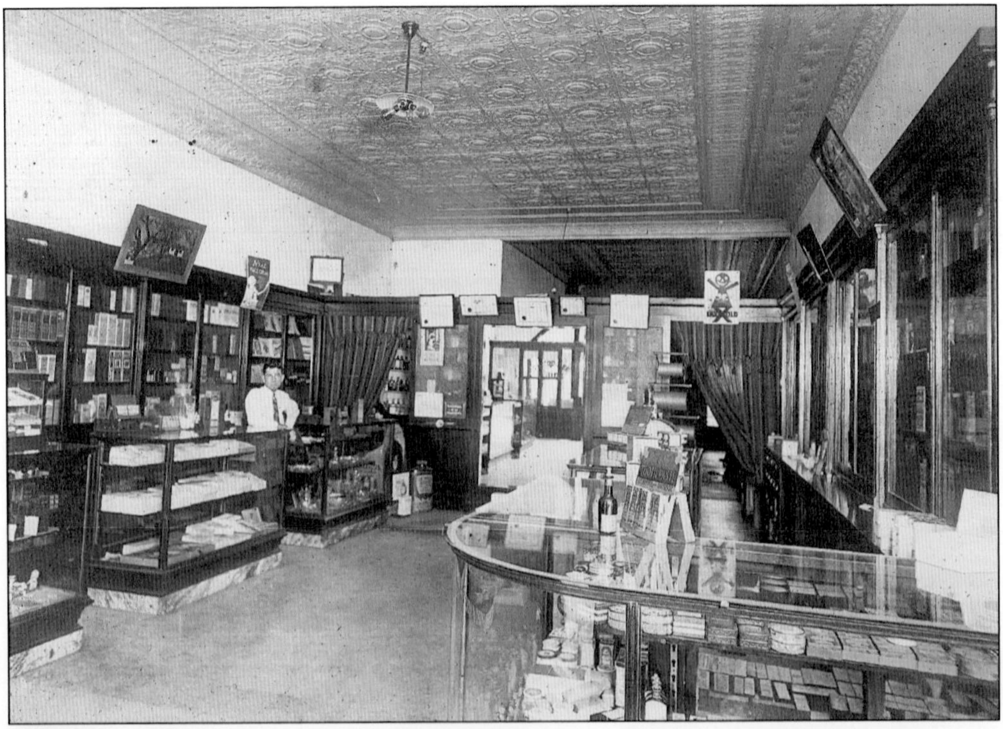

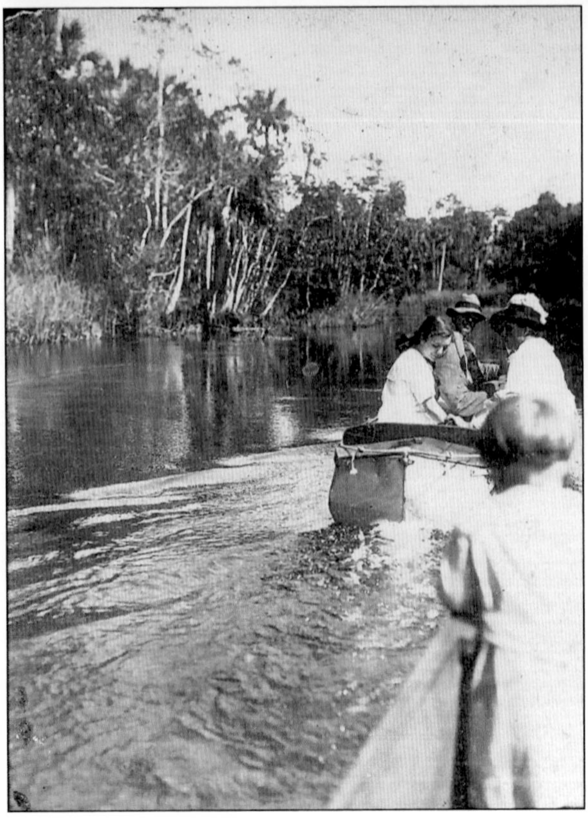

This photograph looks inside Coogler's Drug Store in 1917. Vi Coogler originally opened its doors around 1885 and was just next door to the Hernando State Bank on Jefferson Street.

These locals are cruising up the Weeki Wachee River in 1910. Before it was a mermaid attraction, Weeki Wachee was a popular destination for locals enjoying boating and fishing.

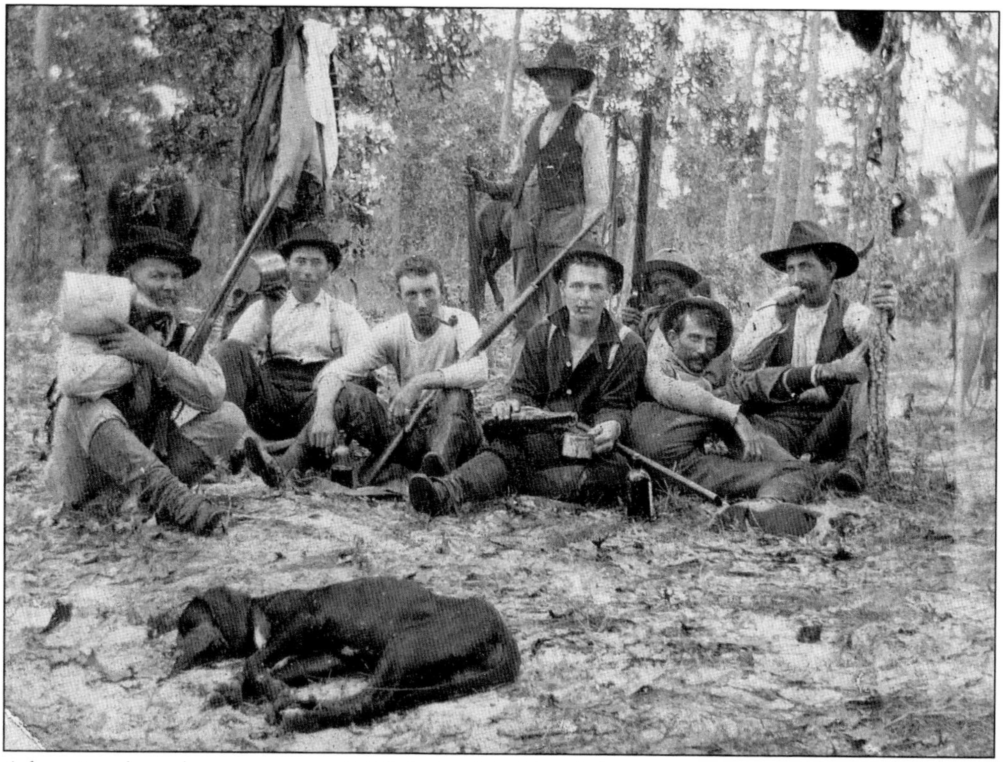

A hunting dog takes a catnap in 1913 during Mr. Hope's hunting trip west of Brooksville as the others pass a jug around.

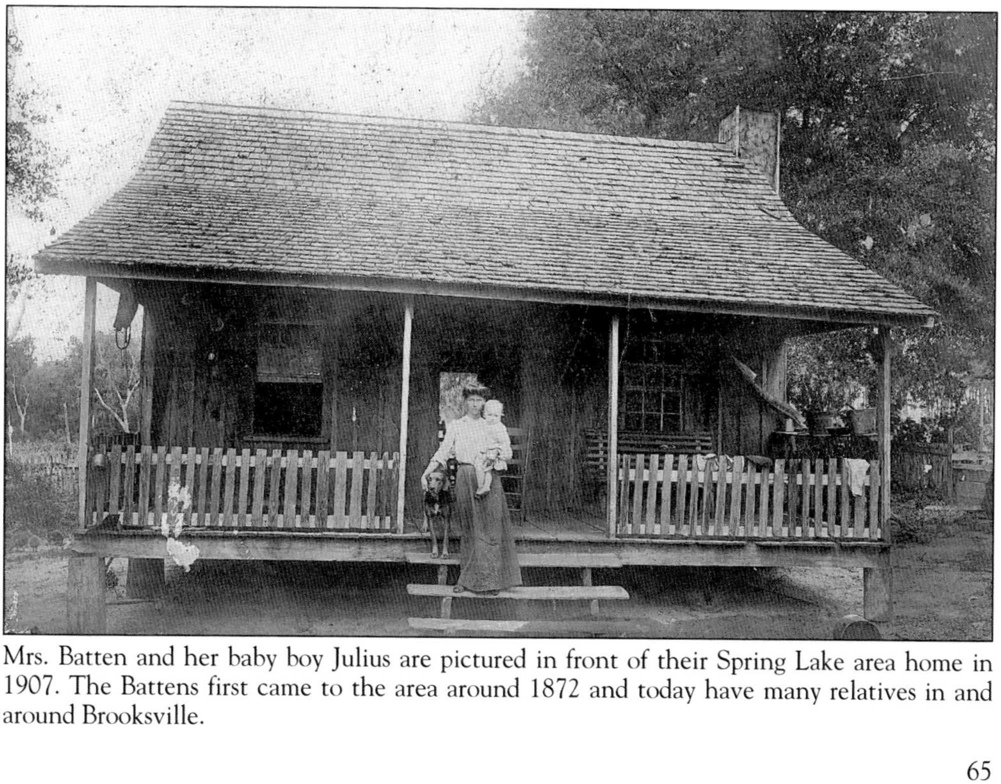

Mrs. Batten and her baby boy Julius are pictured in front of their Spring Lake area home in 1907. The Battens first came to the area around 1872 and today have many relatives in and around Brooksville.

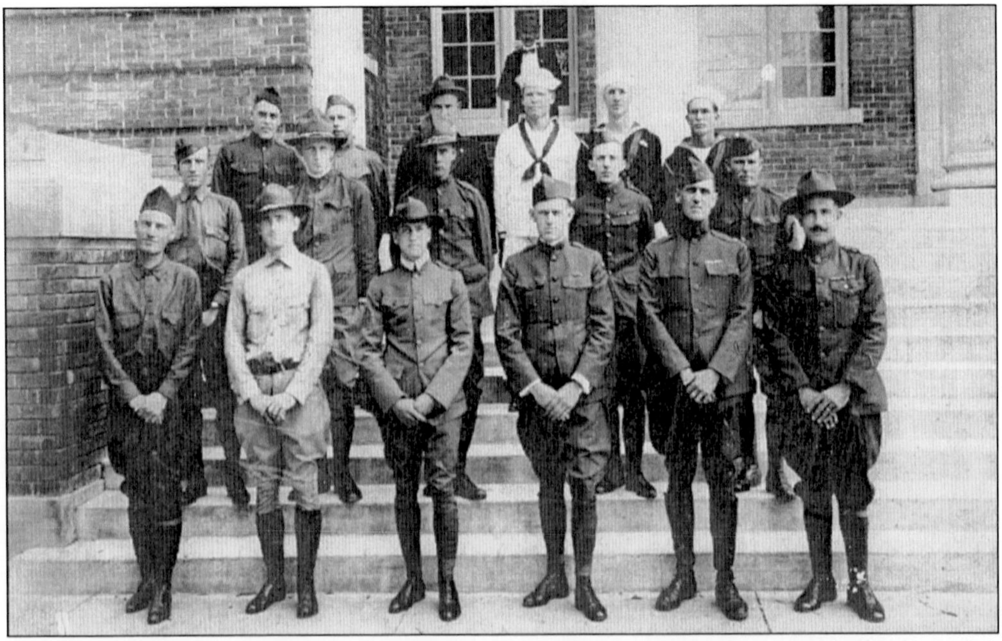

Here is Armistice Day in 1919. World War I veterans pose in front of the court house. From left to right are (front row) Clarence Russell, Charles Gallaway, C. James Law, J.C. Rogers, Capt. Jay Hennig, and George T. Maillis; (middle row) Allan Hawkins, Rainey Martin, Jesse Allen, Ross Clark, and Manning Hayman; (back row) Charlie Sims, Victor Lawrence, Dennis Cason, Bryant Graham, Claude Brown, and Milton Lee.

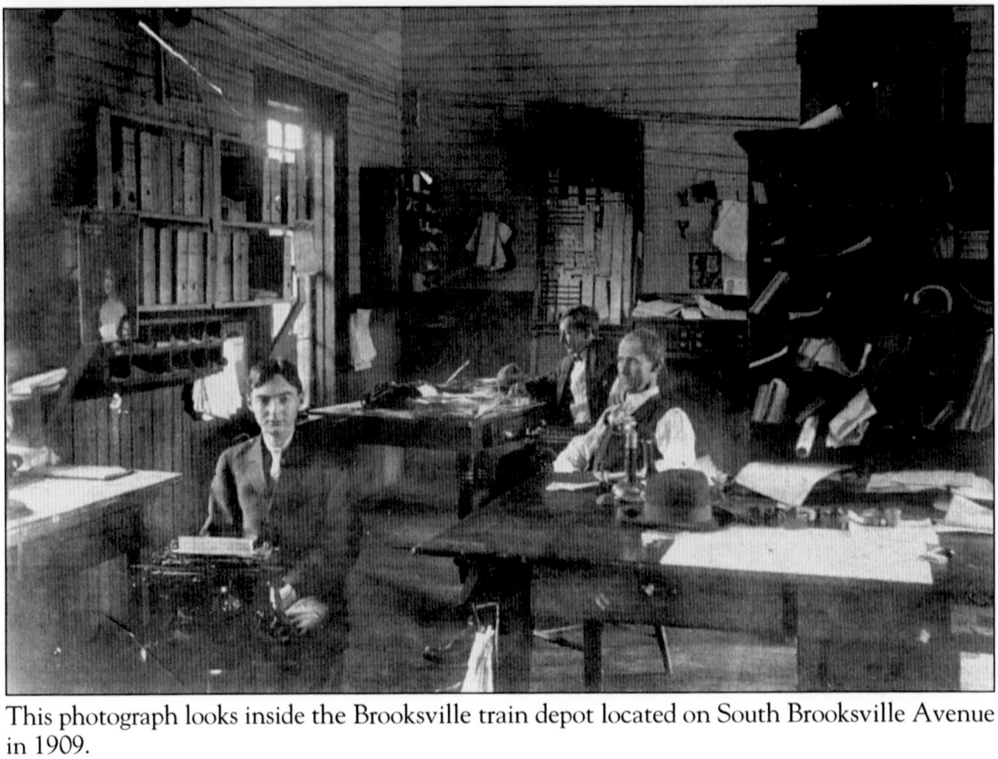

This photograph looks inside the Brooksville train depot located on South Brooksville Avenue in 1909.

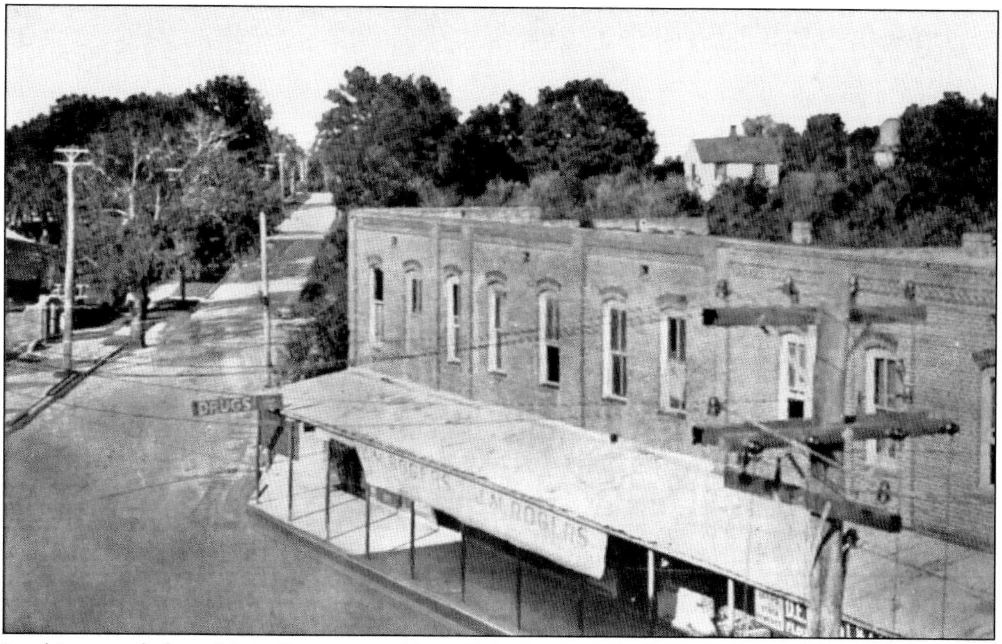

Looking north from Main Street onto Howell Avenue in 1915, one can notice how smooth the streets are by now. On the corner is Thompson's Drug Store, which later evolves into Hope's Drug Store in the 1920s when Mr. Thompson's daughter Margie marries Walter Hope. It stayed in operation until 1963.

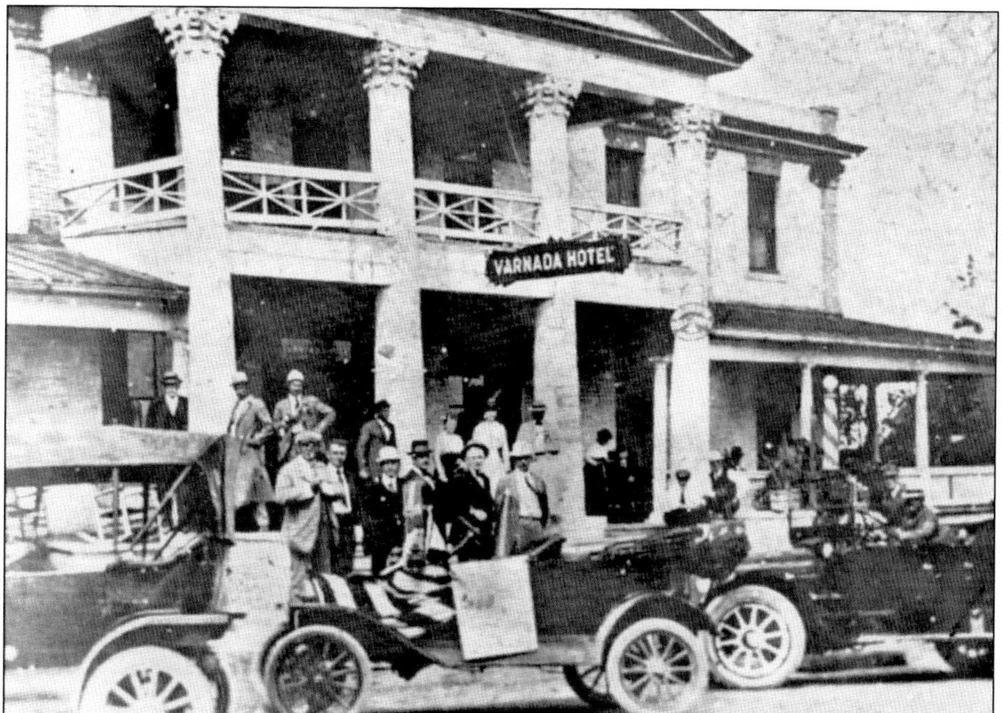

Locals celebrate a Brooksville auto race about 1915 in front of the Varnada Hotel on Jefferson Street.

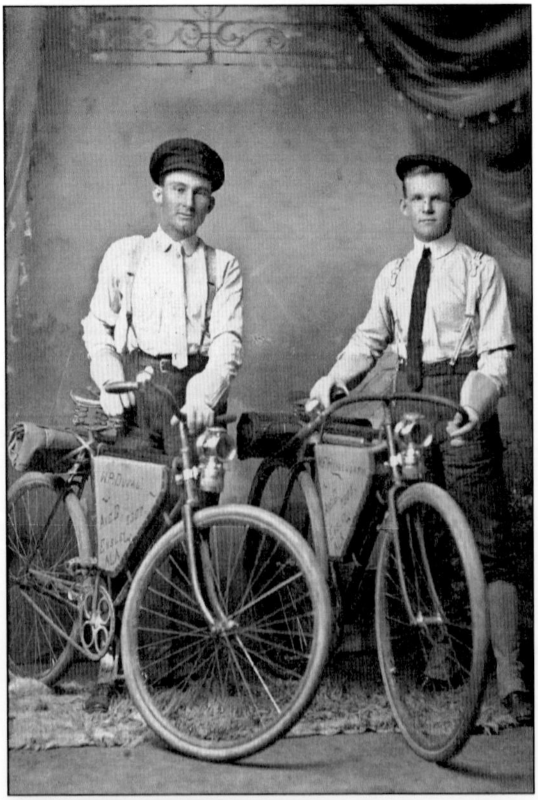

The great bicycle trip of 1903 is pictured here. W.P. Duval and Francis Haynsworth Duval rode from Brooksville to Endsley, Alabama, by bicycle.

A 1908 family reunion is seen in front of the old courthouse. The wooden structure was originally built in 1877, and to this date this is the best photo of the courthouse ever found. A new courthouse was built at the same locale in 1913.

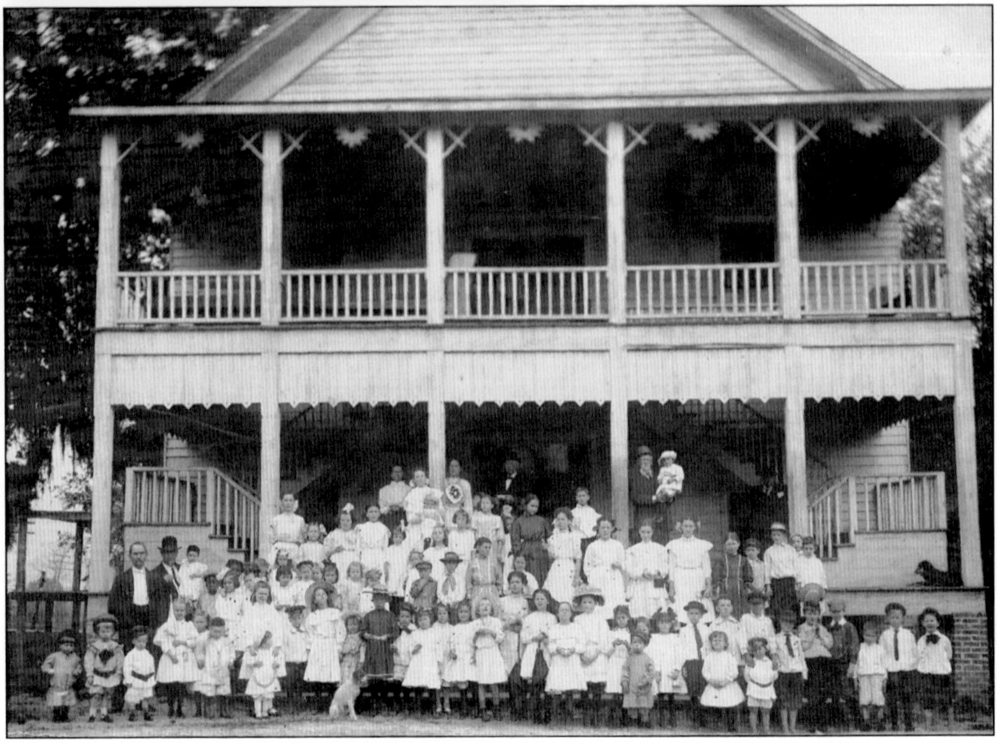

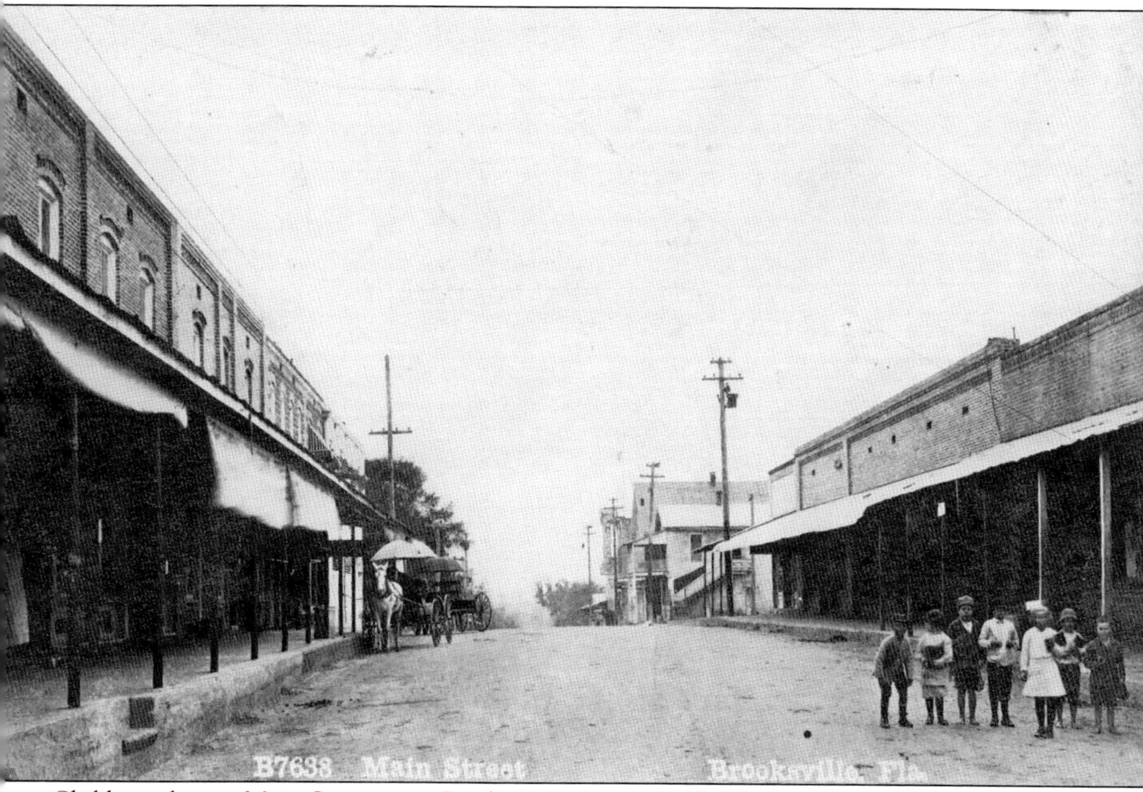

Children play on Main Street on a Sunday morning in 1909. There was very little traffic to worry about.

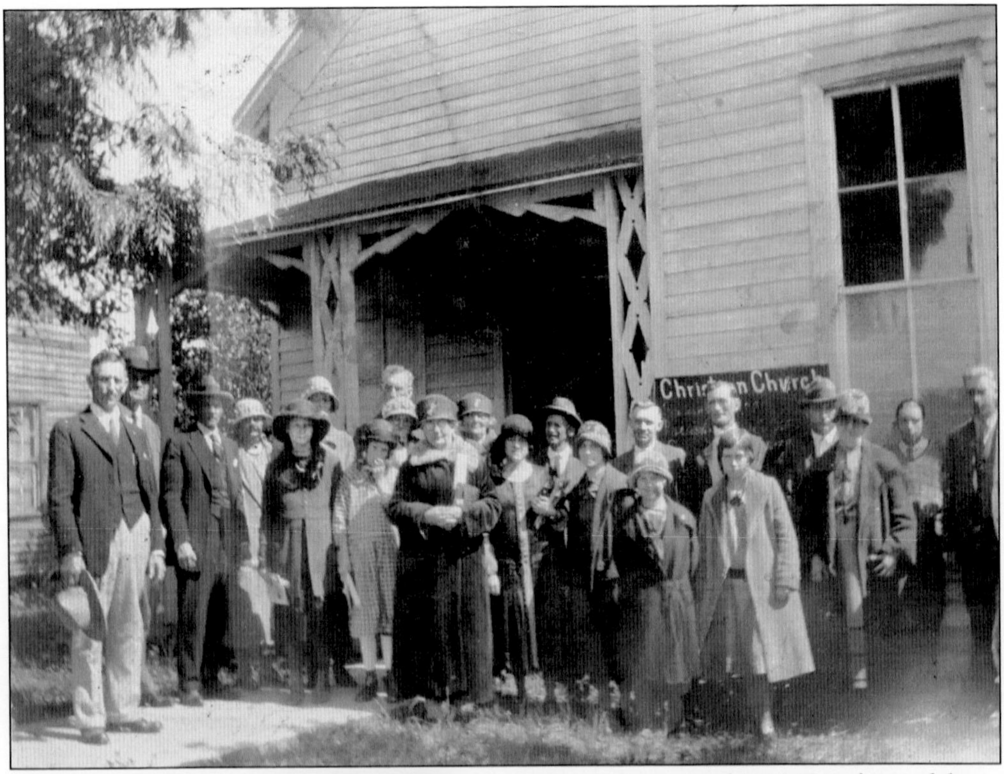

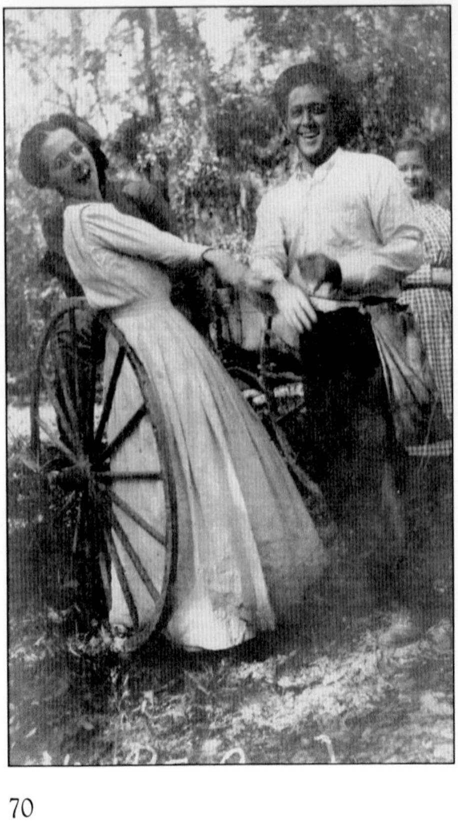

A gathering is pictured in 1910 in front of the First Christian Church at the corner of Liberty Street and Brooksville Avenue where Johnston Law Office is today.

Posturing in the park just north of Brooksville in the Lake Lindsey area in 1910 are Rosalie Bird, David Hedick, and Cora McKeown.

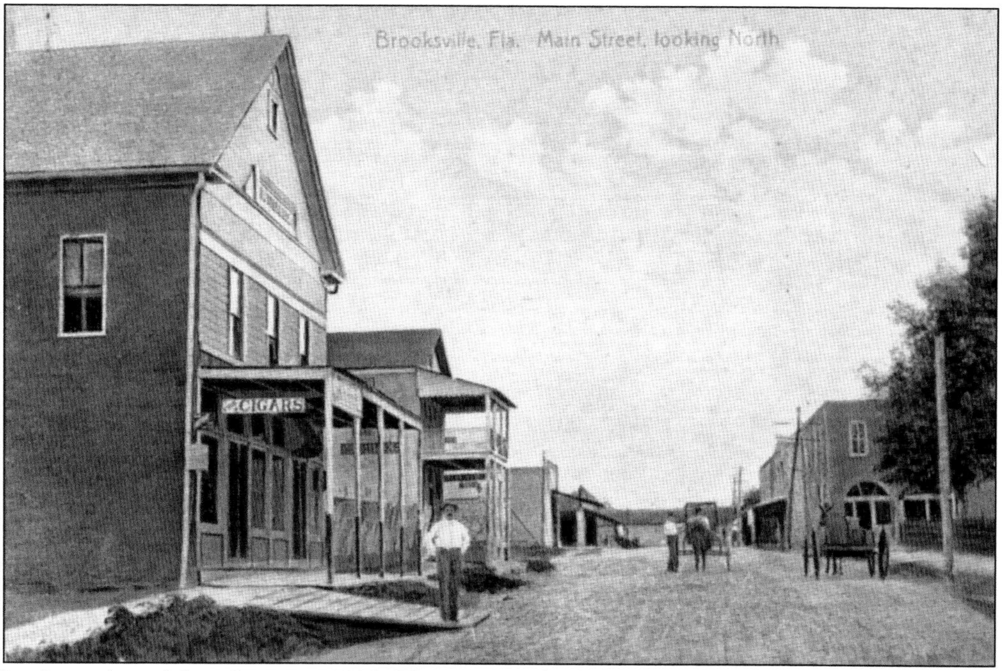

Look north on Main Street in 1905. The man on the left is directly across the street from the old courthouse. The newly completed bank is to the right.

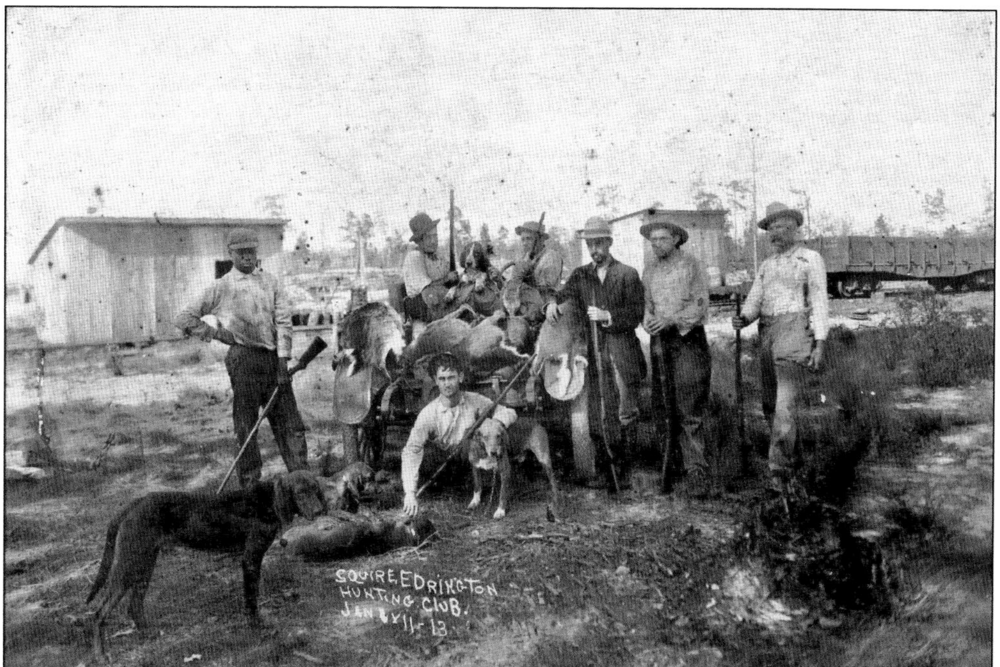

Squire Edrington's Hunting Club, in January 1913, is just north of Brooksville. Squire Edrington was Francis Edrington Jr., whose family first settled on Chinsegut Hill north of Brooksville around 1850. The term "squire" was used facetiously and is an old English title for a country gentleman.

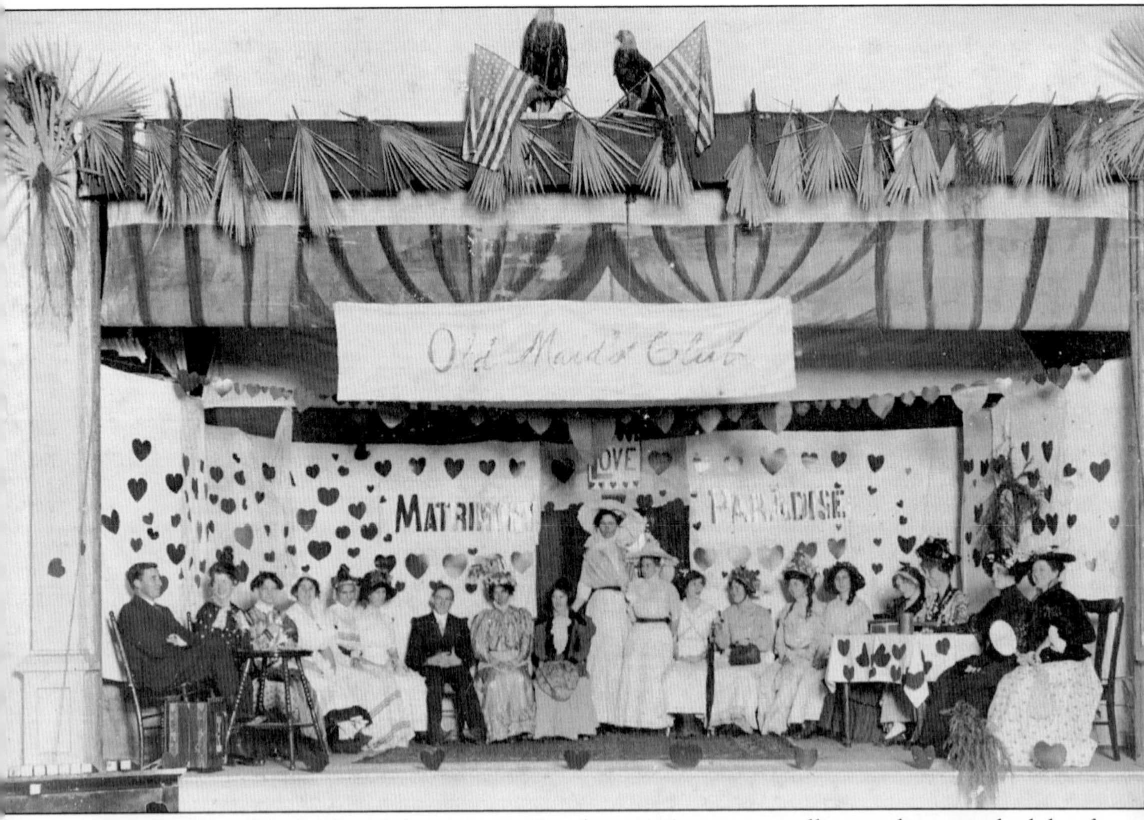

Brooksville Old Maid's Club, seen in October 1913, was actually an elite social club of Brooksville's most eligibles. Pictured are, from left to right, Neil Law, Eunice Cox, Vera Thompson, Cristian Cook, Madora Lowery, Effie Dick, Archie McGeechy, Mildred Martin, Nell Coogler, Leila O'Neel, Mrs. Robert Ellis, Emma Hampton, Ruth Burritt, Mrs. Theo. S. Coogler Jr., Nell Martin, Bernice Billingsley, Helen Martin, Miss Coogler, and Margaret Fulton.

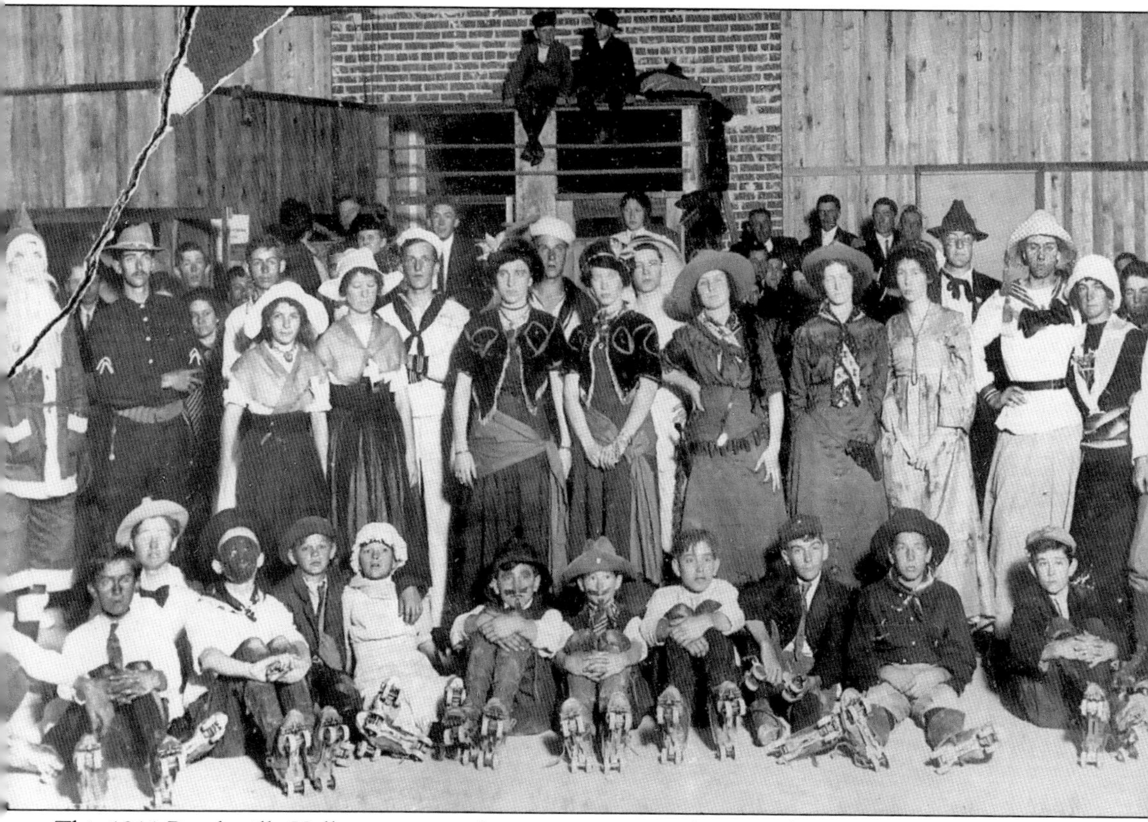

This 1911 Brooksville Halloween party shows some creative homemade costumes.

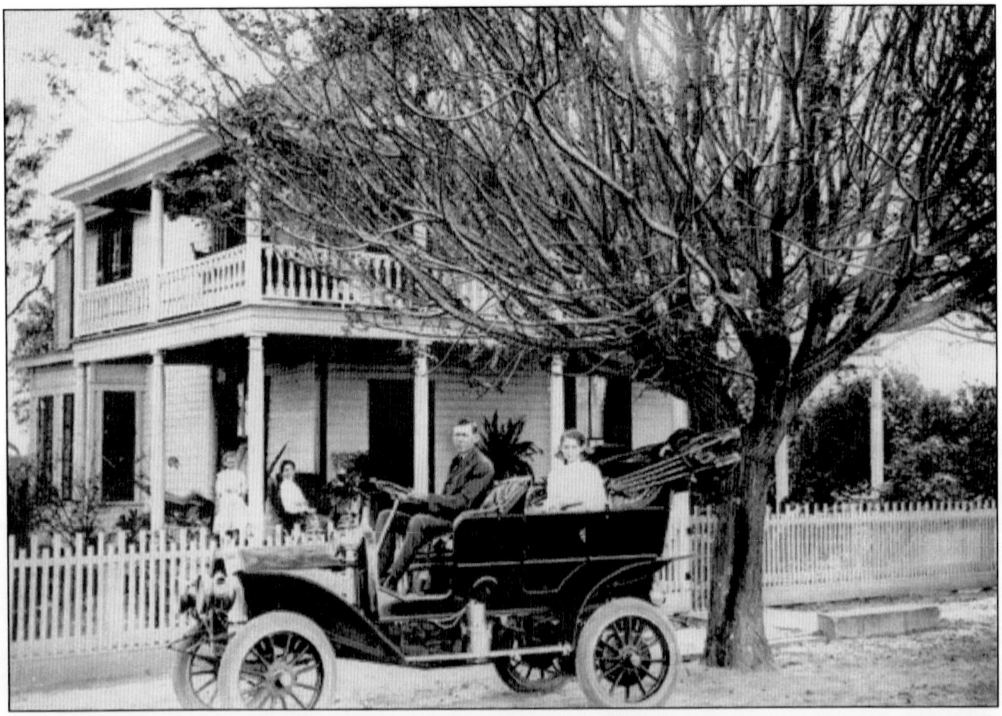

One of Brooksville's first automobiles was this brand new 1908 Buick purchased by John Burwell, pictured here with family members in front of their Olive Street home.

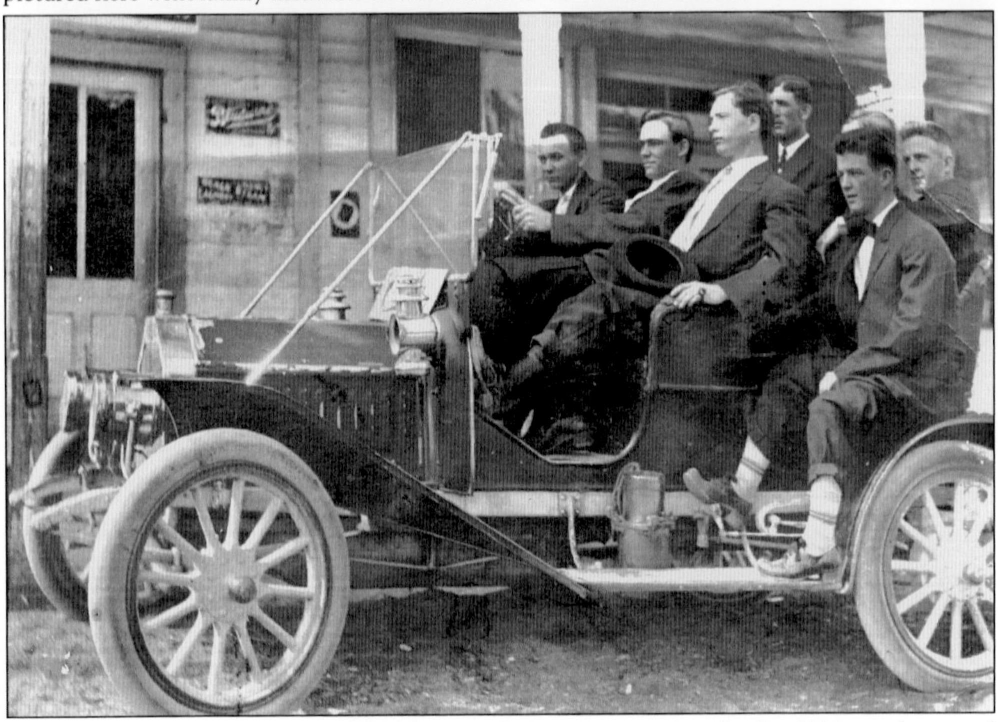

Young men are pictured out on the town in 1914 in a nice new ride. By 1914, roads around Brooksville were beginning to be paved, thanks to $25,000 worth of bonds sold by the county.

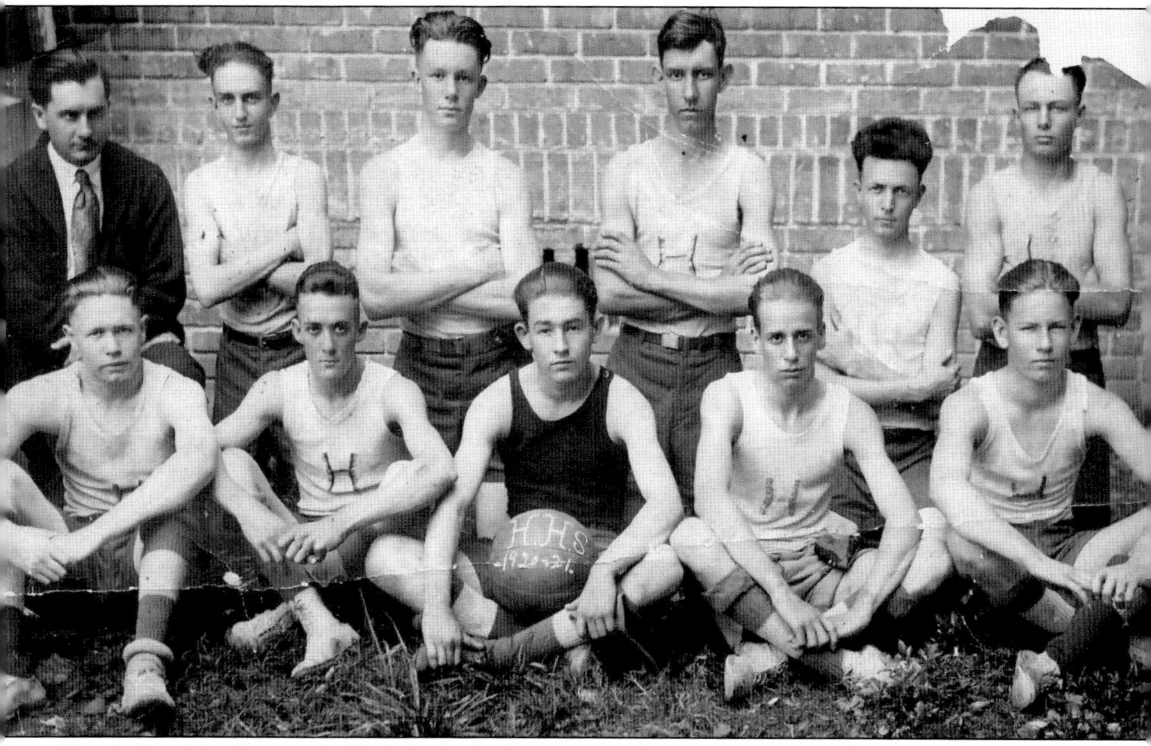

The 1920–1921 Hernando High basketball team was, from left to right, (front row) Marshal Arick, John Law Ayers, Mounger Russell, Mark Edwards, and Miles Russell; (back row) Coach R.A., Lex Green, Gordon Petteway, Lindsey Dawson, Mac Nunn, and Tom Arick.

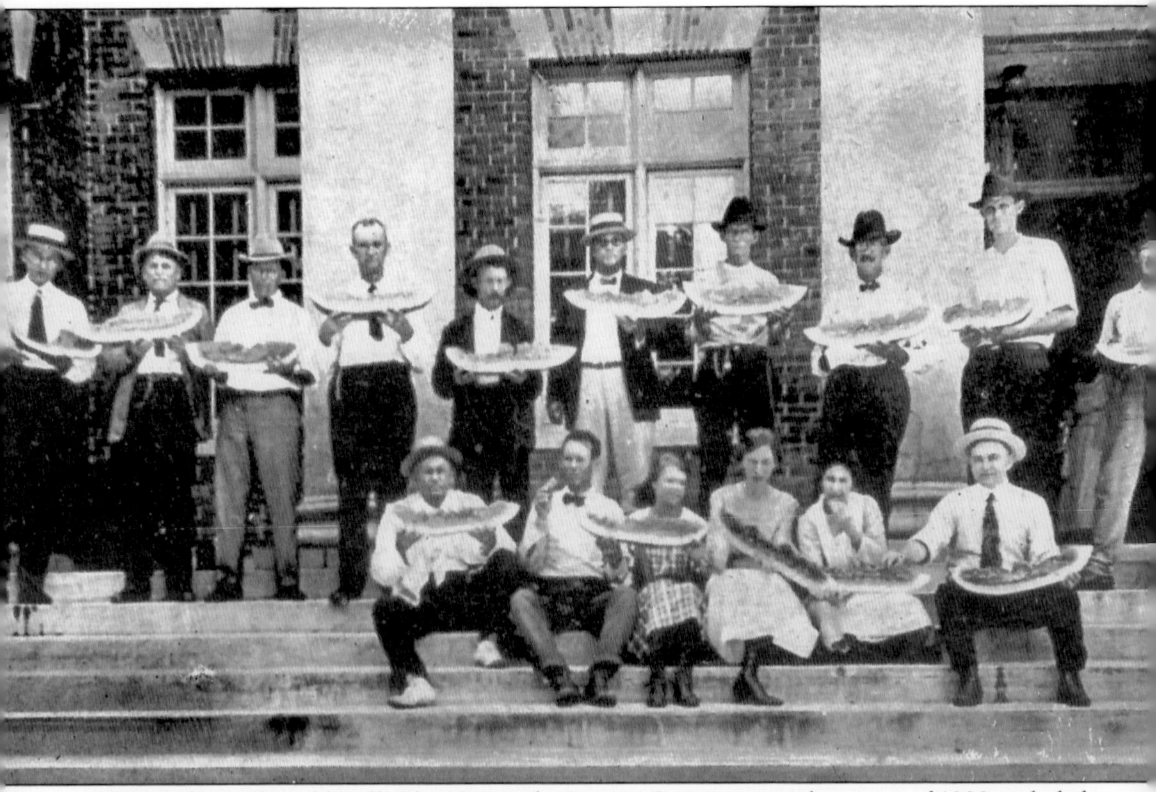

One melon is shared by all. The Hernando County Court watermelon party of 1920 included, from left to right, (front row) J.V. Ramsey, county judge; L.D. Hathaway, secretary of schools superintendent; Lorena Grimsley and Linda Jennings, deputy clerks; and C.C. Kirk, tax collector; (back row) H.C. Mickler, clerk of court; W.P. Tucker, W.E. Barnette, and R.T. Hancock, county commissioners; F.E. Saxon, county tax assessor; W.D. Cobb, sheriff; J.W. Crum, deputy sheriff; and ? Robins, janitor.

Three

1920–1945

Many historians claim that the 20th century really began around 1920. With World War I over, most young Americans sensed a new feeling of adventure and new liberation in literature, music, culture, sports, and style. This period kicks off the Roaring Twenties, a colorful era of jazz, bootleg whisky, tin lizzies, flappers, radio, and movies that talked. Best personified by the works of F. Scott Fitzgerald and the boisterous swagger of Babe Ruth, it would come crashing down in 1929 to be followed by the Great Depression and then World War II. It was only a 25-year period, but it was a roller-coaster ride of emotions that may never be equalled. Brooksville was just another small-town example of the giddy euphoria,the disappointments, the fears, the tragedies, and the triumphs most Americans encountered during that time.

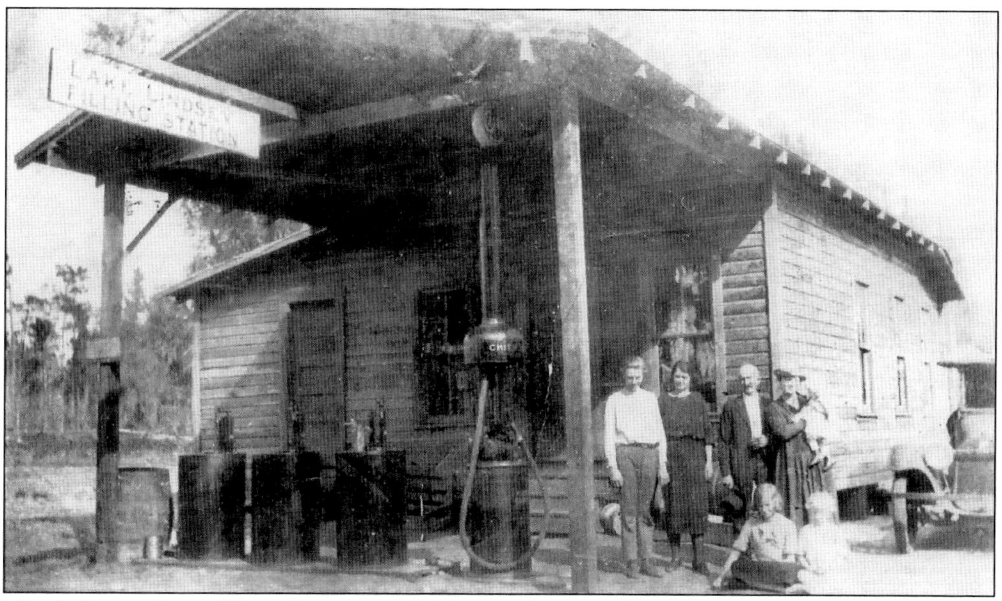

The Lake Lindsey Filling Station in 1923 provides us with a view of how most gas stations looked in that era.

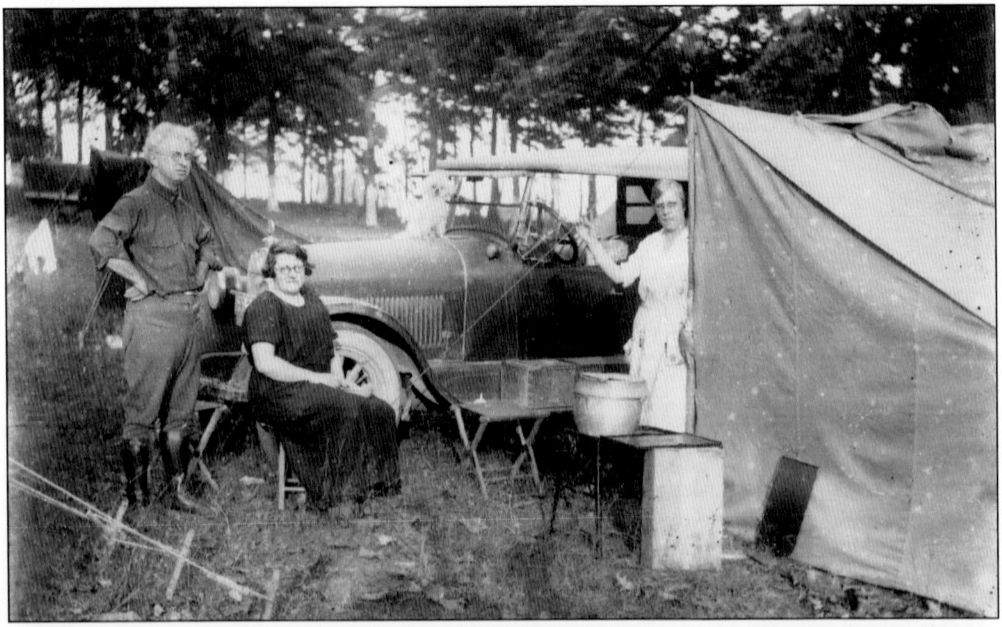

Tin-can tourists in 1929 north of Brooksville stayed at the Shady Rest Tourist Resort. During the 1920s, tourism really took off thanks to a renewed optimism and the automobile. As one writer put it, "these tourists . . . they ride in tin cans, eat out of tin cans, and leave a trail of tin cans behind . . . these tin can tourists."

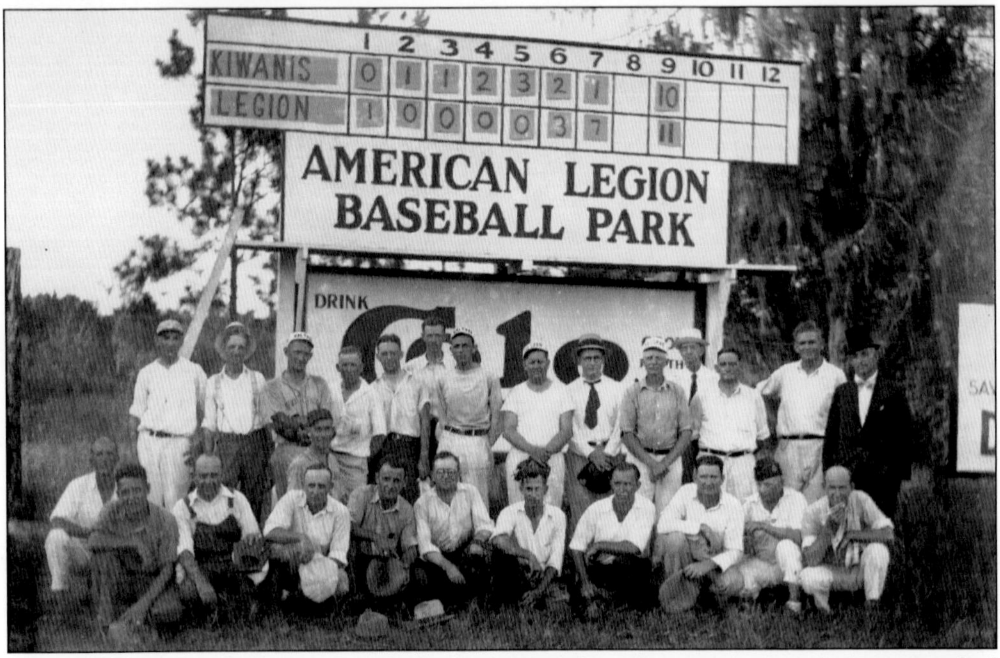

This Brooksville baseball team took the field in 1929. The only experience most Americans had with baseball, unless you lived in a big city, was their hometown team. Before most folks had radio and way before television, this was the only game in town. The fan support in many towns was just as rabid as in big cities, and the rivalries against neighboring towns was even more intense. During the early 1930s, a local game against a Tampa team drew 2,000 spectators.

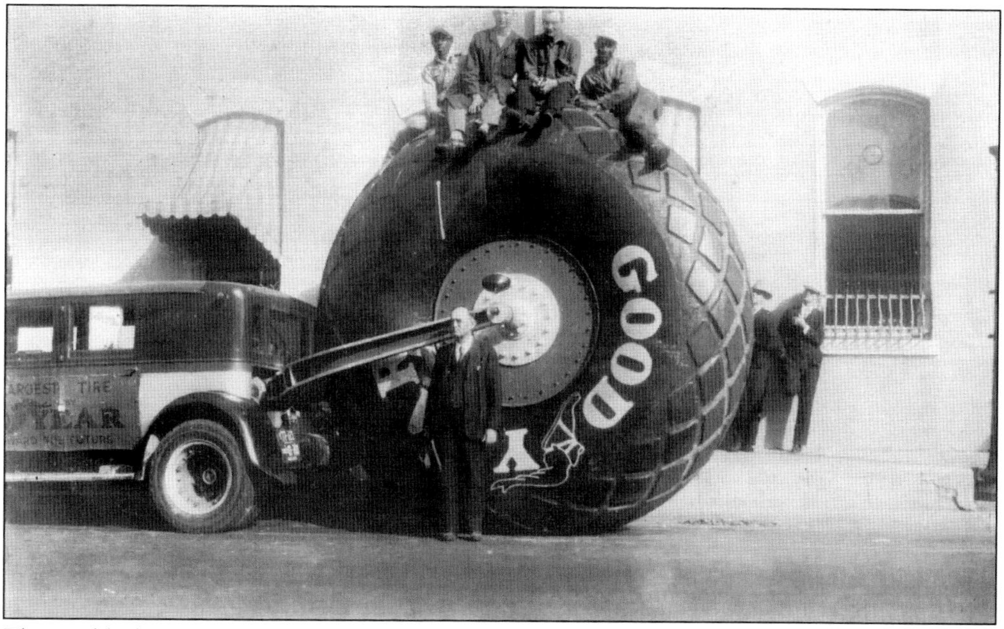

The world's largest tire, seen in 1929, made its appearance as a promotional stunt for Simpson Chevrolet, located at the corners of Broad and Main Streets.

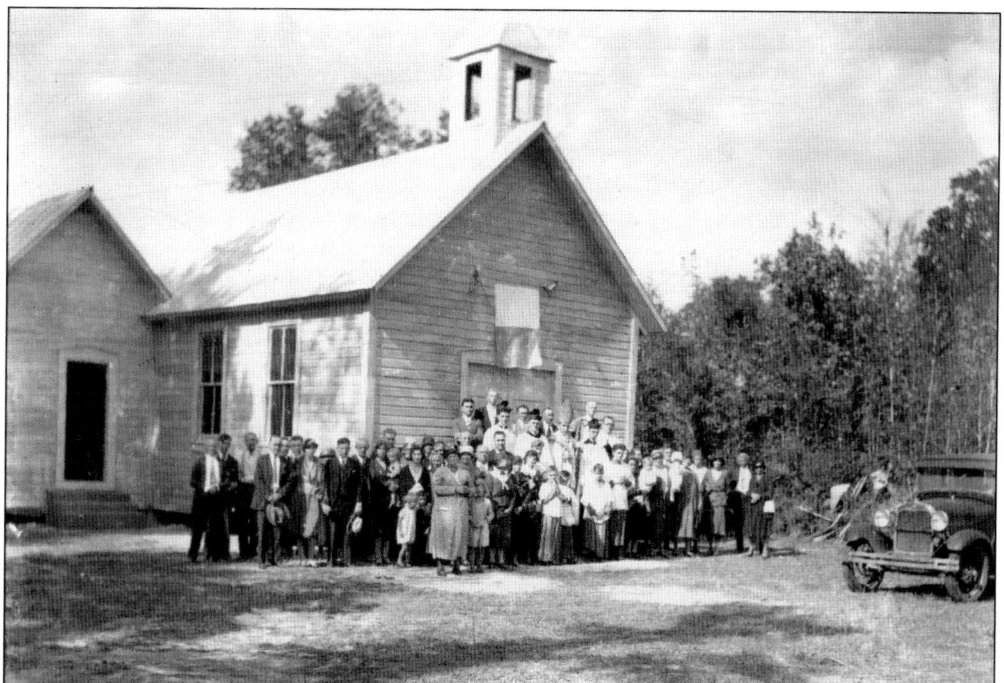

St. Stanislaus Catholic Church was located north of Brooksville in 1926. This must have been a very special day, since it appears a cardinal is present.

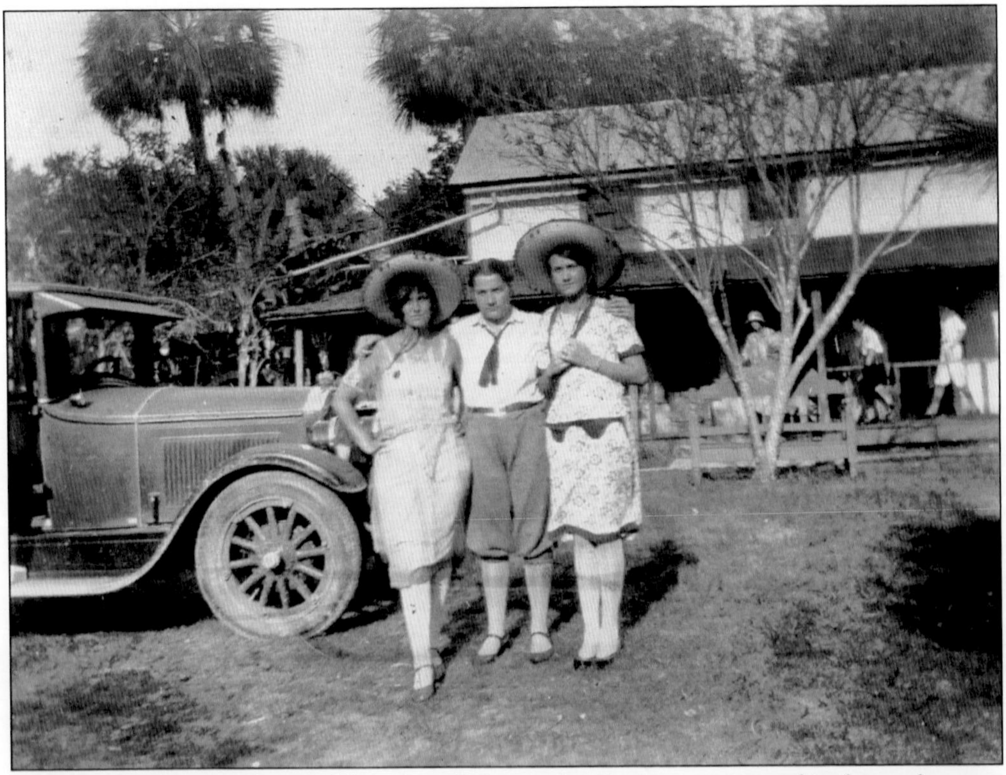

Ruth Hancock, an unidentified friend, and Verona Creekmore are pictured in front of a camp in 1926 during some good times.

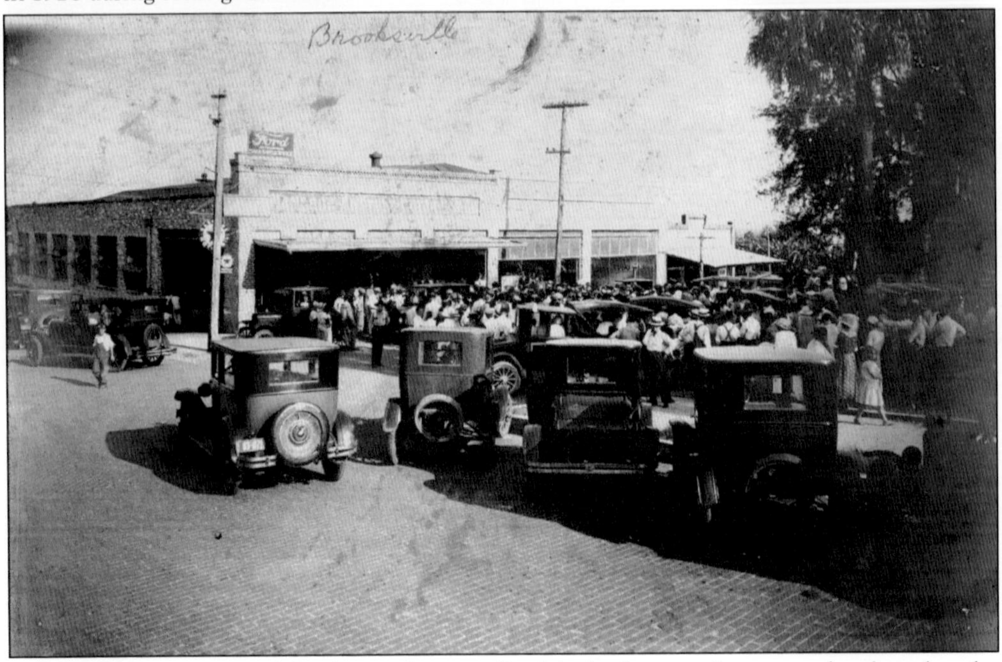

Hancock/Amstutz opened the doors of its new Ford dealership to a large crowd gathered at the corner of Brooksville Avenue and Jefferson Street in 1925.

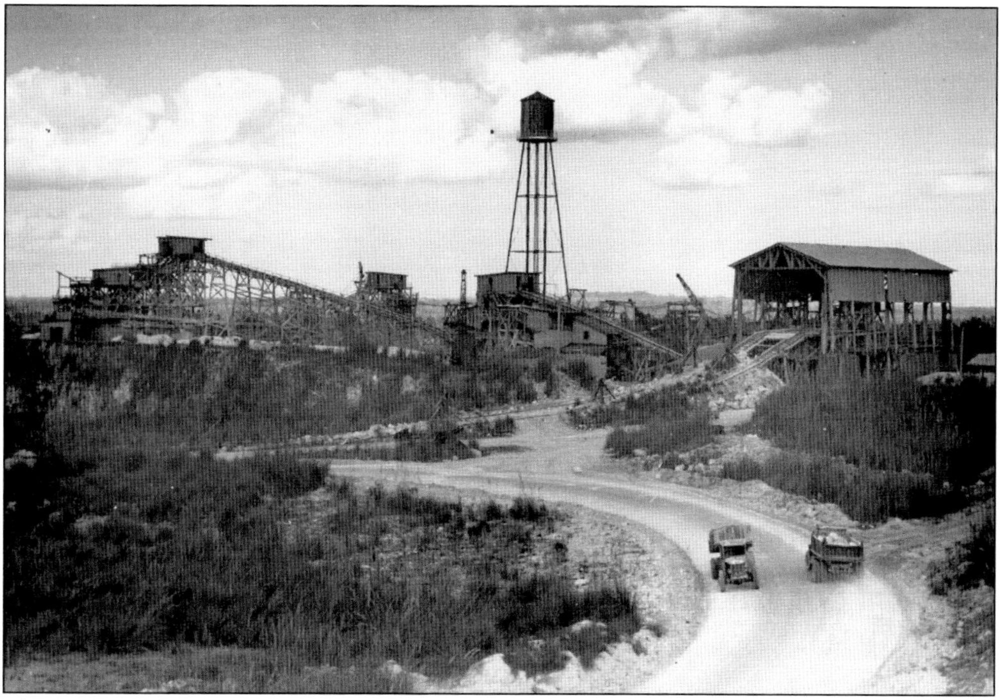

The McDonald Mine is seen here in 1929. During the 1920s, rock mining began to take off as a major industry in Hernando County; now it is huge. This mine, located on Mondon Hill Road about two miles east of Brooksville, closed down in the 1960s.

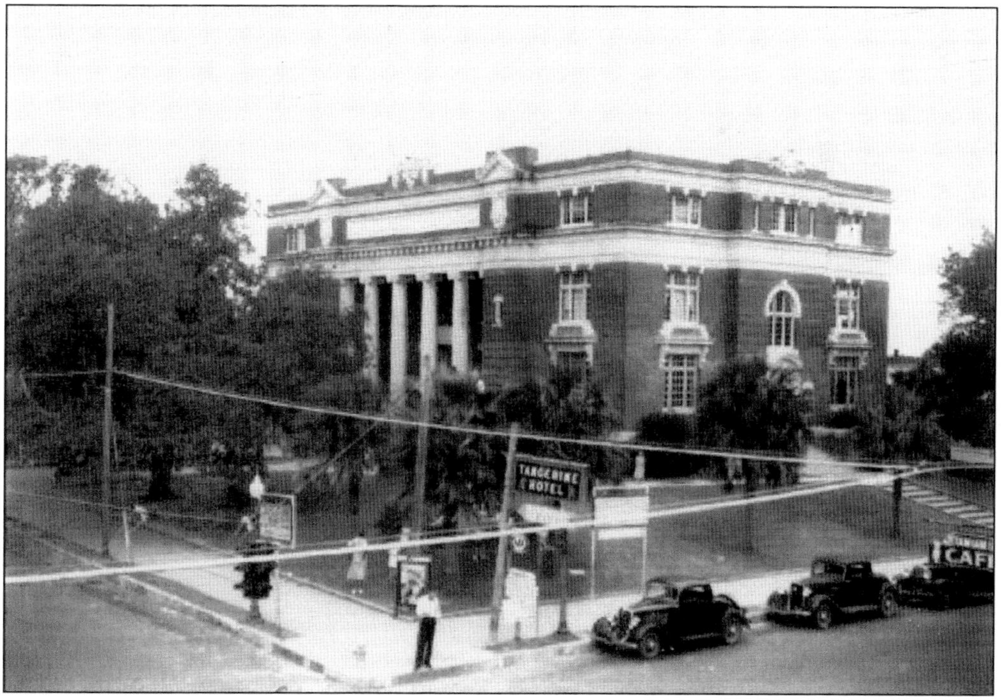

Shown here is Courthouse Square in 1938. This is the corner of Broad Street (U.S. 41) and Main Street. The Tangerine Hotel sign directs tourists to its location a few blocks away.

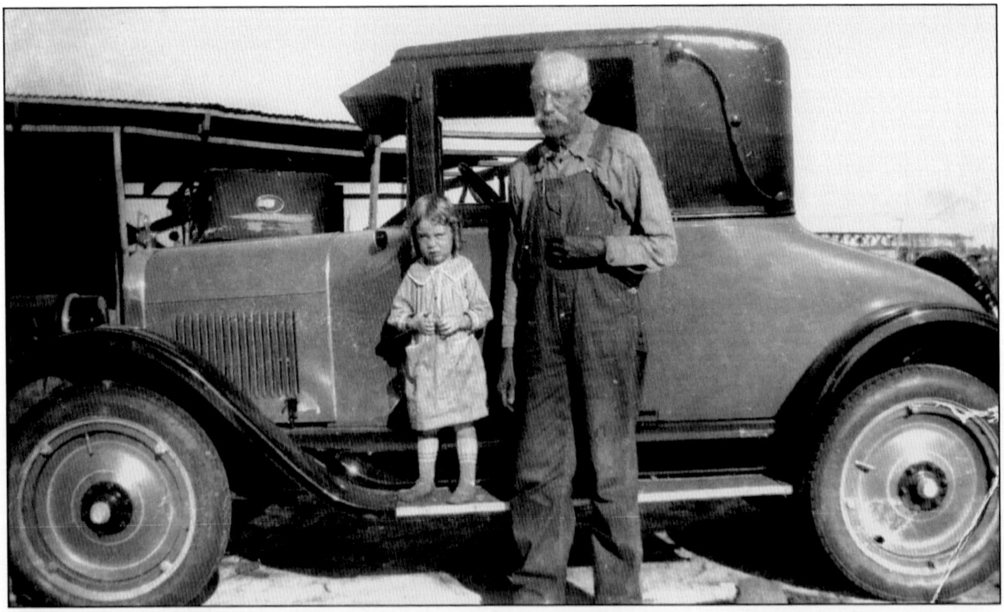

Evelyn Sisk and her grandfather John Sisk are seen in 1926, just north of Brooksville. John Sisk came from a farming family.

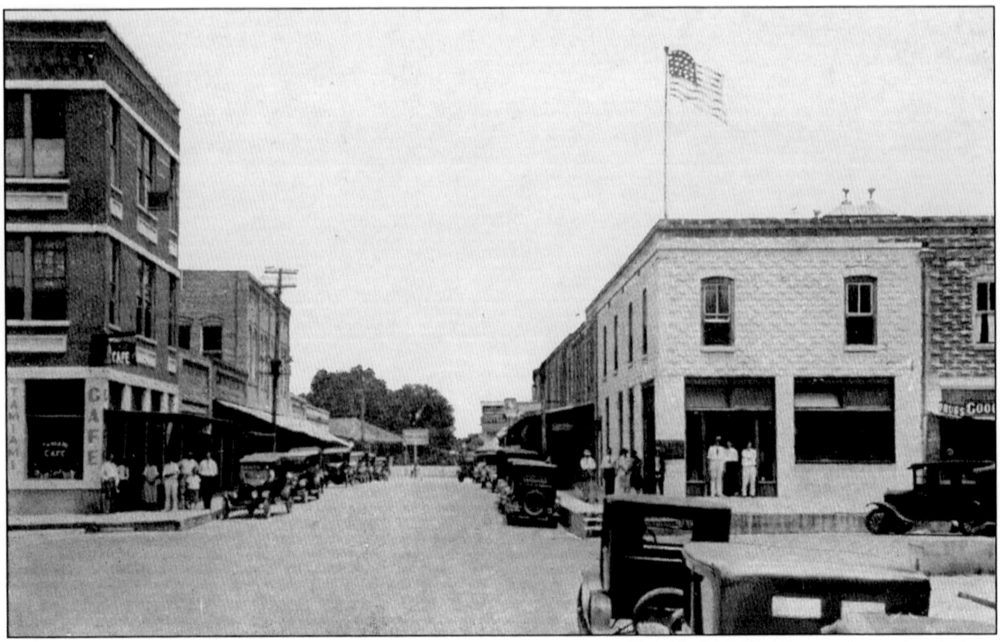

Look north on Main Street in 1925; to the right is Hernando State Bank, and to the left is Tamiami Cafe.

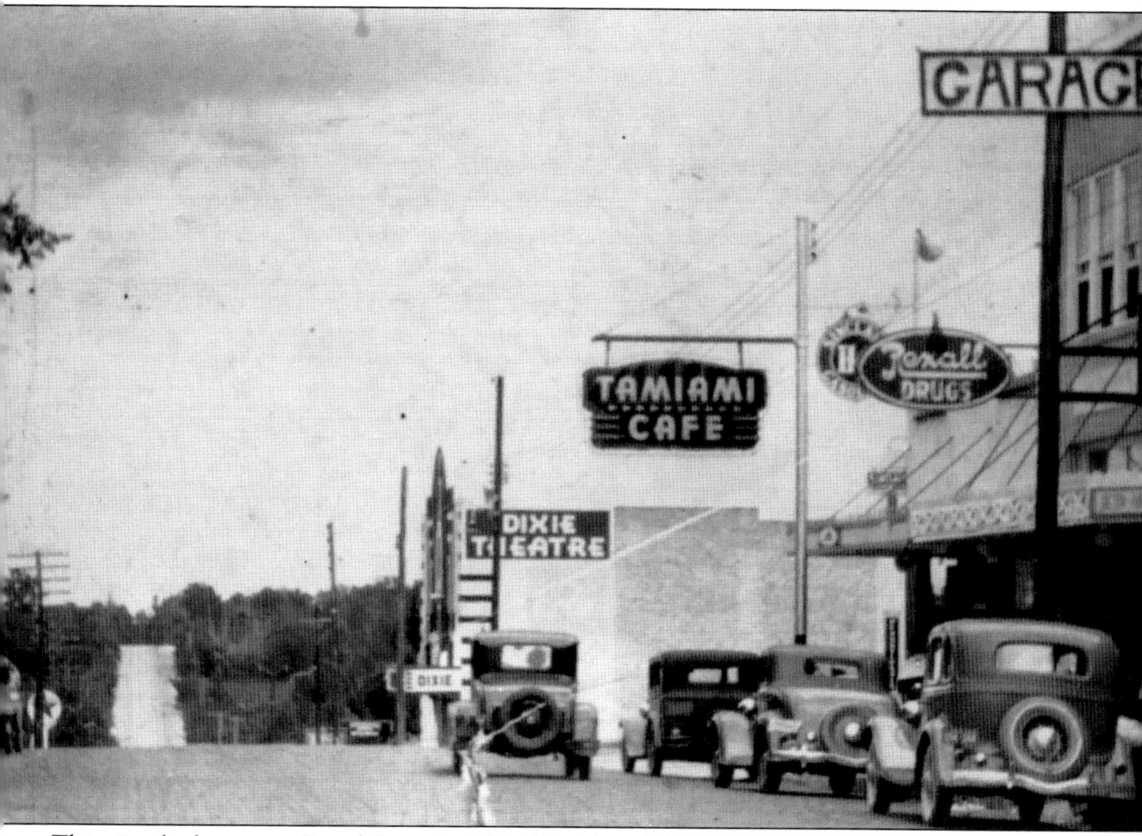

This view looks east on Broad Street in 1938. The Dixie Theatre was a favorite at this location until 1964.

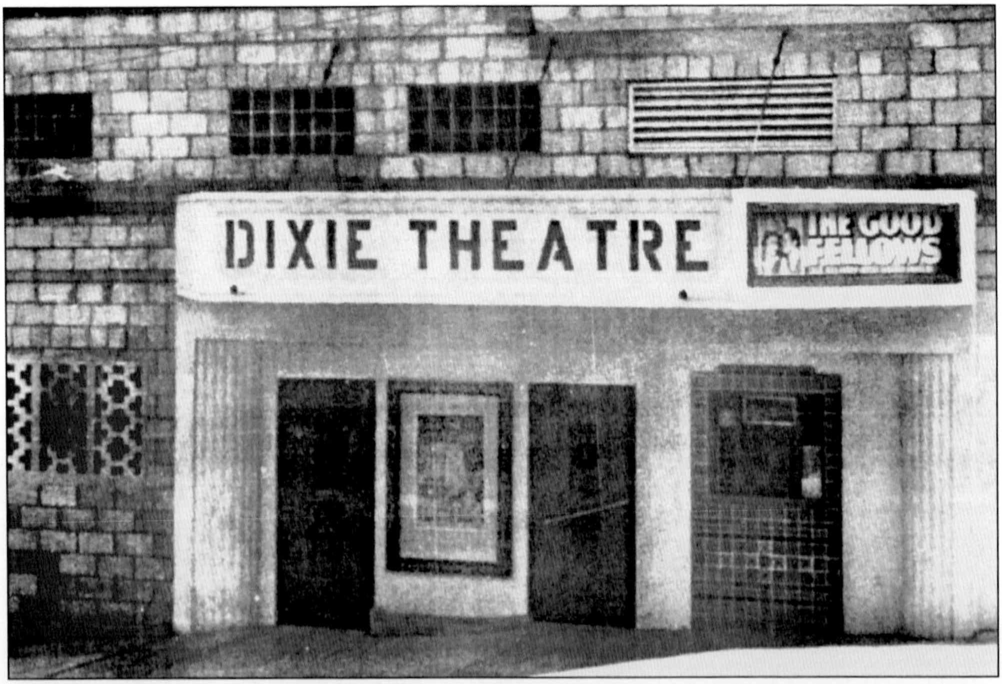

The Dixie Theatre is seen here in 1943. Anyone who lived in Brooksville from the 1930s to the 1960s has fond memories of the Dixie. Times have changed since one could get Saturday afternoon shoot-em-ups, jujyfruits, popcorn, and a coke all for about a quarter.

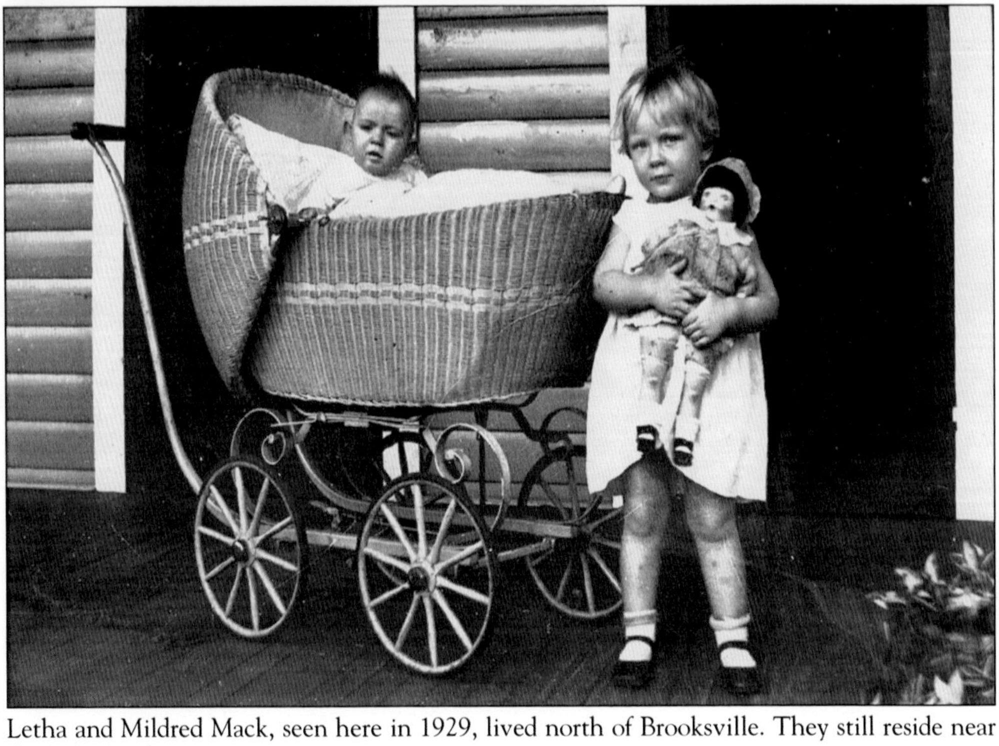

Letha and Mildred Mack, seen here in 1929, lived north of Brooksville. They still reside near the Lake Lindsey area.

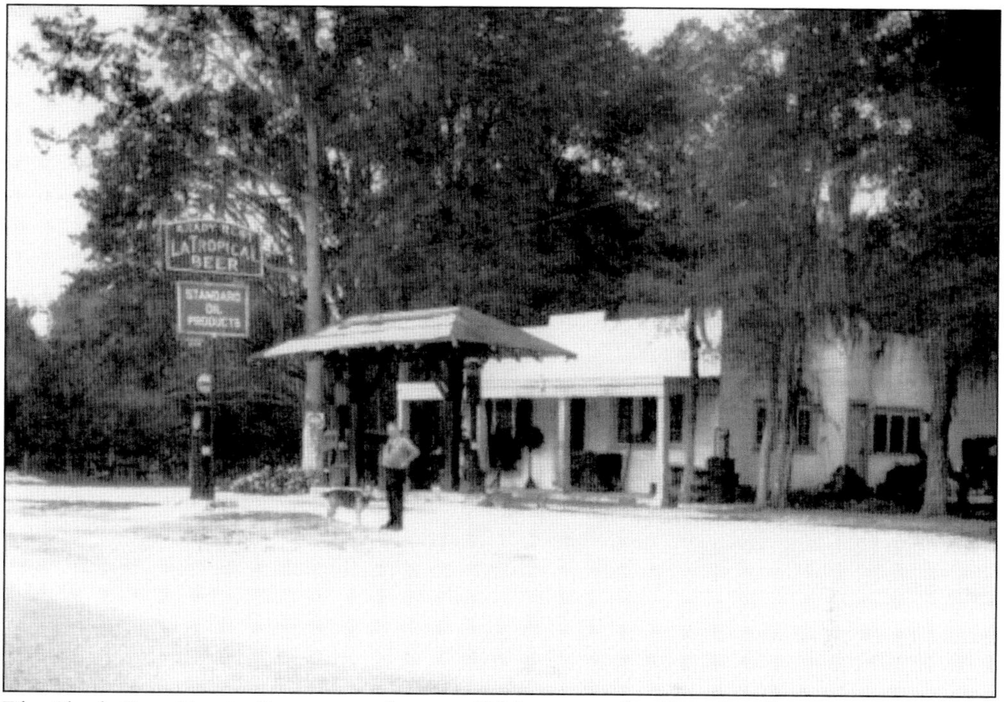

The Shady Rest Tourist Resort, seen here in 1938, was north of Brooksville on U.S. 41. It was a very popular tourist stop featuring Tropical Beer, a mild beer brewed in Tampa.

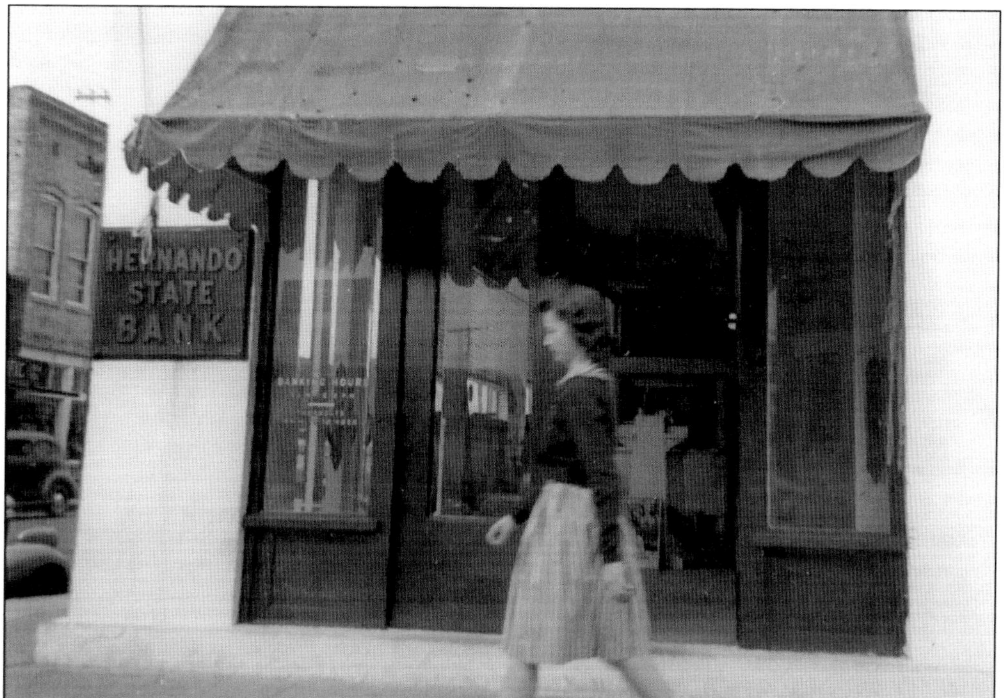

Pedestrians walking downtown in 1940 pass the Hernando State Bank on Jefferson Street

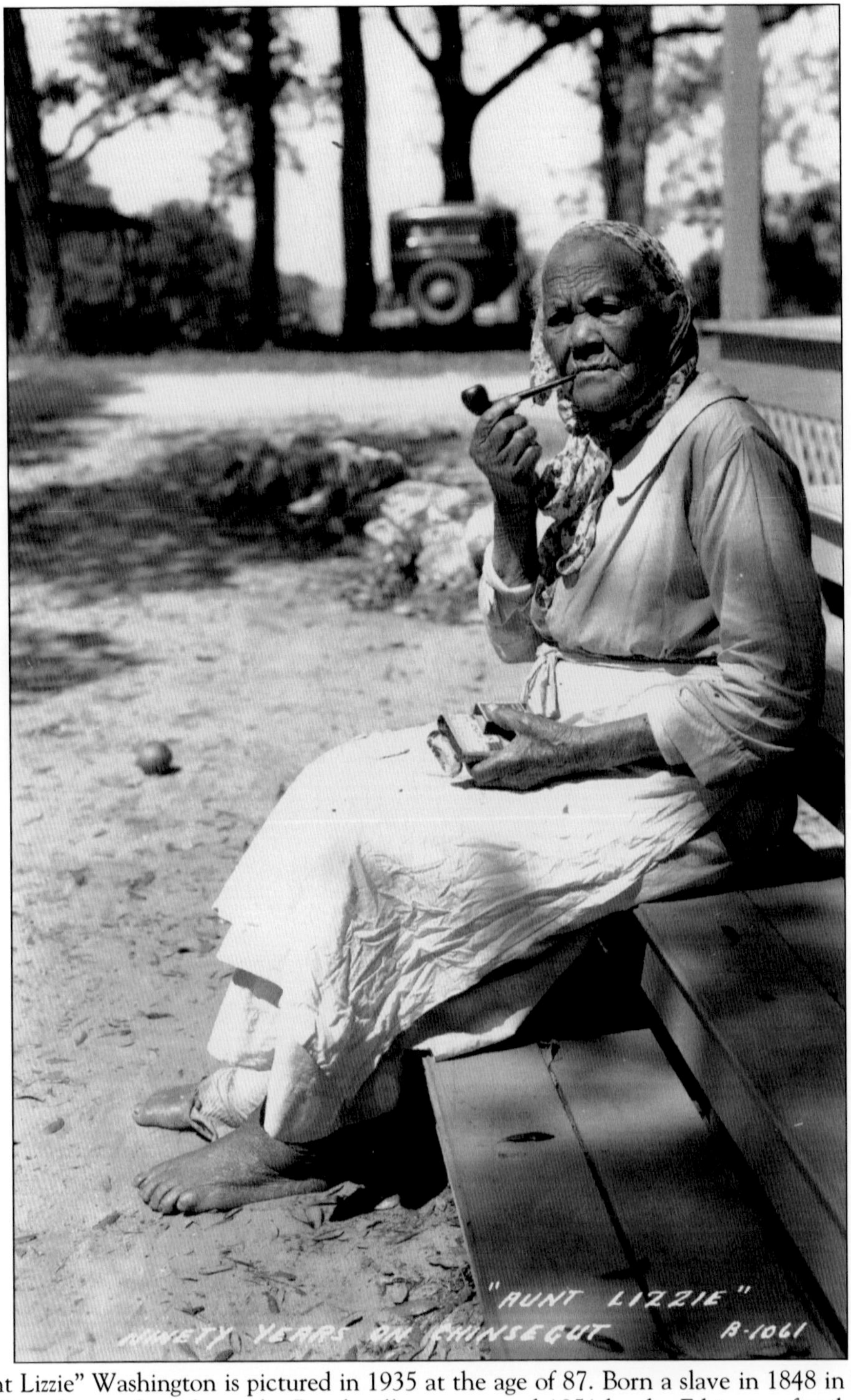

"Aunt Lizzie" Washington is pictured in 1935 at the age of 87. Born a slave in 1848 in South Carolina, she was brought to the Brooksville area around 1851 by the Edrington family to be their help at the big house on Chinsegut Hill, north of Brooksville near Lake Lindsey. It was said she helped deliver more babies than any doctor. When she died in 1938, she had won the respect and admiration of everyone who ever knew her.

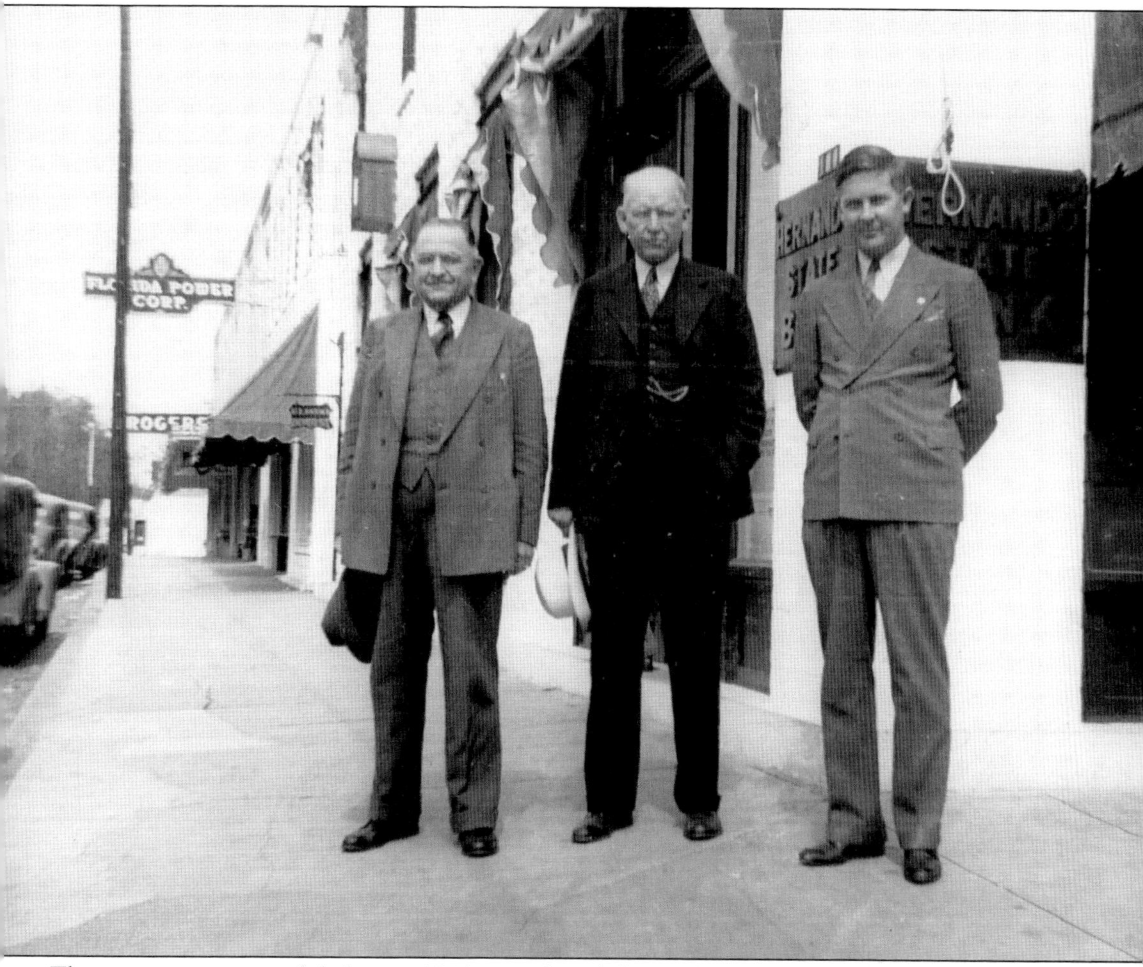

Three major movers and shakers in 1940 were, from left to right, Dr. Creekmore, who practiced medicine in Brooksville for nearly 70 years; Frederick Lykes, scion of the Lykes Brothers family cattle empire; and Alfred McKethan, one of Hernando County's most influential bankers and businessmen. McKethan later became a noted philanthropist. The University of Florida's baseball field is named after him. Lykes's donations and contributions to area hospitals helped relieve their debts. Today, the Lykes Memorial Hospital bears his name.

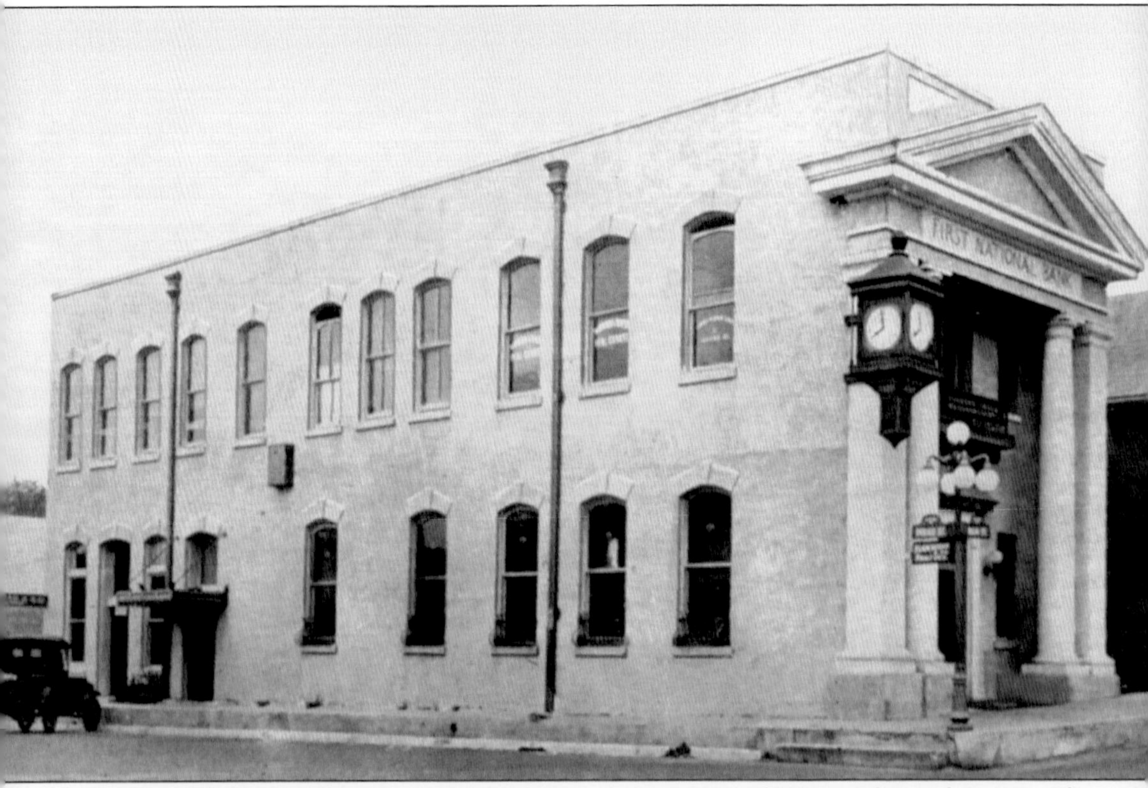

First National Bank Building is seen in 1923 at the corner of Main and Broad Streets. The building was built originally in 1906 and is now occupied by Browning Insurance.

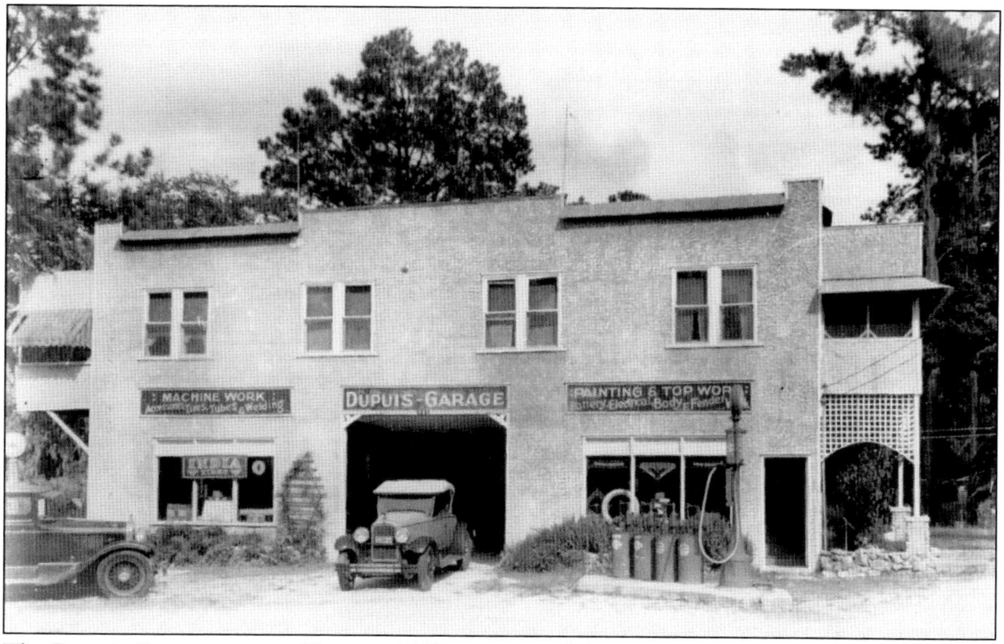

The Dupuis Garage, pictured here in 1927, was one of the city's finest. It was located on North Howell Avenue, near where the high school is today.

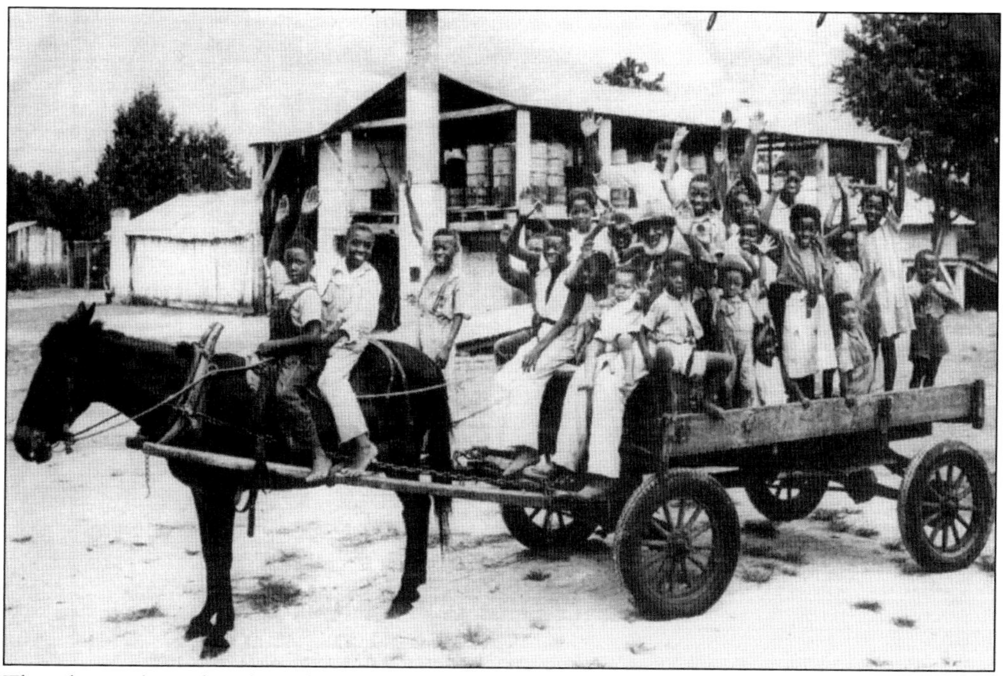

This photo of a mule ride at the Lewis Plantation Resort is from 1938. The resort was one of the area's most popular tourist attractions. During its heyday in the 1930s, it was a popular stopover featuring cabins as motel rooms and African-American entertainers, mule rides, and music. The entertainment centered around the stereotyped behavior expected during those times.

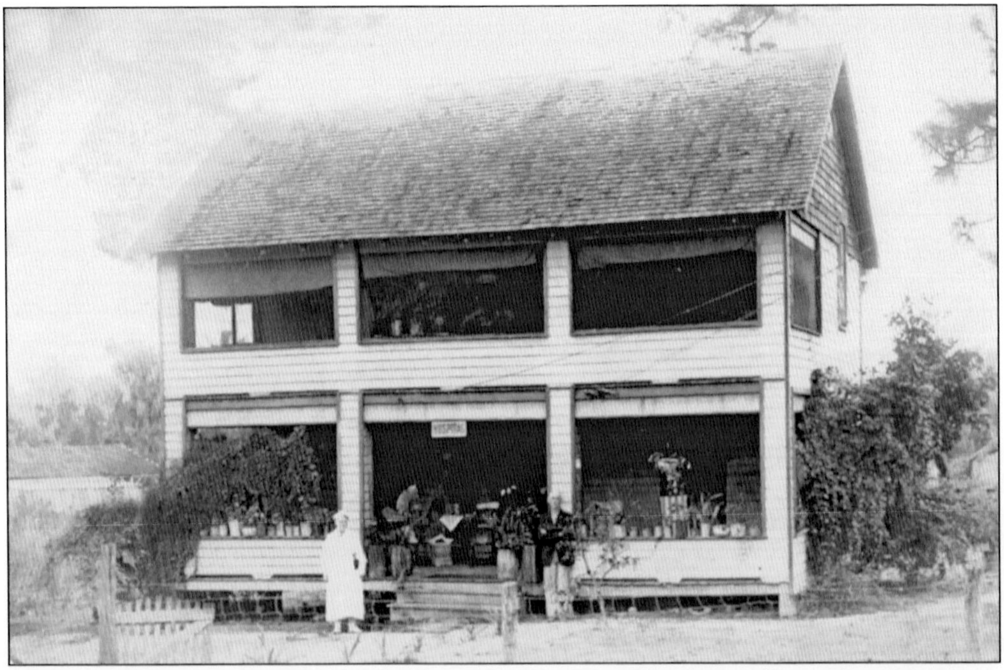

The first Brooksville hospital, pictured in 1921, was operated by Mr. and Mrs. Boggess and was on Summit Road. Its early doctors were Dr. Coogler, Dr. Hancock, and Dr. Creekmore.

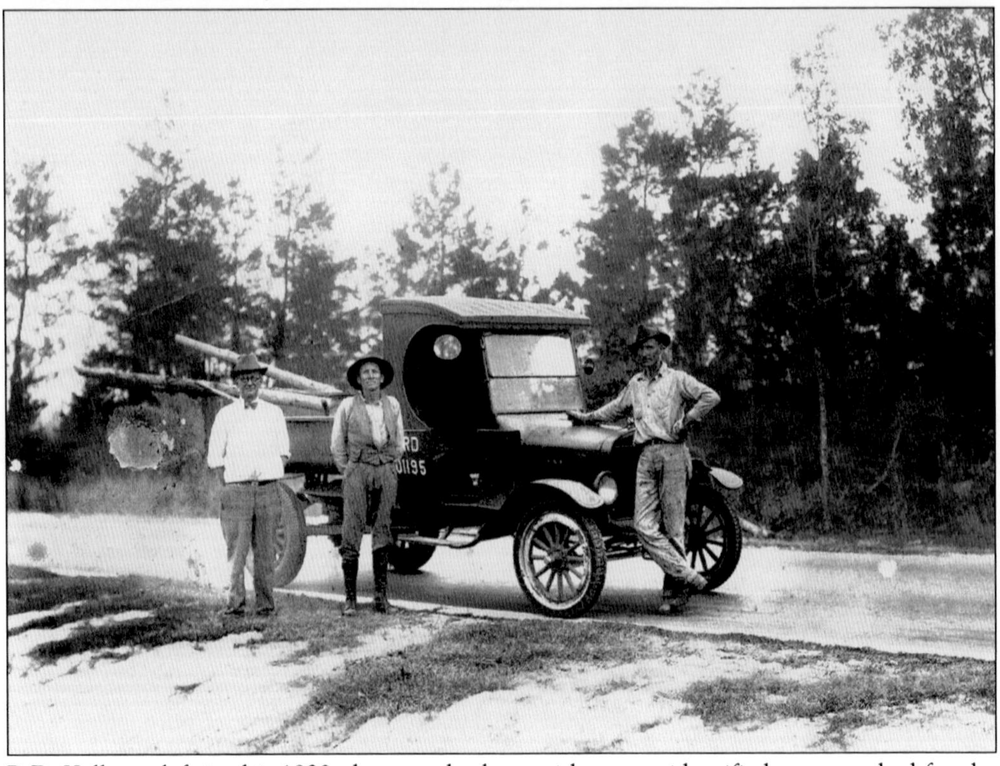

R.D. Kelly, at left in this 1930 photograph along with two unidentified men, worked for the State Road Department on a job site along a Brooksville street.

The three Brooksville girls in this 1926 photograph are, from left to right, Delma Crum, Ella Mae Weeks, and Nell Underwood. These are three prominent Brooksville family names and are still quite common today.

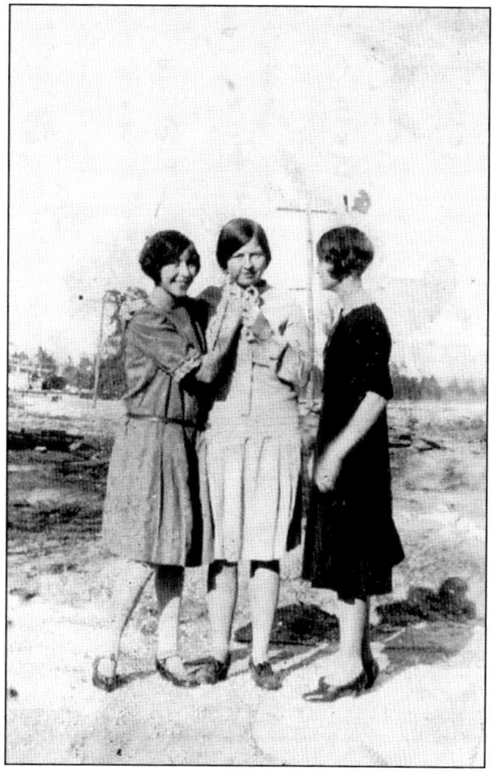

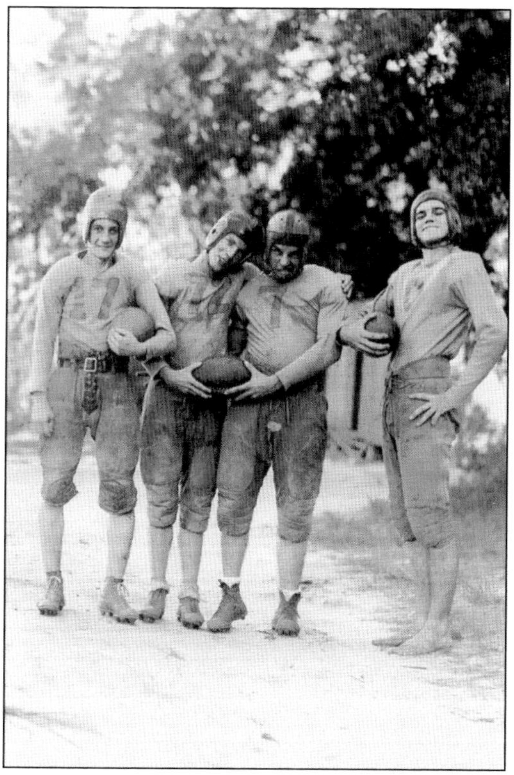

Four star players from the 1937 Hernando Leopards football team are caught during a lighter moment. The players are, from left to right, Vernon Webb, Franklin Emerson, C.H. Luke, and Eddie McIntyre.

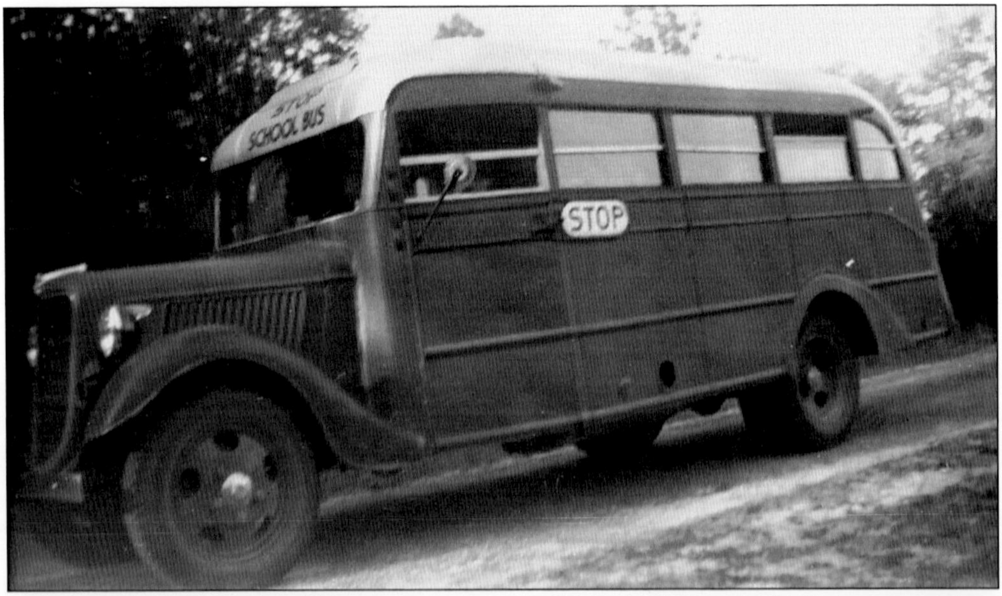

This early Brooksville school bus, seen in 1935, was driven by Jimmy Graham for many years.

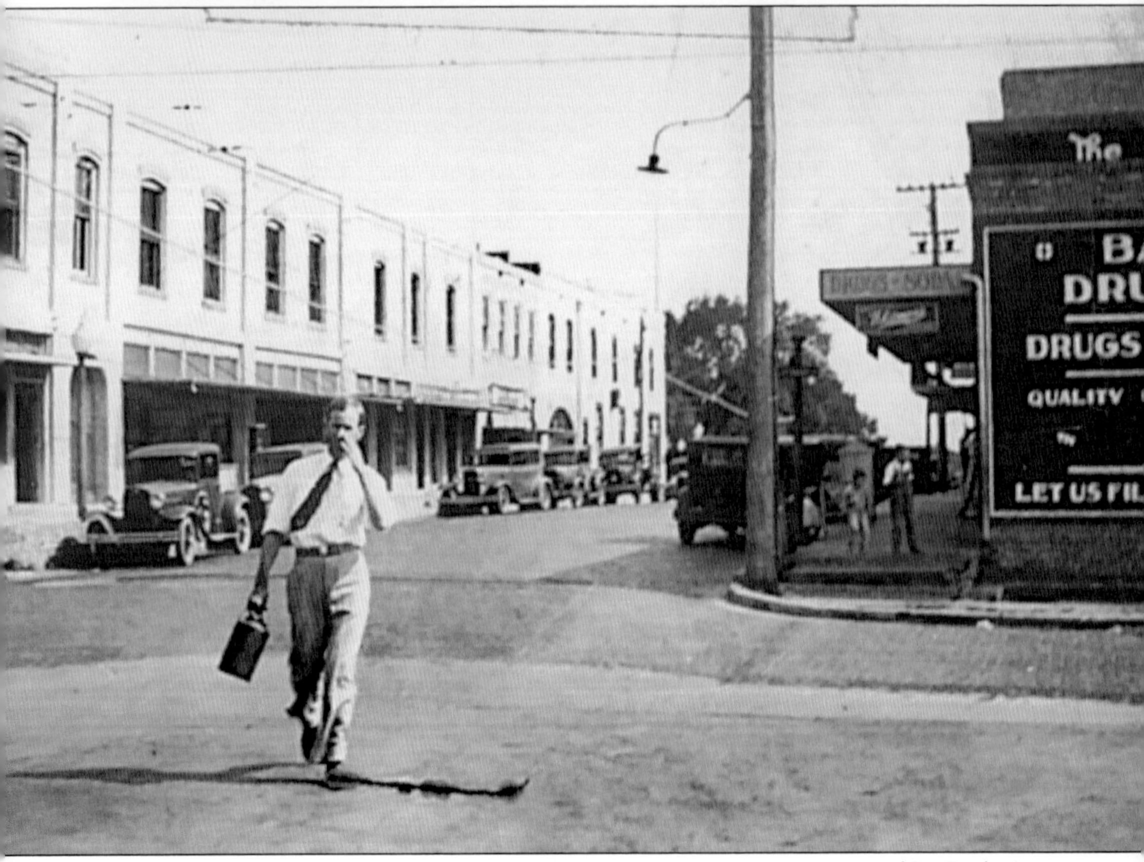

This panoramic 1929 shot shows Brooksville at the corner of Main Street and Ft. Dade Avenue. It was common back then for ads to appear on the side of buildings. Celo was a popular soft

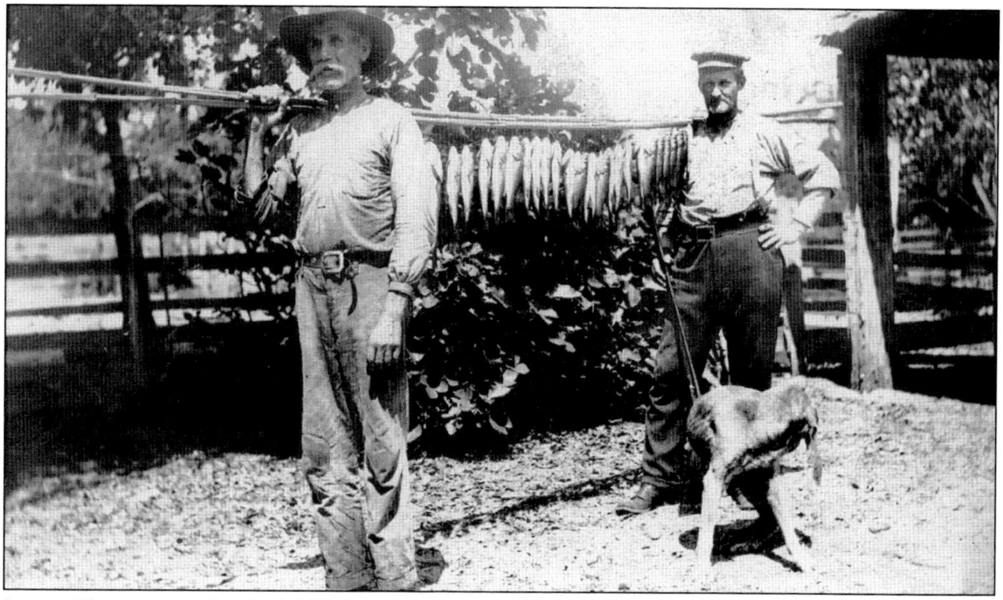

James Chapman and A.P. McKeown pose in 1920 after a good day of fishing at Lake Lindsey.

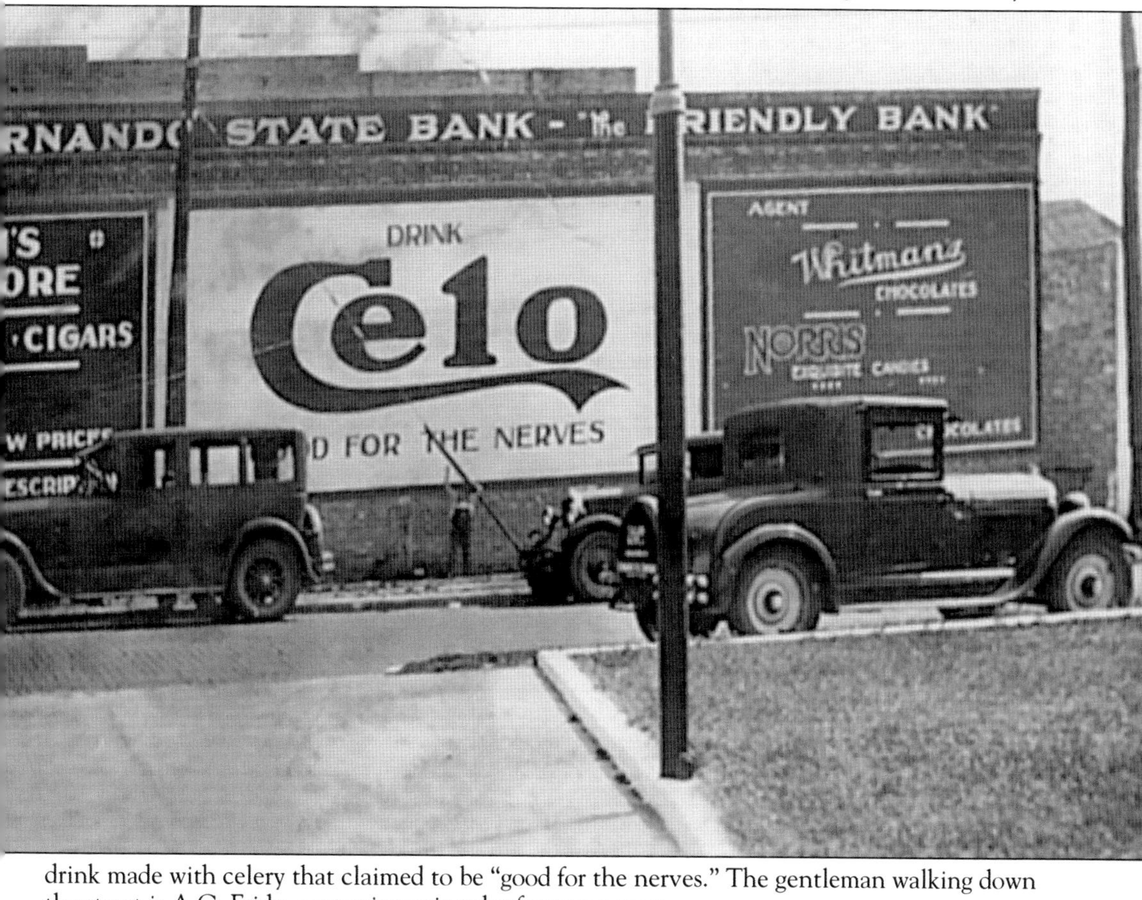

drink made with celery that claimed to be "good for the nerves." The gentleman walking down the street is A.G. Fridy, a prominent jeweler for many years.

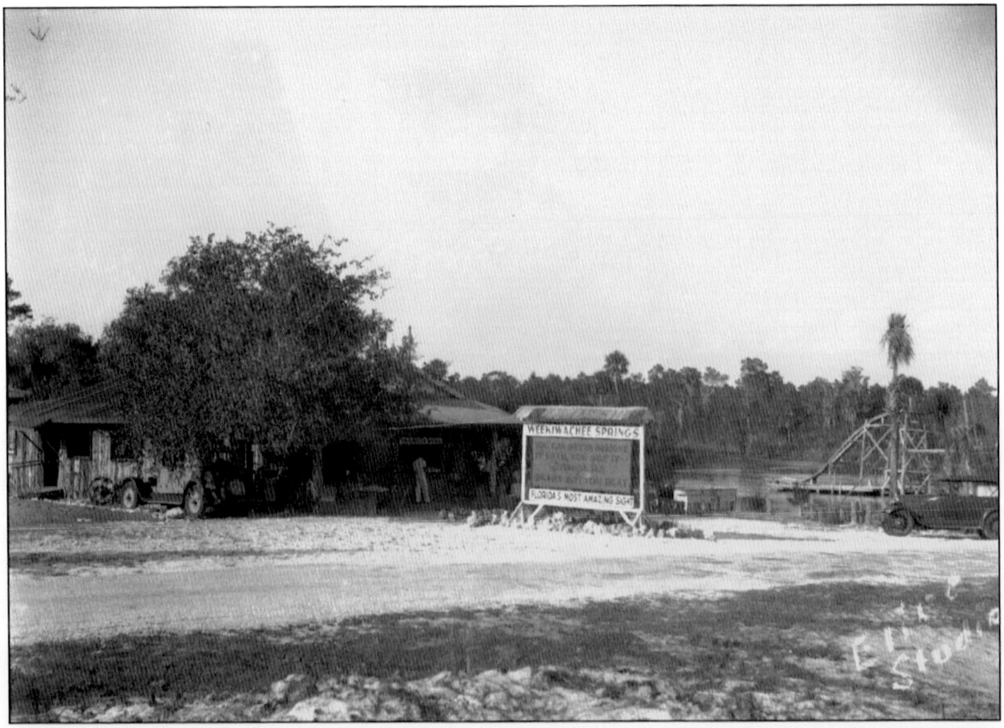

This early Weeki Wachee attraction is from 1929. Before mermaids, all Weeki Wachee had to offer was a glass-bottom boat ride and a concession stand. Back then, that was enough to draw tourists from miles around.

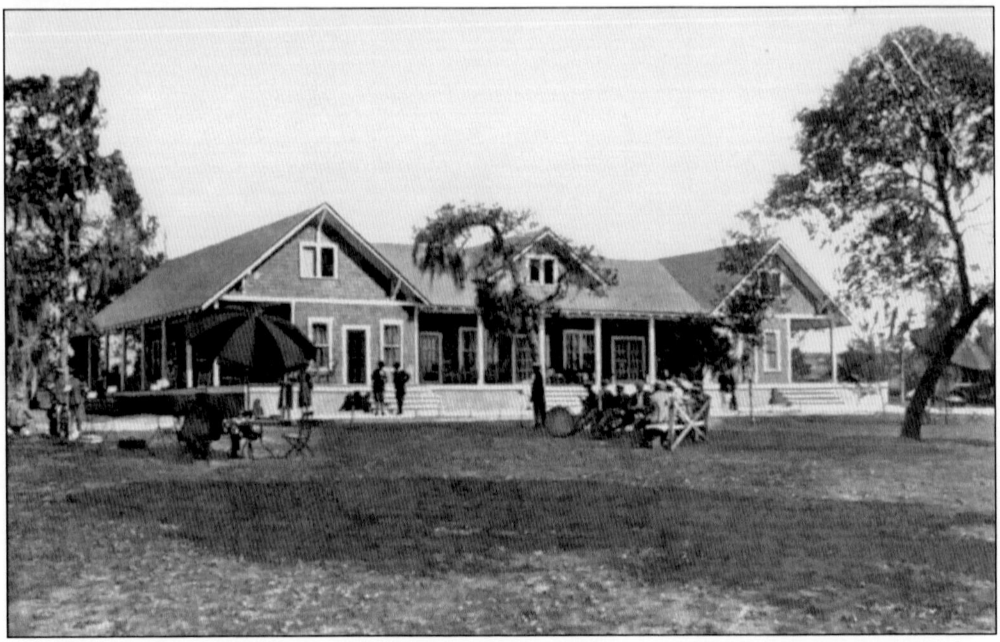

The Hickory Hills Golf Course Club House, seen in 1926, was at Brooksville's first golf course. First opening its doors in 1926, Hickory Hill closed in the early 1930s because of the stock market crash and never reopened. It was located about seven miles east of Brooksville near Spring Lake.

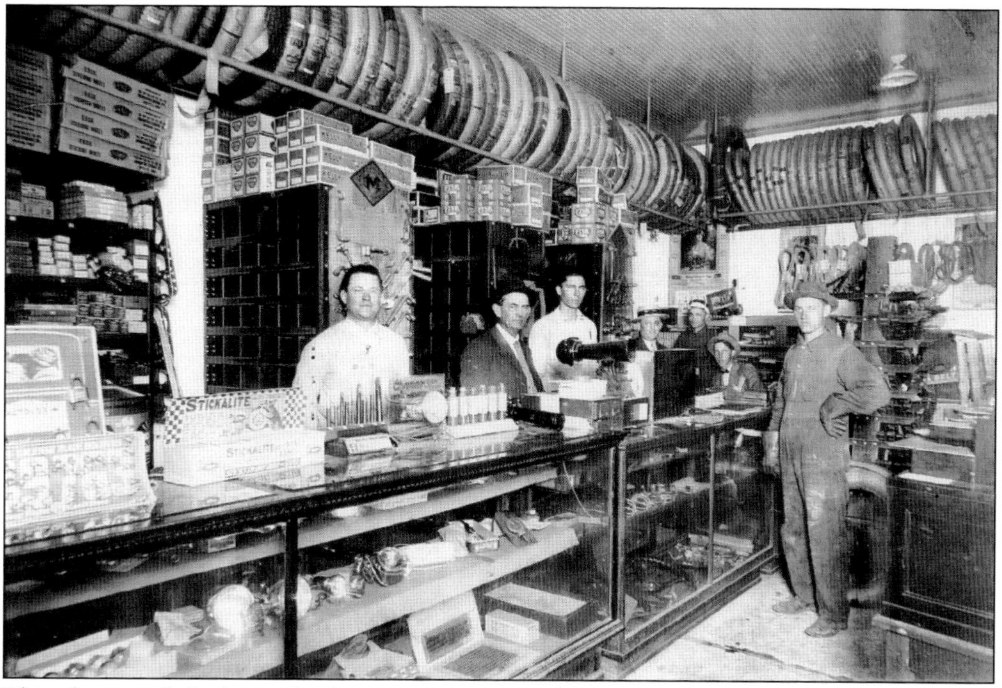

This photograph looks inside the auto parts store of Simpson Chevrolet in 1932. Notice the innertube tires. Located at the corner of Main and Broad Streets, the dealership would later move down the block.

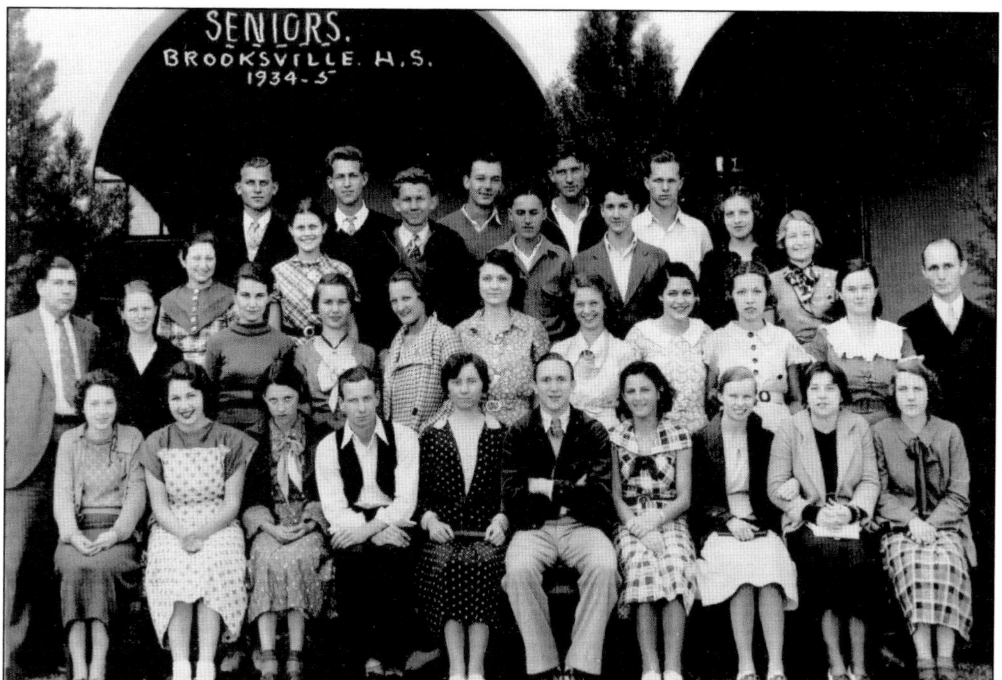

Pictured here is the 1934–1935 Hernando High senior class. The high school was by then located at the top of the hill on Bell Avenue.

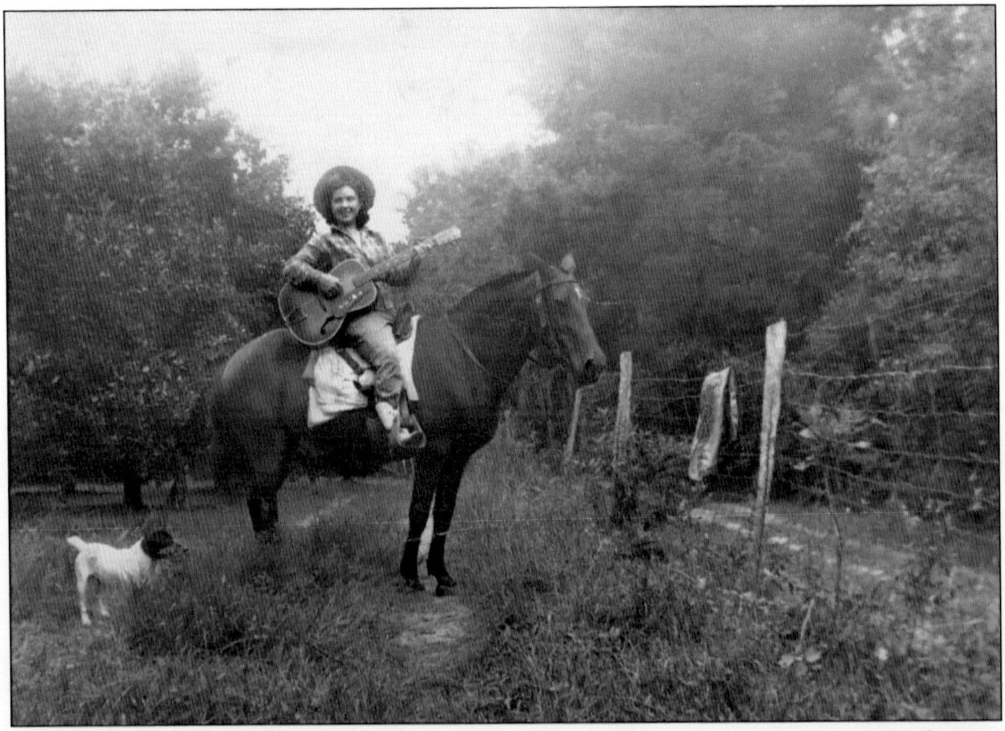

This cowgirl in the groves is pictured in 1943. Olivia McPherson, from the Spring Lake area near Brooksville, serenades two of her friends.

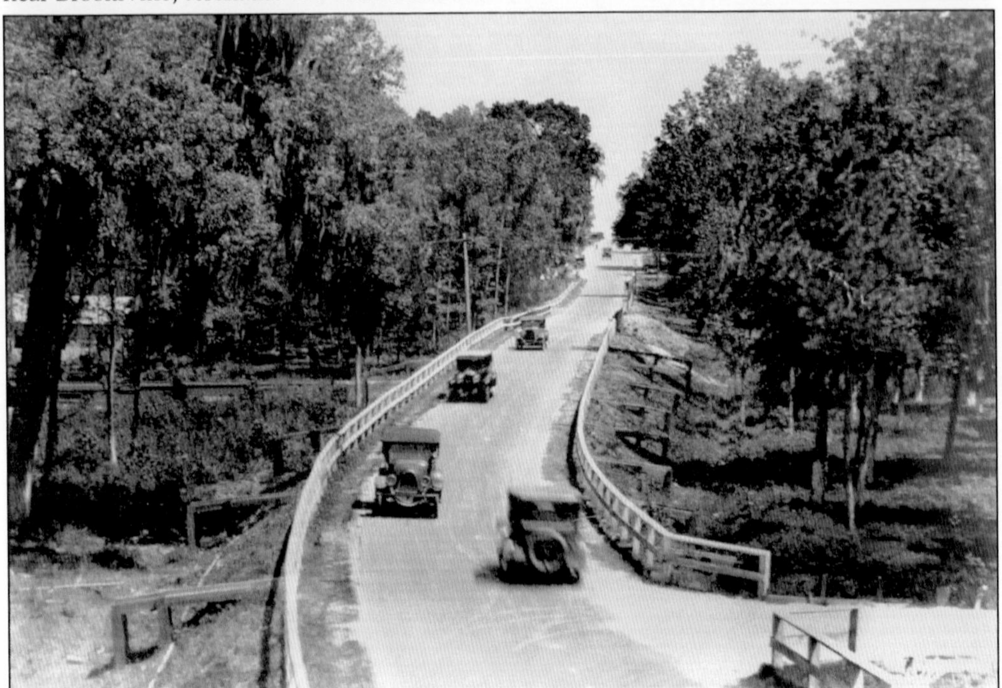

Brooksville was entered from the south on State Road 5 in 1925. The road was later designated U.S. Highway 41.

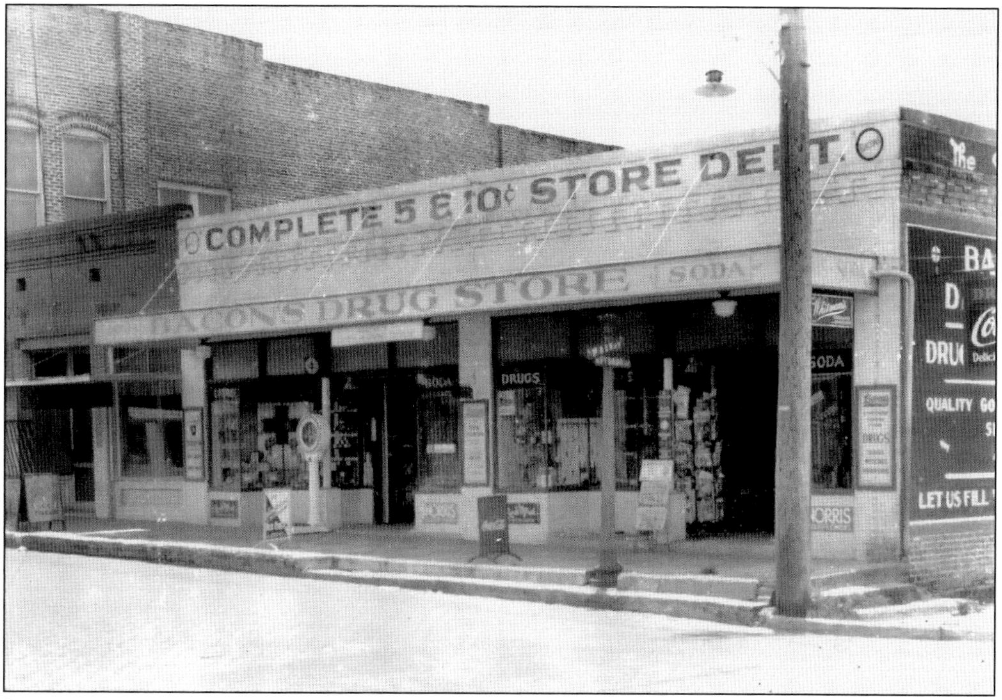

Bacon's Drug Store, seen in 1929 at the corner of Main and Ft. Dade, would later move to the other corner.

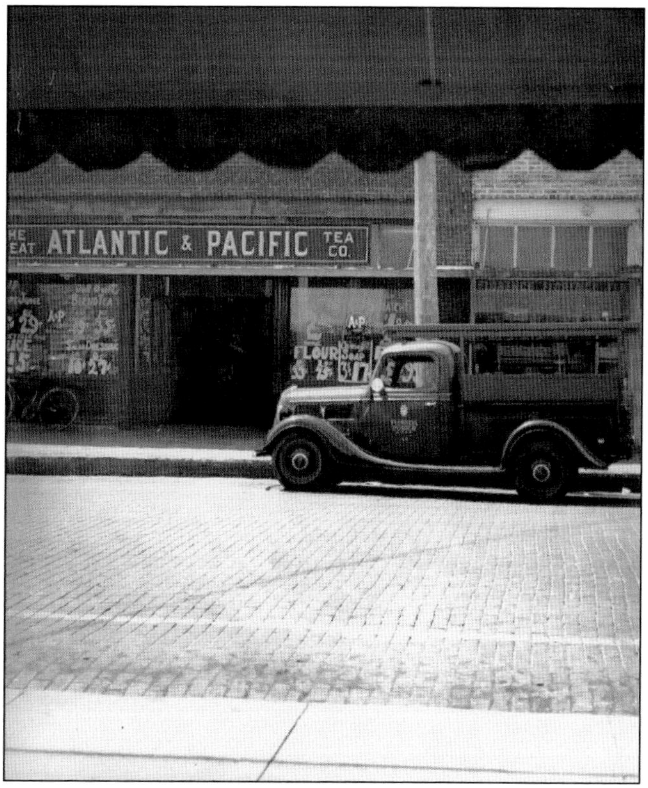

The old A&P Grocery Store on Main Street was one of the city's most popular groceries in 1938. A&P was the Publix of its day and it had a great national reputation.

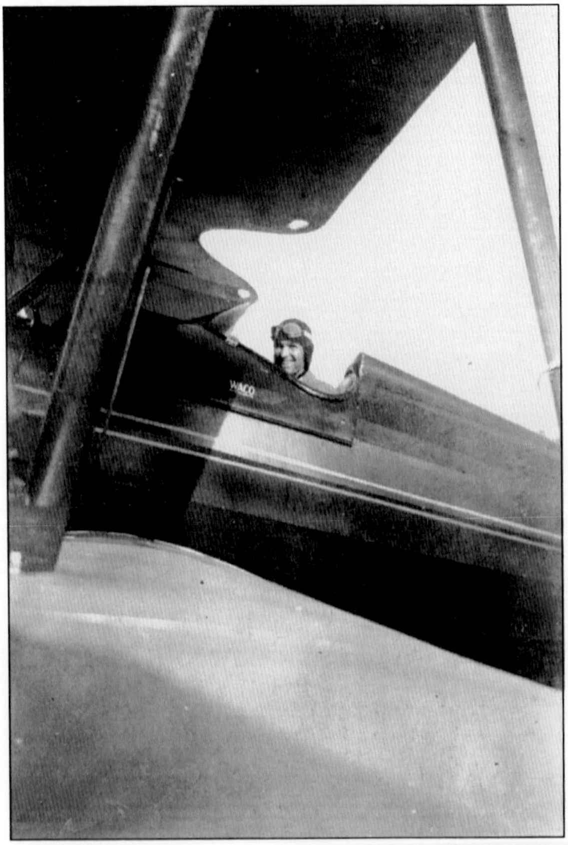

Pilot extraordinaire Jack Endsley takes off at the old Brooksville Airport in 1933. The old airport was nothing more than a landing strip for small planes and helicopters. This airport was just east of downtown Brooksville. It faded out right before the war, and a new and improved airport was built south of the city large enough to accommodate bomber planes to practice landing on aircraft carriers in World War II.

The corner of Jefferson and Main Streets is seen in 1940. By then, Bacon's Drug Store had moved from the other corner and would remain here until about 1970.

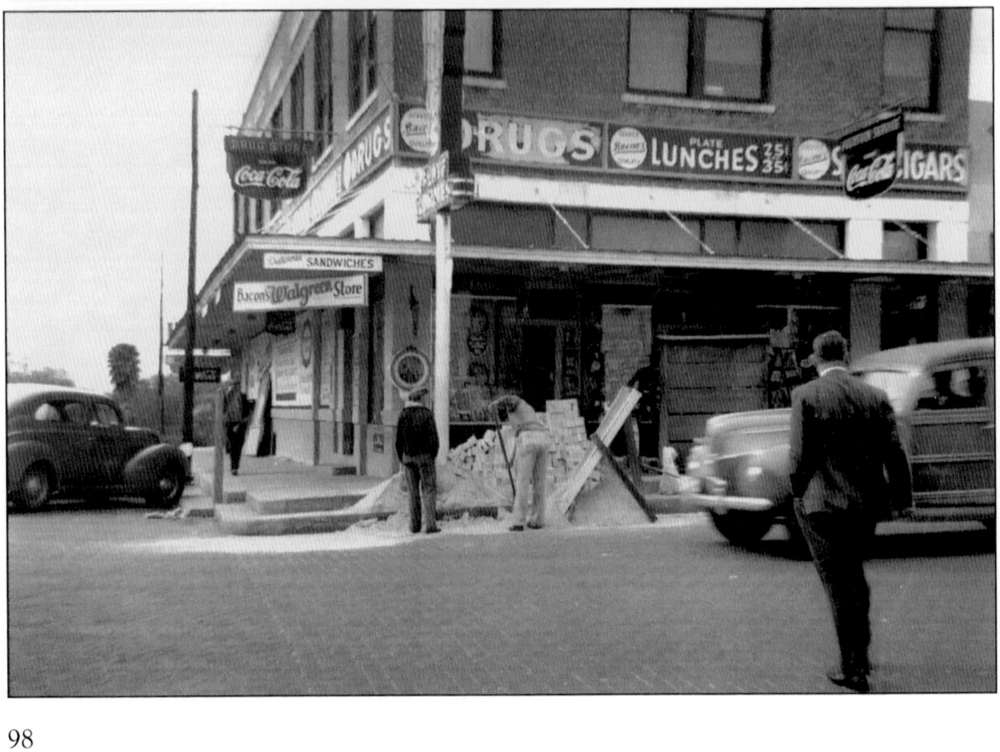

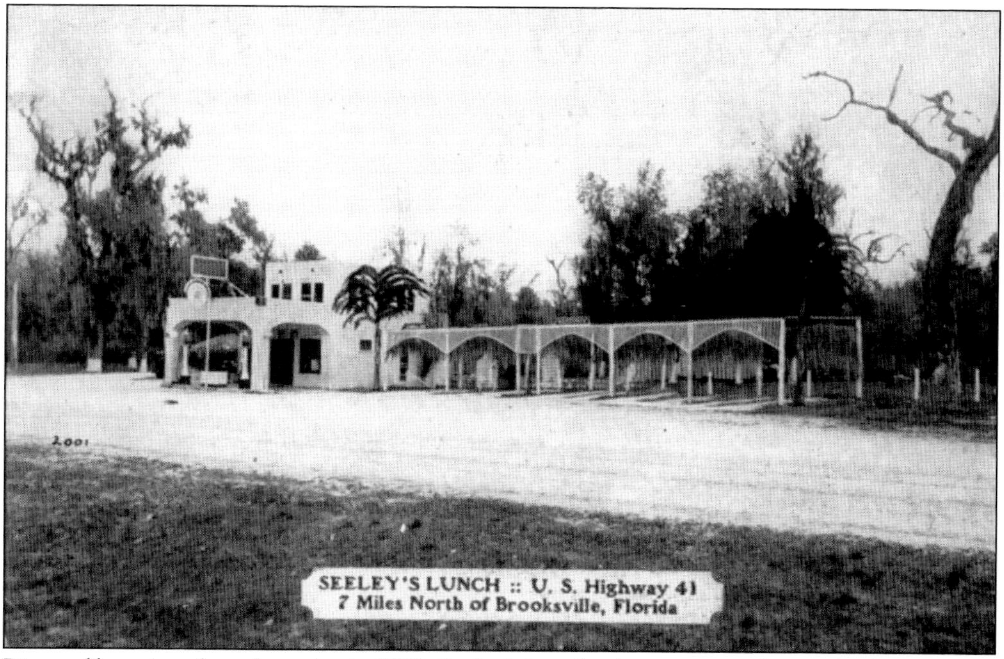

Pictured here is early curb service in 1927. Seeley's Lunch, about seven miles north of Brooksville on U.S. Highway 41, was one of the very first drive-in restaurants.

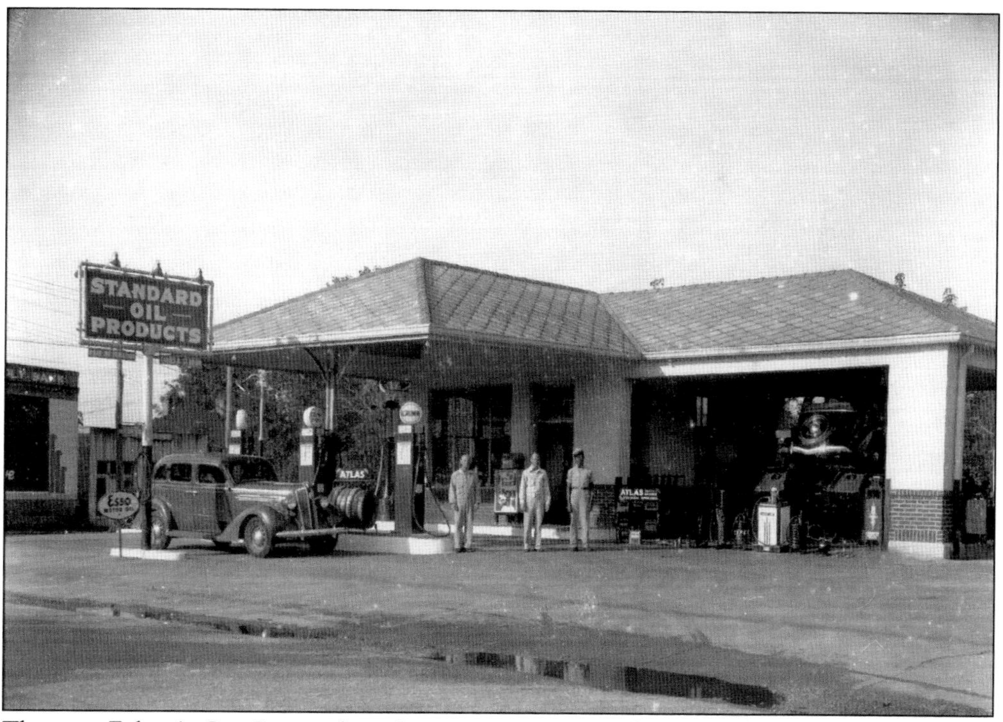

The new Fulton's Gas Station brought gas stations toward a more modern look in 1938. It would later be known as McGee's and was on the corner of Ft. Dade and Howell, where the city hall is today.

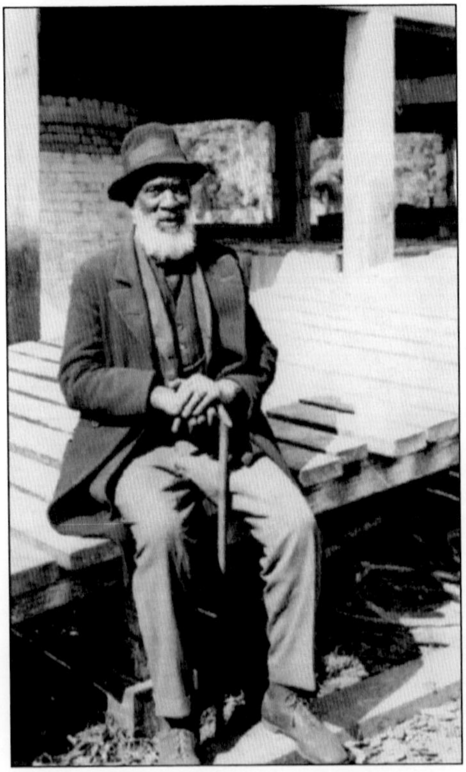

Uncle Ambrose, seen here in 1938, was a popular "Uncle Remus"–type entertainer and storyteller at the Lewis Plantation Resort and Motor Lodge. Legend has it that he fathered 39 children with only two wives.

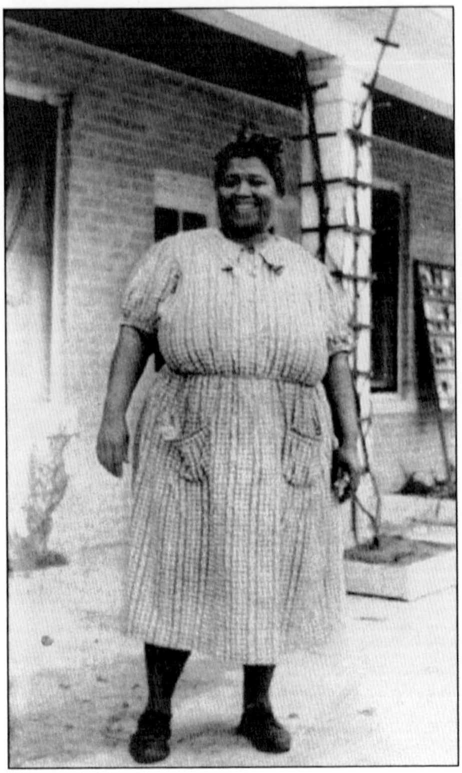

The food must be good here. Blanche, a popular cook at the Lewis Plantation in 1938, was a mainstay there for many years.

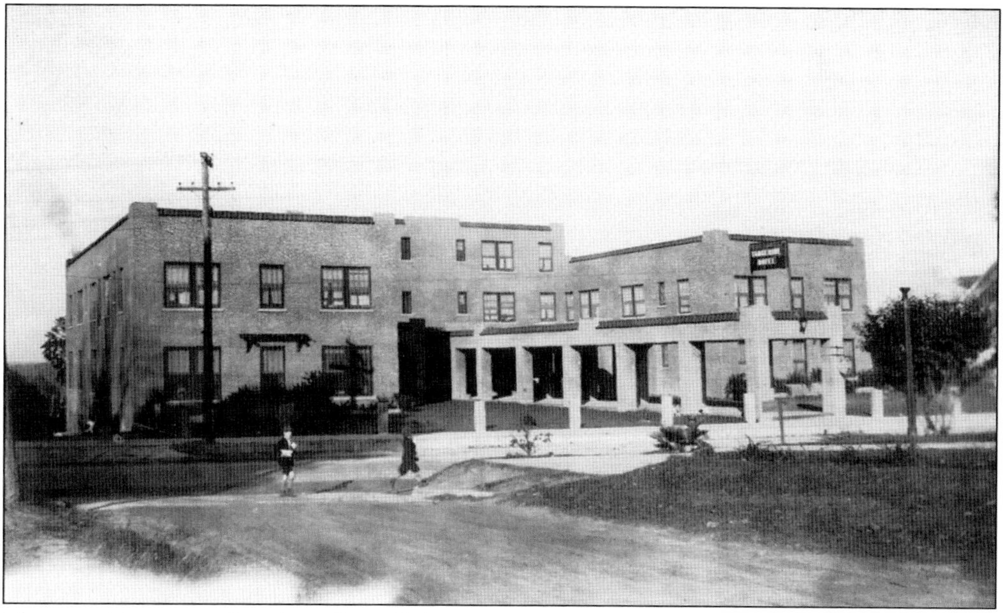

The new Tangerine Hotel on Howell Avenue, seen here in 1925, was Brooksville's premier hotel up through World War II.

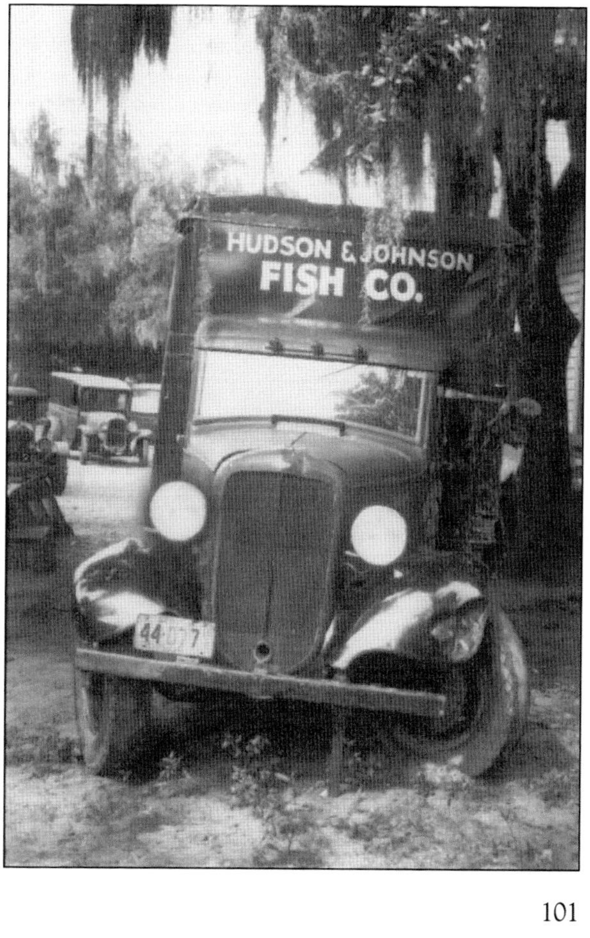

This fish delivery truck drives through the streets of Brooksville in 1929. Most of the fish was caught at Bayport, Aripeka, or Homosassa, so it was sure to be fresh.

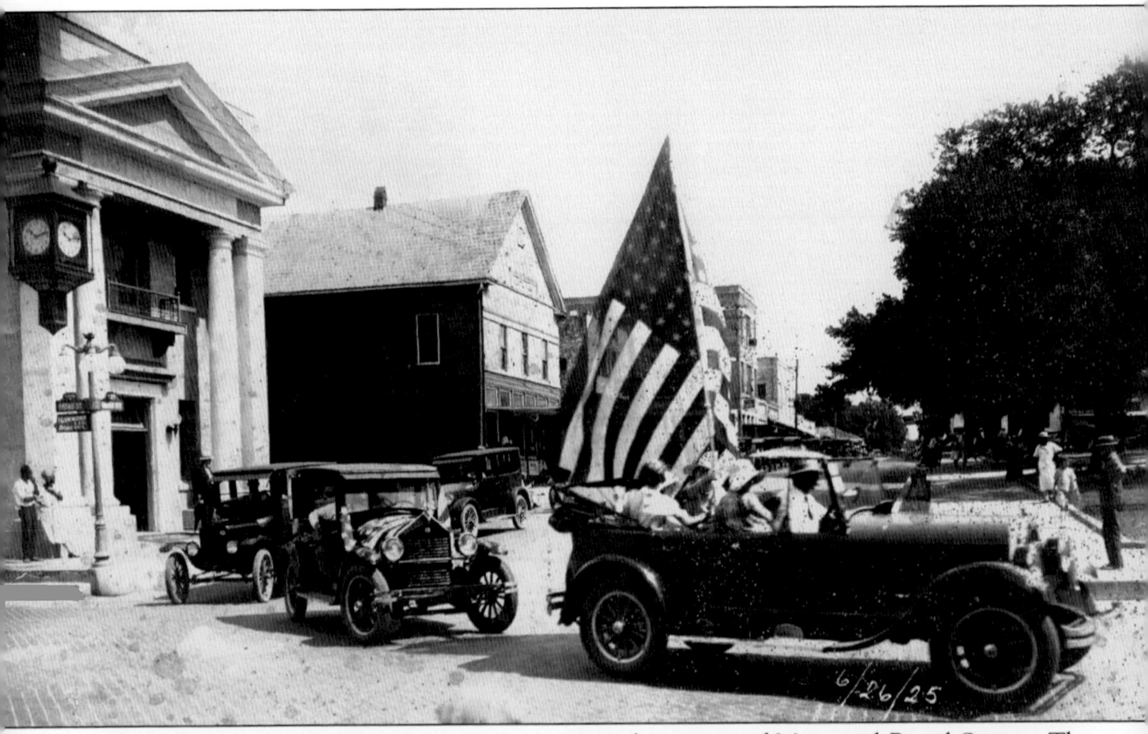

This 1925 Brooksville funeral procession crosses the corner of Main and Broad Streets. The service was conducted by Garnett Funeral Home for a departed war veteran.

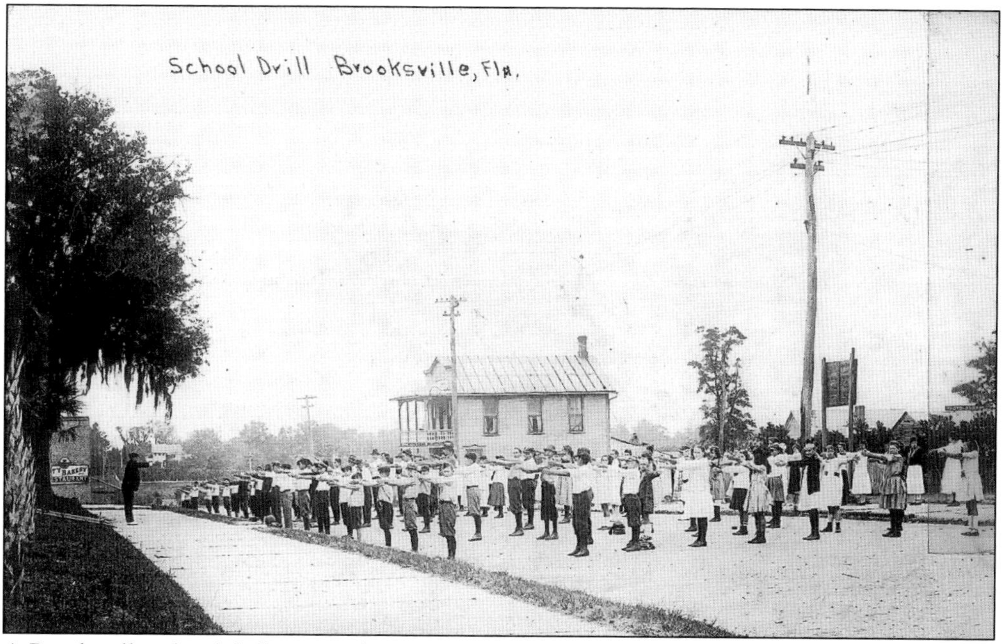

A Brooksville school drill on South Main Street in 1917 looks more like a fitness exercise.

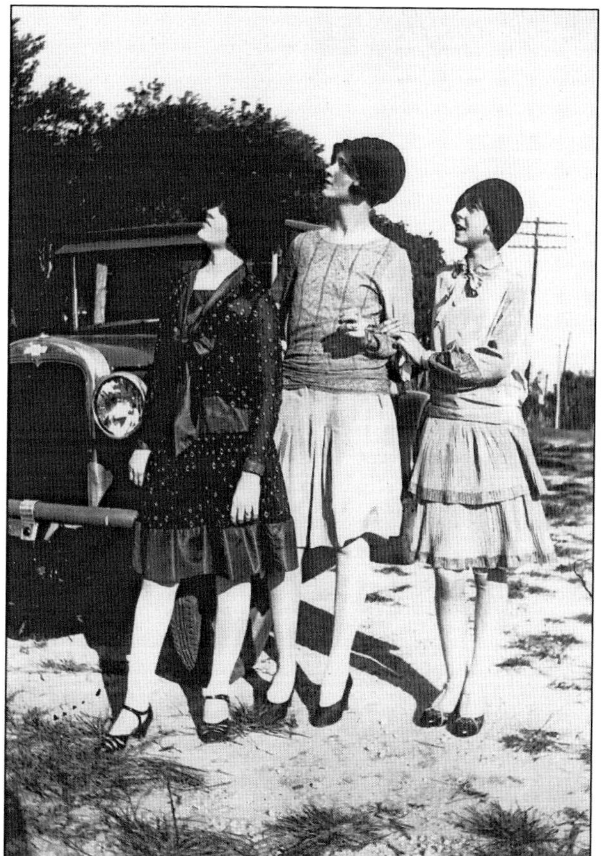

Flapper styles were at their peak when this 1926 photo was taken in Brooksville. The three young ladies are Dot McKethan, Ruth Weeks, and Millie Amstutz.

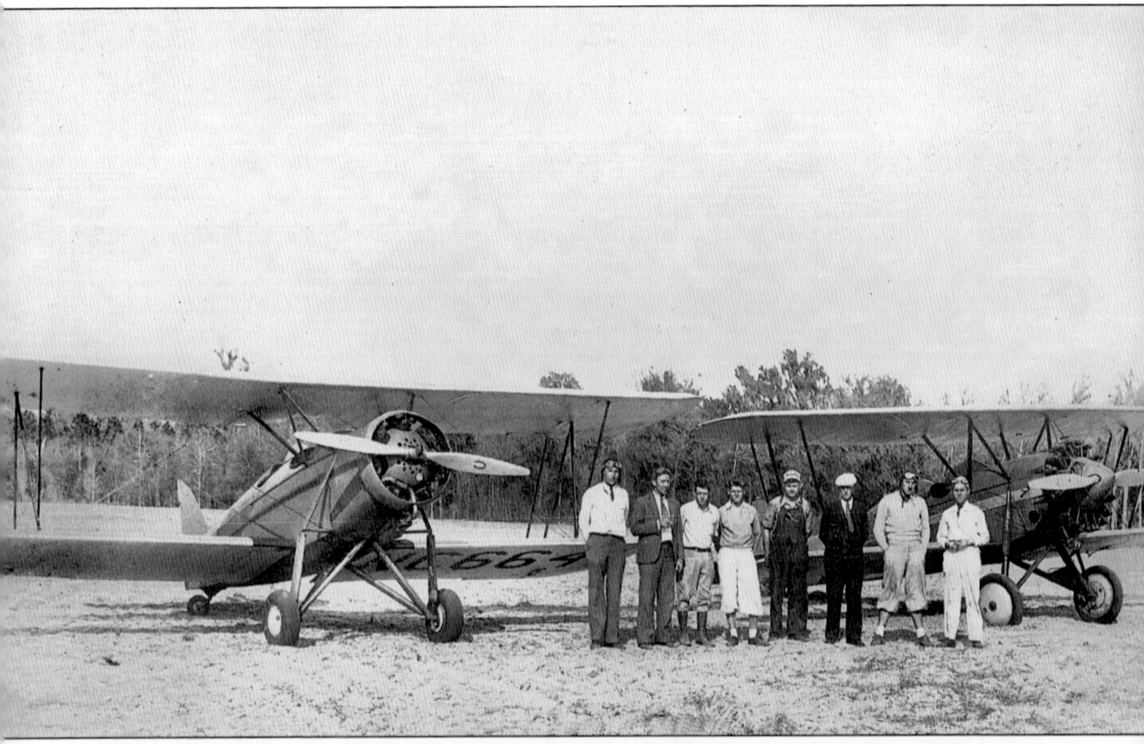

Brooksville Airport is pictured here in 1931. The first airport was just east of downtown on what is now Highway 50. Barnstormers would charge 25 cents for those brave enough to take a quick spin.

Four

1945–THE PRESENT

The overall landscape of America changed dramatically after World War II. American was once again feeling carefree and the road was calling. People were more than ever on the move and it reflected in and around Brooksville with more motels, tourist attractions, gas stations, and the development of the suburbs.

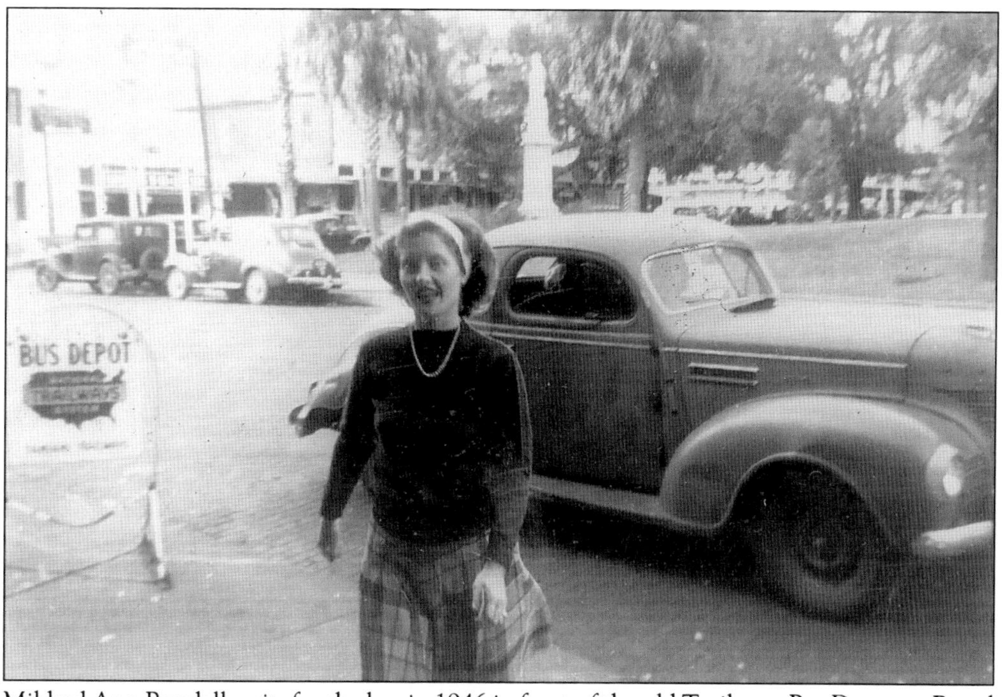

Mildred Ann Randall waits for the bus in 1946 in front of the old Trailways Bus Depot on Broad Street. Bus travel was much more common during the 1940s and 1950s than today.

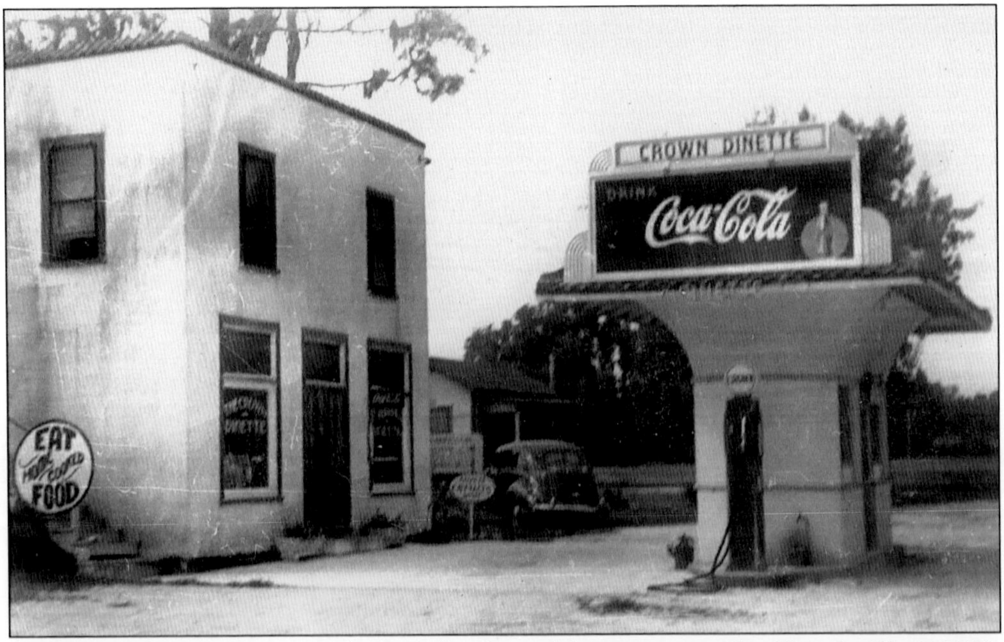

The Crown Dinette was a popular little honky-tonk/restaurant north of Brooksville in 1949. About this time *Grand Ole Opry* stars Grandpa Jones and Minnie Pearl made a surprise visit one evening.

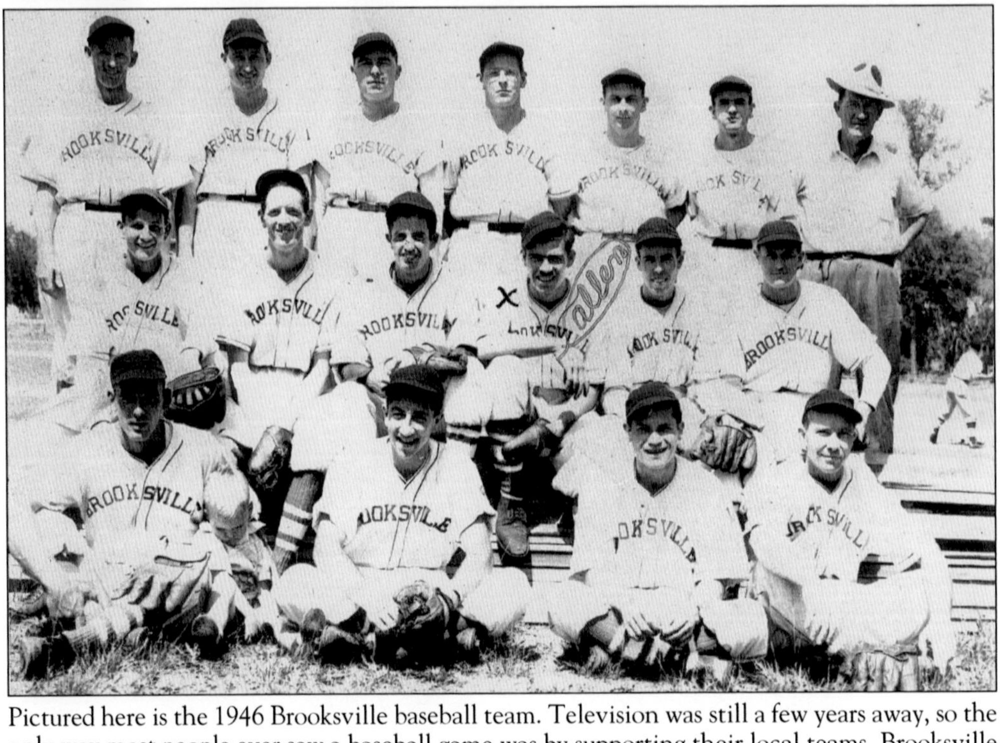

Pictured here is the 1946 Brooksville baseball team. Television was still a few years away, so the only way most people ever saw a baseball game was by supporting their local teams. Brooksville was close to some major league spring training teams, but during the season, teams such as the one pictured above had a following not seen in today's era.

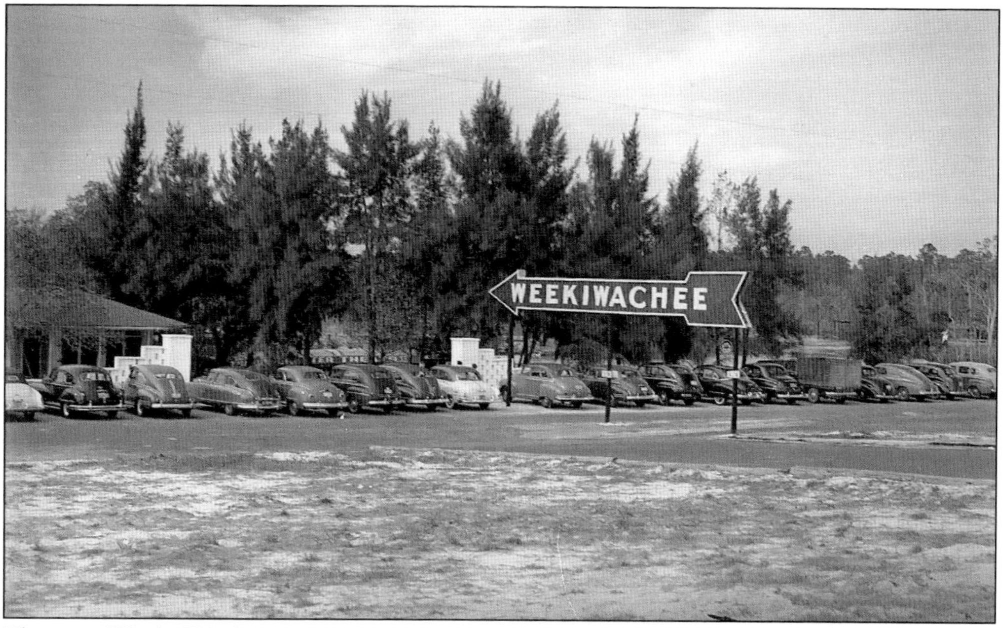

The new Weeki Wachee attraction, now featuring mermaids, opened in 1947. Twelve miles west of Brooksville on U.S. Highway 19, it became one of the nation's most popular tourist attractions during the 1950s, advertising as far as New York and Detroit. Notice the rather generic sign—that would soon change.

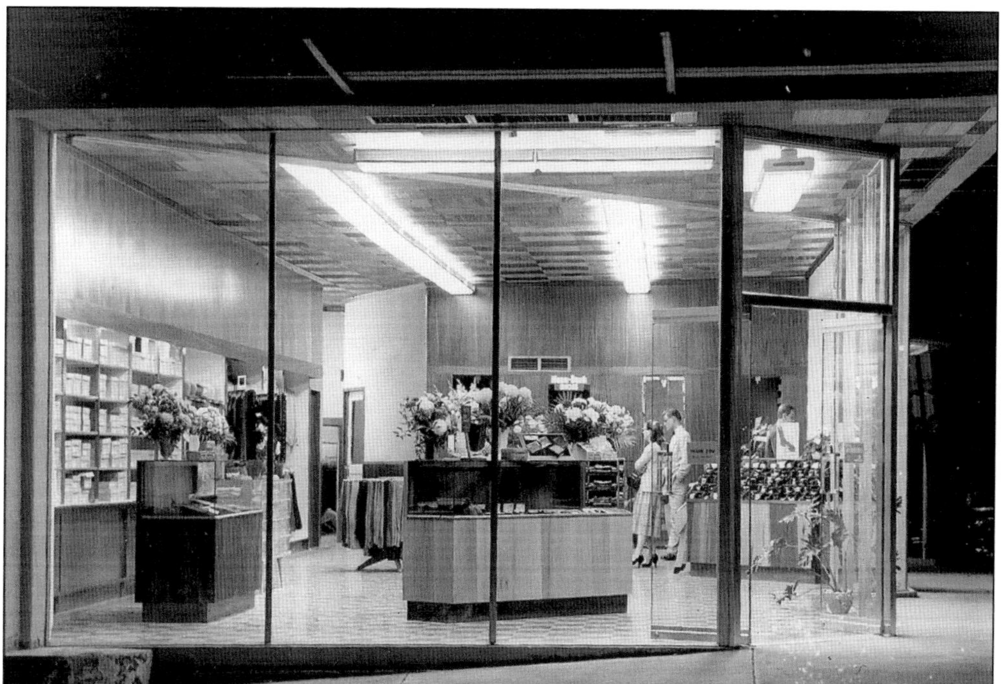
This photo looks inside a Brooksville department store at night in 1959. The Quality Shop was at the corner of Broad and Main Streets and was a popular department store up to the 1980s.

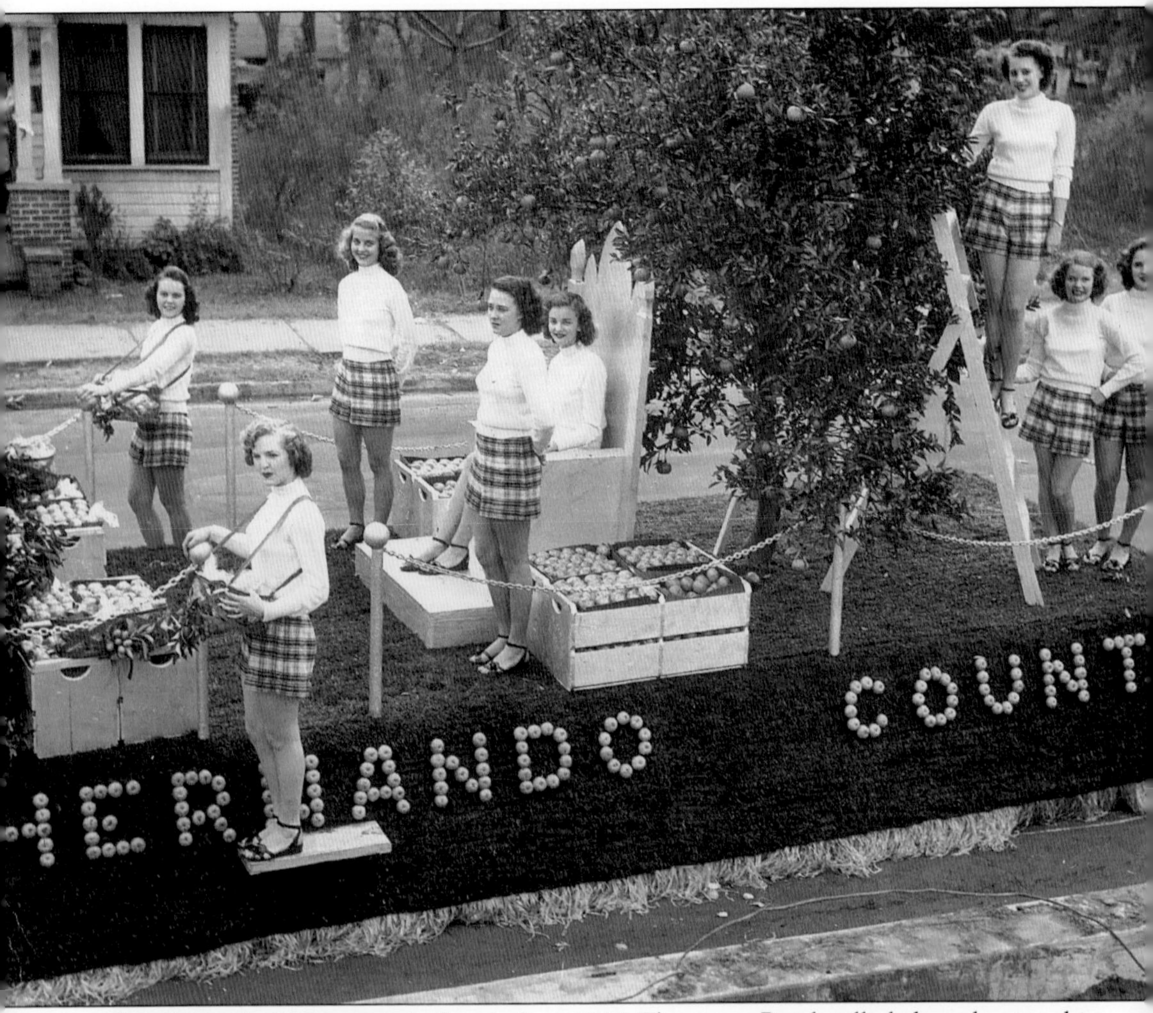

This Hernando County parade float is from 1948. The pretty Brooksville ladies adorning this float emphasize Hernando County's citrus industry during a Tallahassee parade celebrating the election of Gov. Fuller Warren. Brooksville was once known as "the Home of the Tangerine" and as you entered the city you would see signs advertising the claim. It provided the New York–Philadelphia area with more tangerines than any other area.

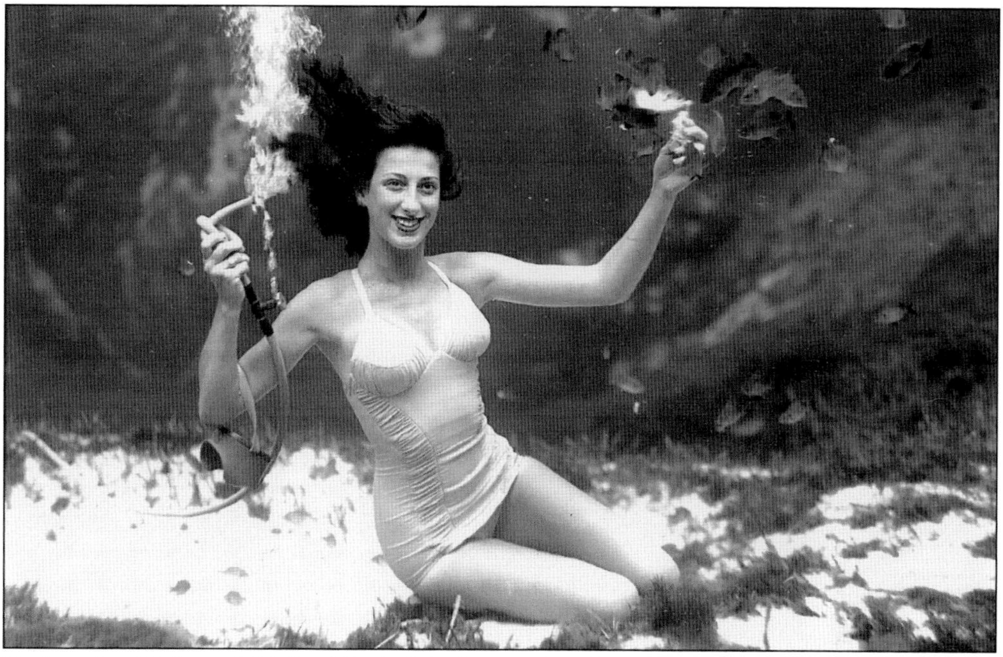

During the 1950s and 1960s, Weeki Wachee and its live underwater mermaid shows drew tourists from all over the world. This 1954 photo shows how a typical performance could draw oohs and ahhs.

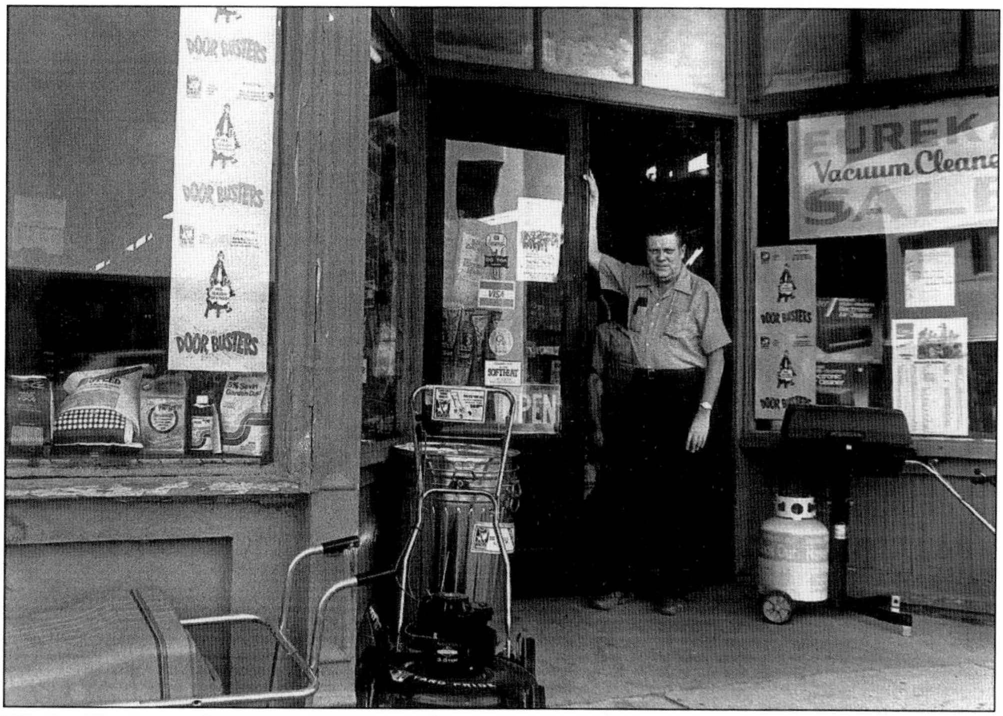

Weeks Hardware Store, pictured in 1970, has occupied the same location since 1916. Joe Weeks, seen above, still manages the store on North Main Street. It is the oldest retail store in the county, and it has been owned by the same family for 88 years.

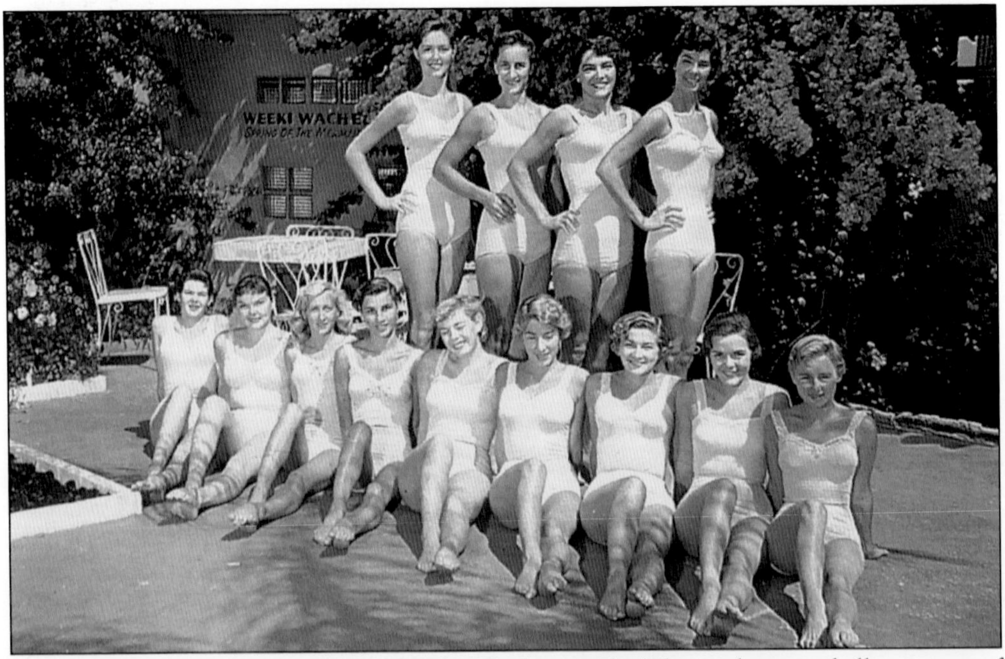

This 1955 souvenir postcard from Weeki Wachee reads "The underwater ballet troupe of shapely maidens who perform feats of grace and endurance in the crystal clear waters of Weeki Wachee Springs, Florida."

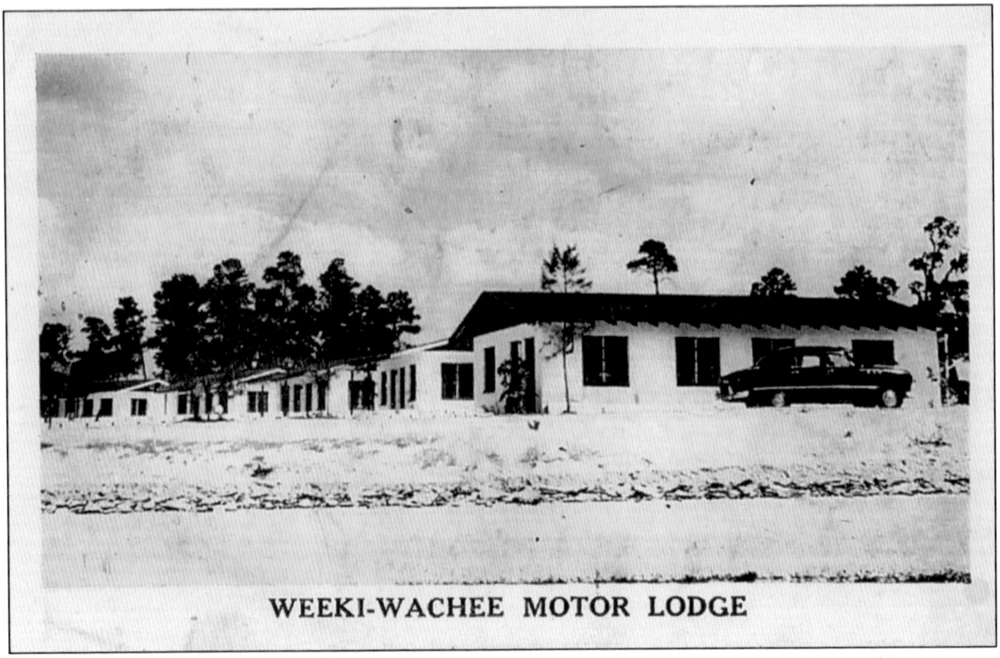

Weeki Wachee Motor Lodge was the closest place to stay near the attraction in 1956.

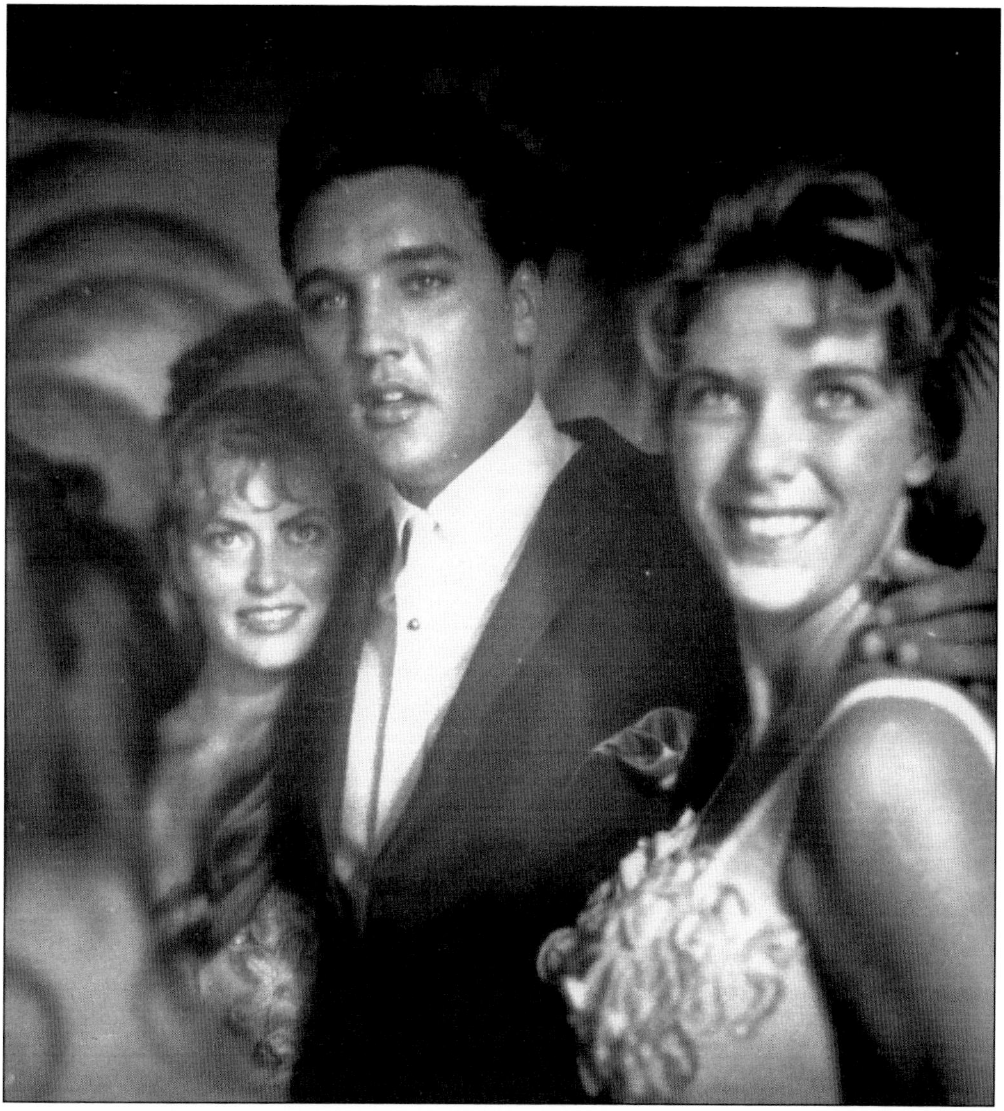

Seen here are Elvis and the mermaids in 1961. Elvis Presley would ask to visit Weeki Wachee while filming *Follow That Dream* 30 miles north in Crystal River. His visit one Sunday afternoon drew over 2,000 visitors to the attraction, some to get autographs, and some just to get a glimpse of "the King." He did not disappoint them.

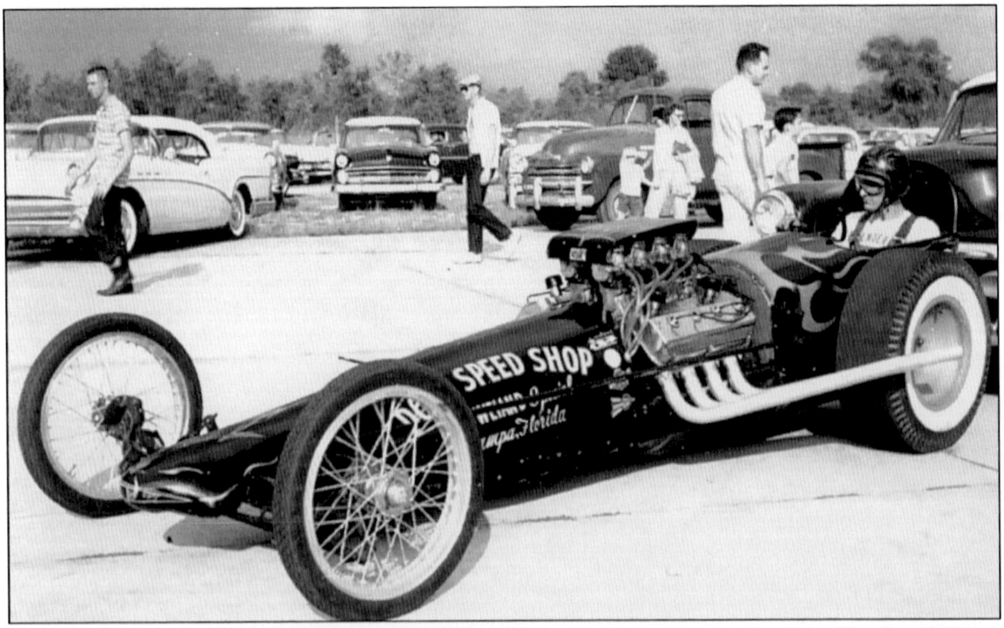

On November 10, 1957, a new drag racing speed record was set at the Brooksville Airport, when "Big Daddy" Don Garlits from Tampa hit 176 miles-per-hour in a quarter-mile before 3,000 race fans. He had beaten a record set in California a few months earlier. In 1959, Art Arfons would beat that record once again at the Brooksville Airport with a speed of 180.9 miles per hour. During the late 1950s, drag racing events were held on a regular basis at the airport about five miles south of Brooksville.

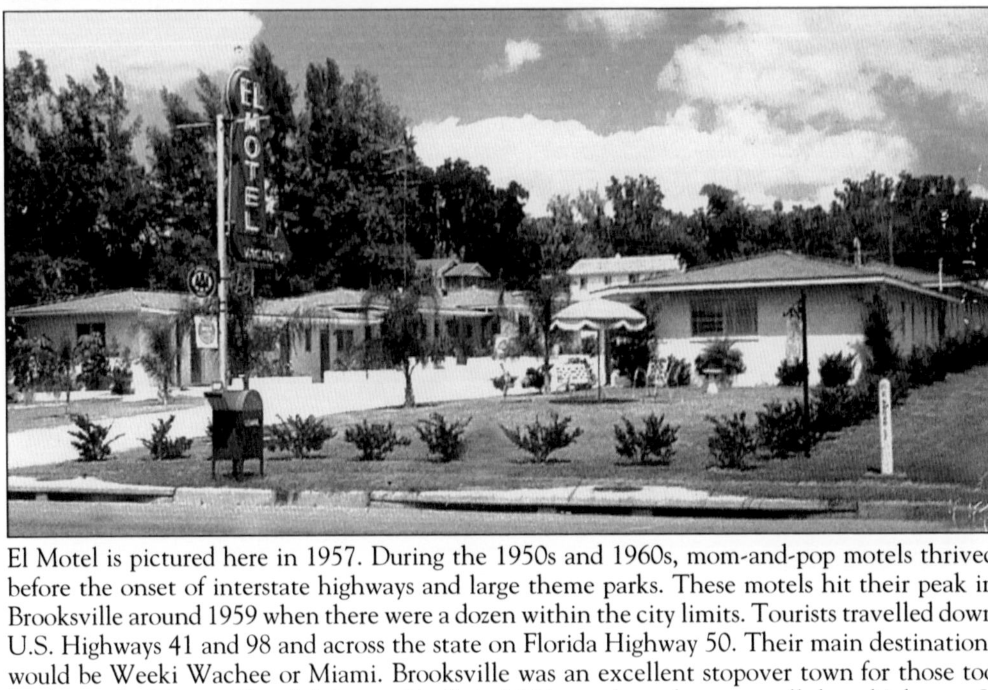

El Motel is pictured here in 1957. During the 1950s and 1960s, mom-and-pop motels thrived before the onset of interstate highways and large theme parks. These motels hit their peak in Brooksville around 1959 when there were a dozen within the city limits. Tourists travelled down U.S. Highways 41 and 98 and across the state on Florida Highway 50. Their main destinations would be Weeki Wachee or Miami. Brooksville was an excellent stopover town for those too tired to make Miami. This AAA motel built in 1954 was the only one on all three highways. It was torn down in 1987.

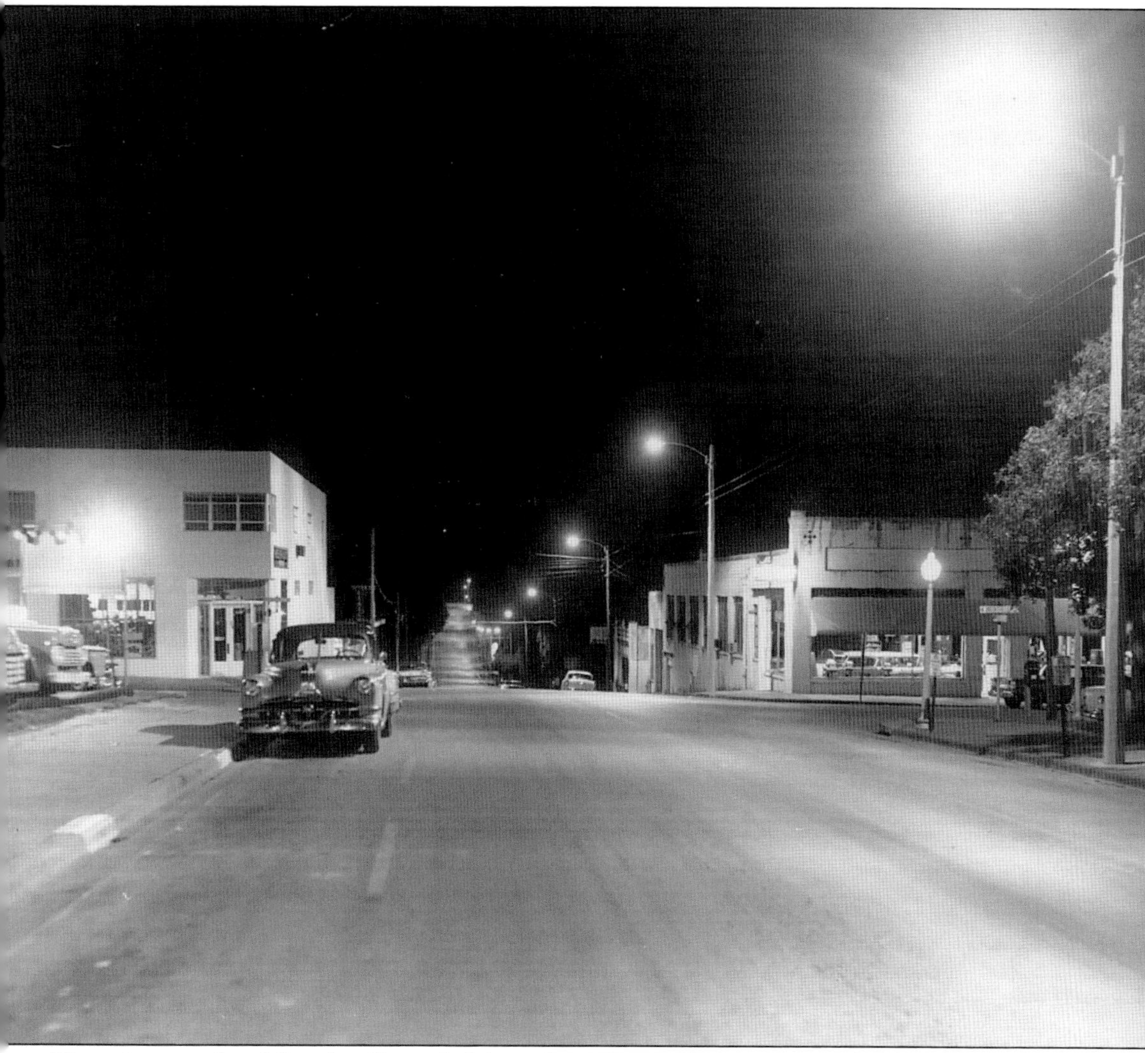

This photograph of Brooksville nightlife is from 1959. The streets are bright and clean. Brooksville at the time had a population of about 3,500, but during a weekday, night traffic was very light. To the right is an auto dealership, to the left is Western Auto, and down the street is an old ice plant.

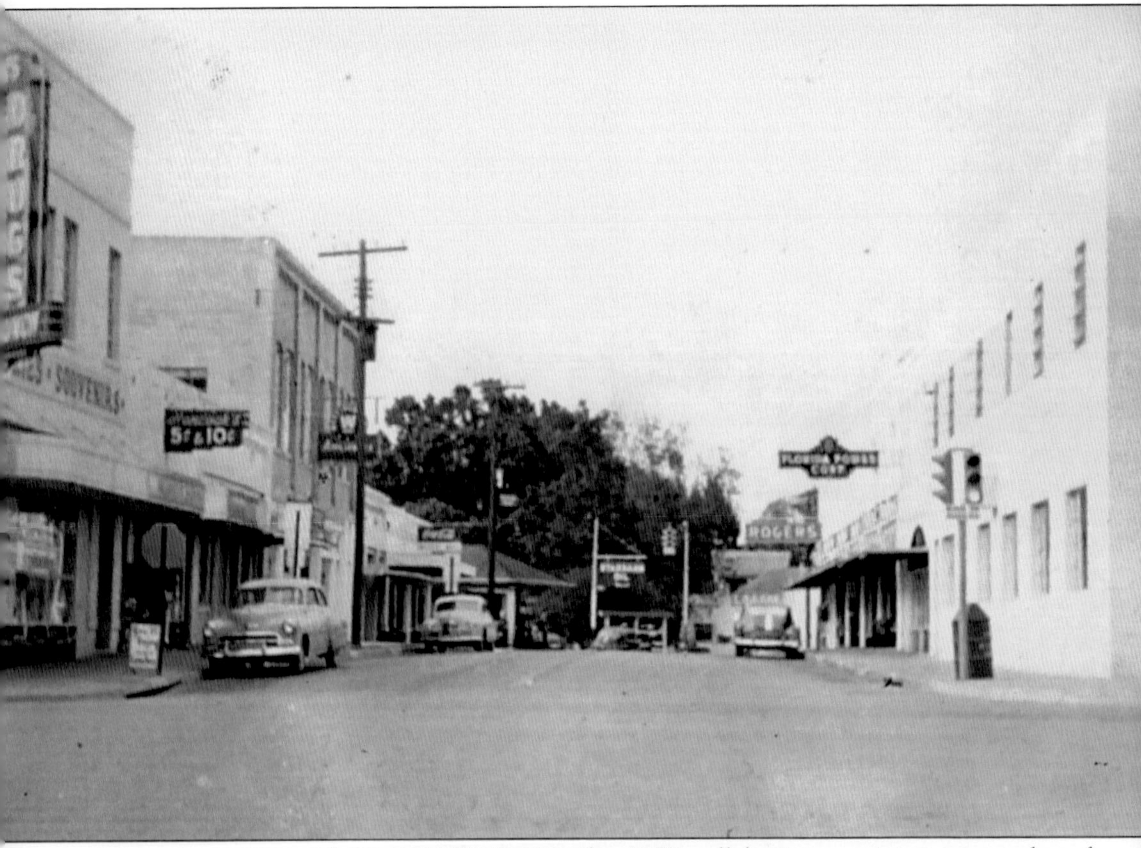

Main Street is seen here in 1953. During the 1950s, all business activity was conducted downtown. Shopping centers and strip malls would not make their appearance until 1965.

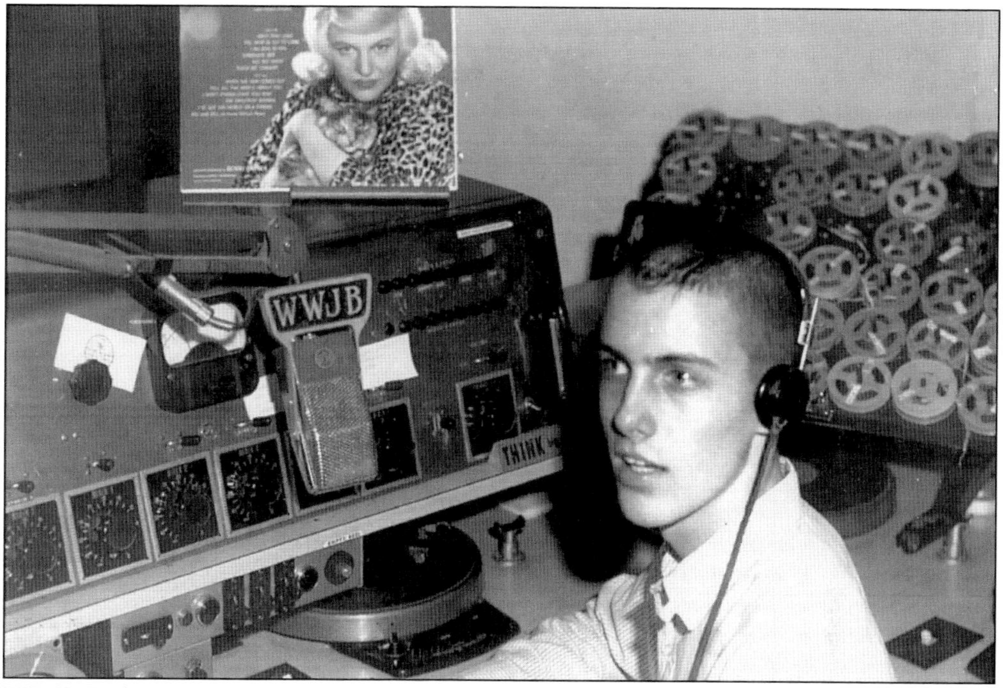

WWJB Radio Station is on the air in 1963, as young deejay Steve Manuel spins "the sound of Peggy Lee on 1450." WWJB went on the air in 1958 to replace WKTS. WKTS was the first radio station in Brooksville, beginning in 1956, but it burned down in early 1958. During the 1950s and 1960s it featured a middle-of-the-road format mixed with local live sports and school club programs. Today, Manuel is a co-owner of the station.

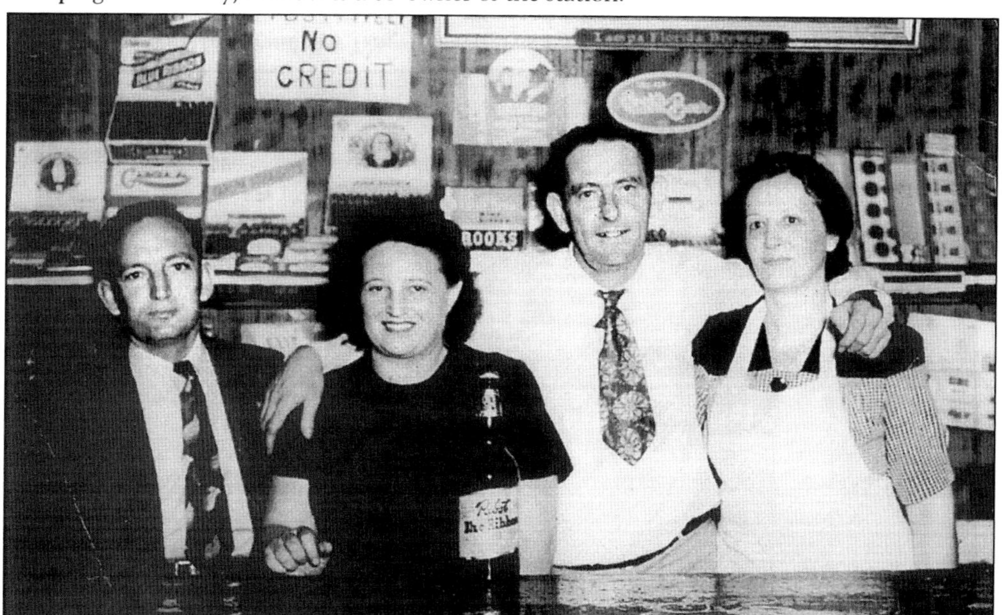

Pictured here is some honky-tonk fun from 1947. The All States Inn was a popular dance hall north of Brooksville. Pictured are Ben E. Smith, Mary the barmaid, owner "Slim" Adams, and his wife Neola.

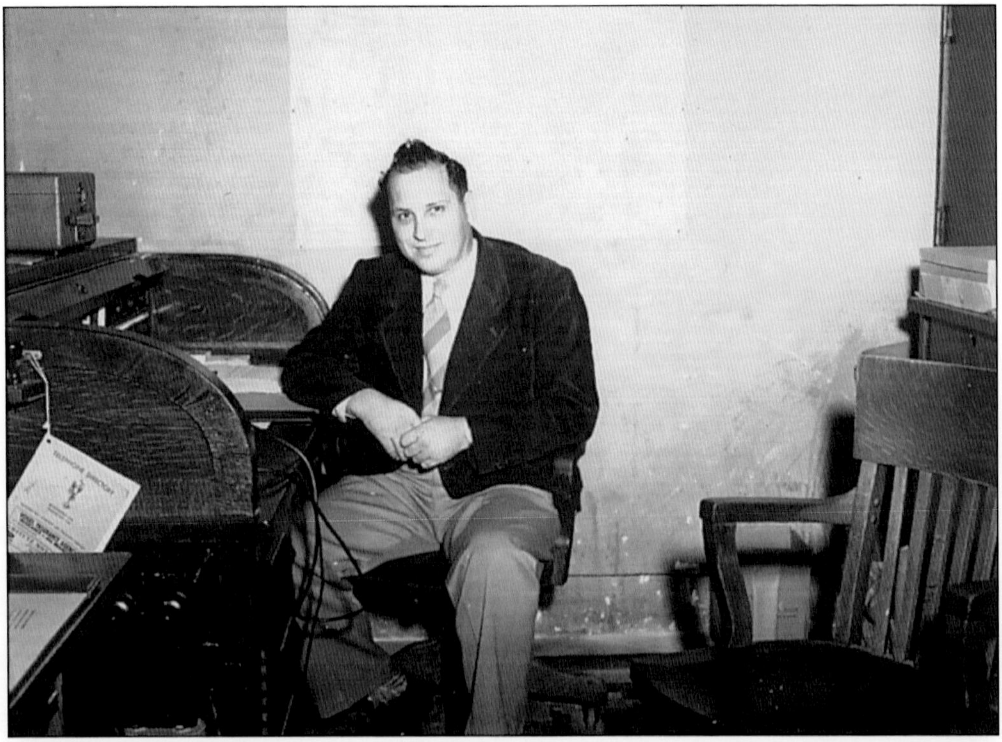

Sheriff Sim L. Lowman was popular throughout the state. He served from 1949 to 1970. The sheriff's office was then located near downtown on Jefferson Street along with the jail.

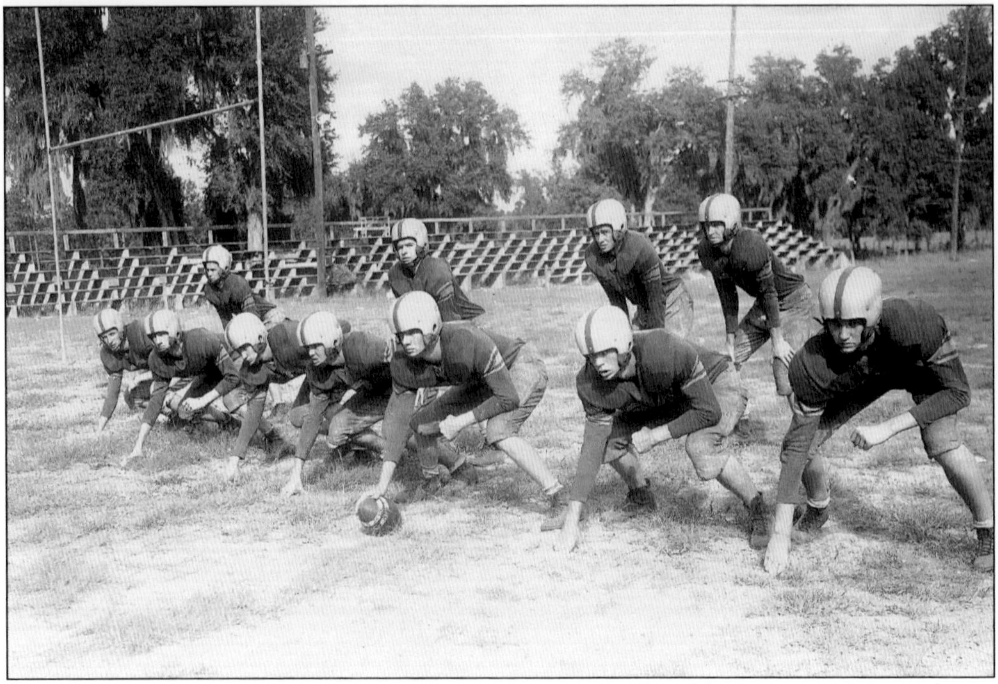

The 1951 Hernando Leopards had a lean, mean, and streamlined look. Leopard teams during the late 1940s and early 1950s were some of the best teams in the state.

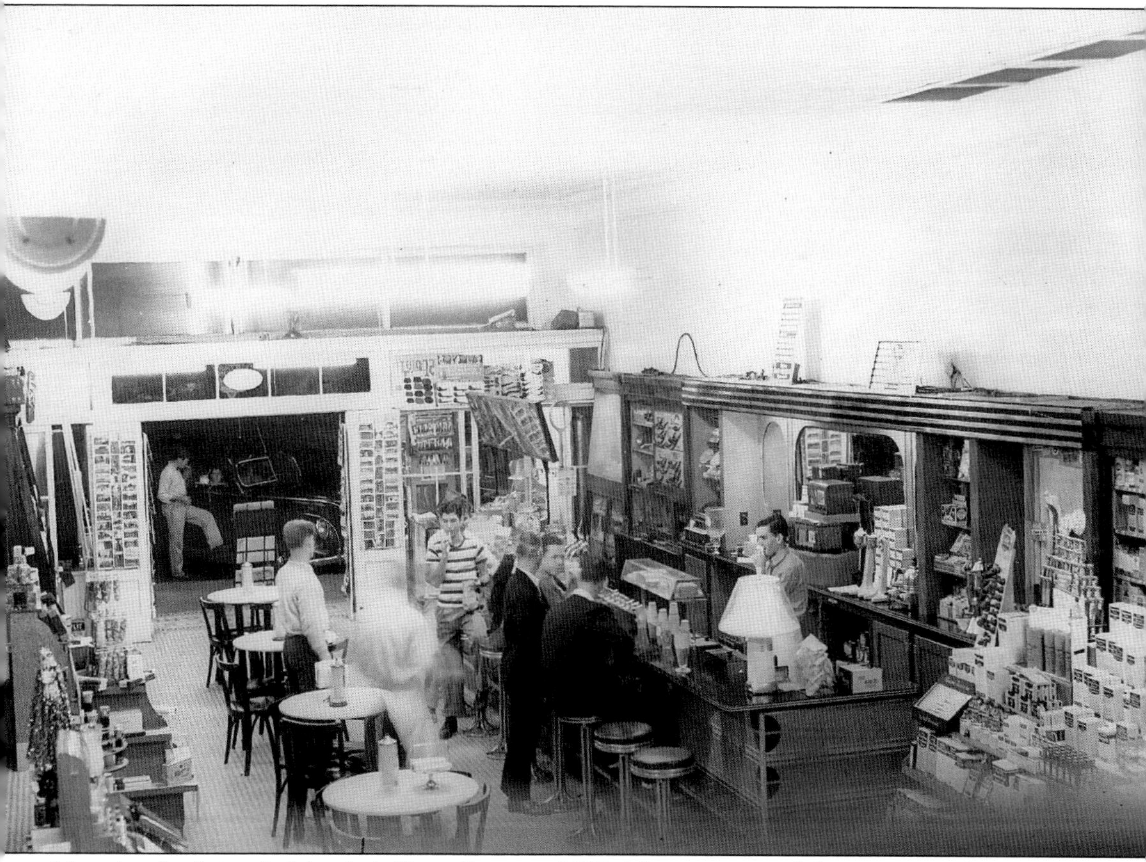

Here is a look inside Murphy's Drug Store in 1950. This was one of the most popular teen hangouts during the 1950s and early 1960s, featuring cherry cokes, comics, and magazines.

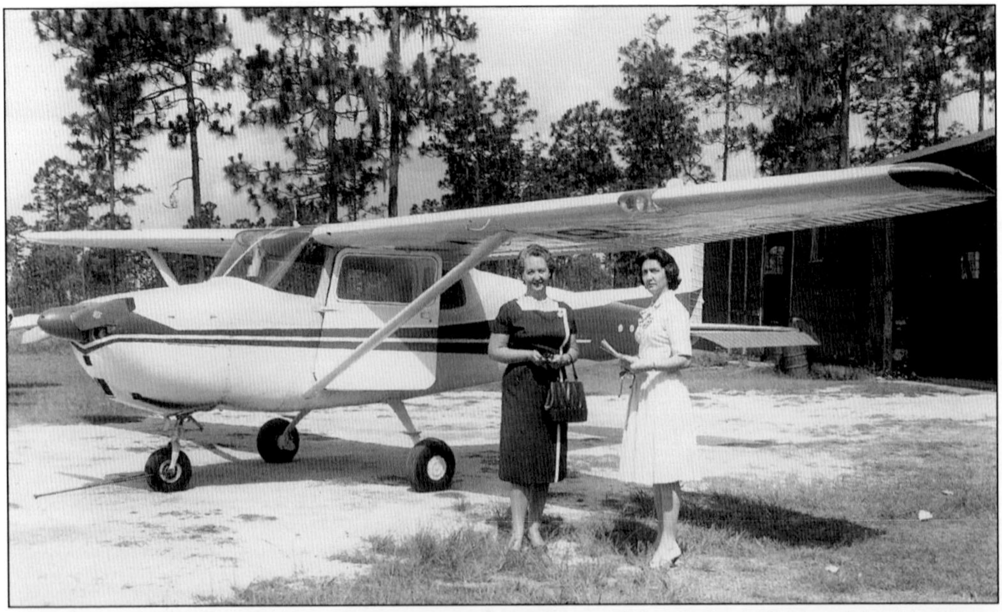

"Dutch" Endsley and Thelma Dawson, two members of the ladies' flying club the Flying Grasshoppers, look like they're ready to go shopping in this 1963 photograph. This would be a good way to beat the traffic.

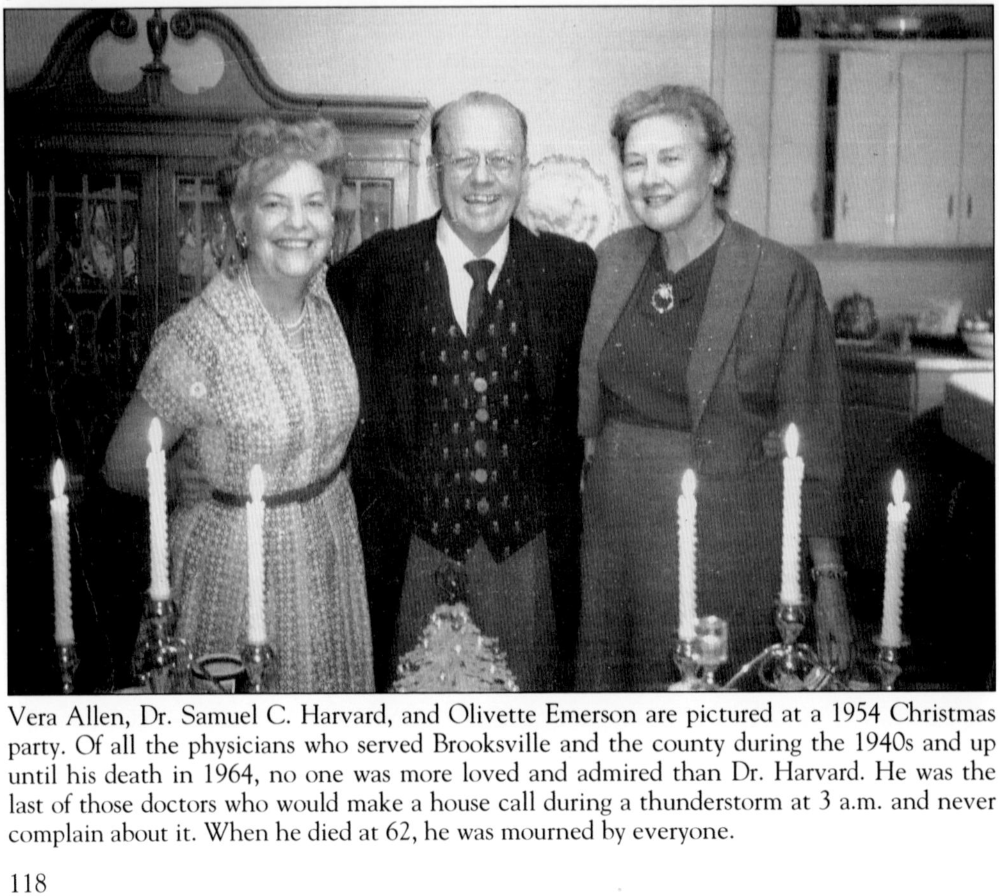

Vera Allen, Dr. Samuel C. Harvard, and Olivette Emerson are pictured at a 1954 Christmas party. Of all the physicians who served Brooksville and the county during the 1940s and up until his death in 1964, no one was more loved and admired than Dr. Harvard. He was the last of those doctors who would make a house call during a thunderstorm at 3 a.m. and never complain about it. When he died at 62, he was mourned by everyone.

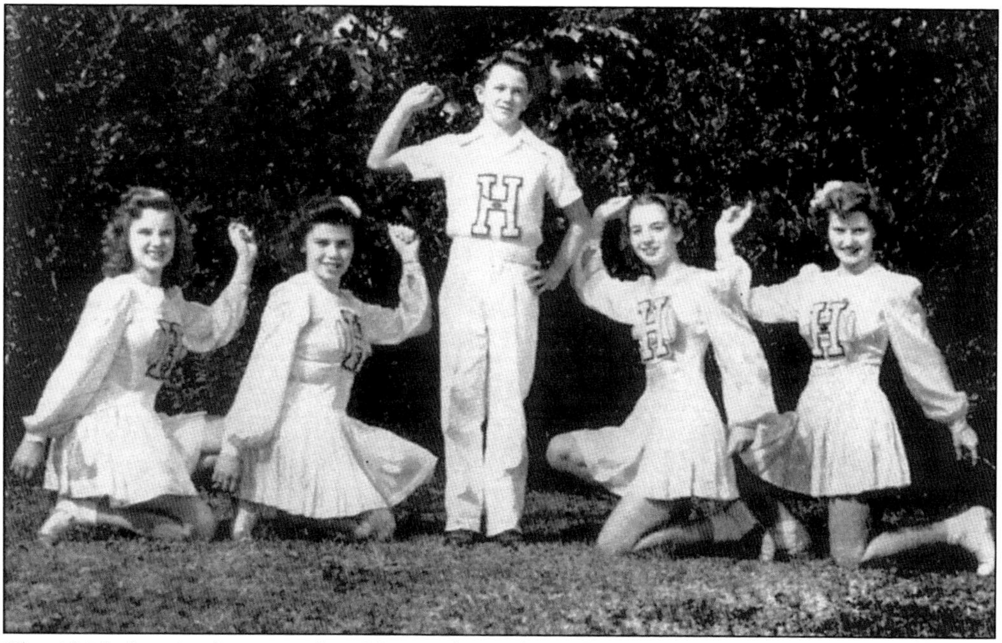

The 1946 cheerleading squad at Hernando High is, from left to right, Betty Griffen, Edna Stevens, Kenneth "Button" Bray, Patsy Murphy, and Mildred Ann Randall. Miss Griffen was later a top model in New York.

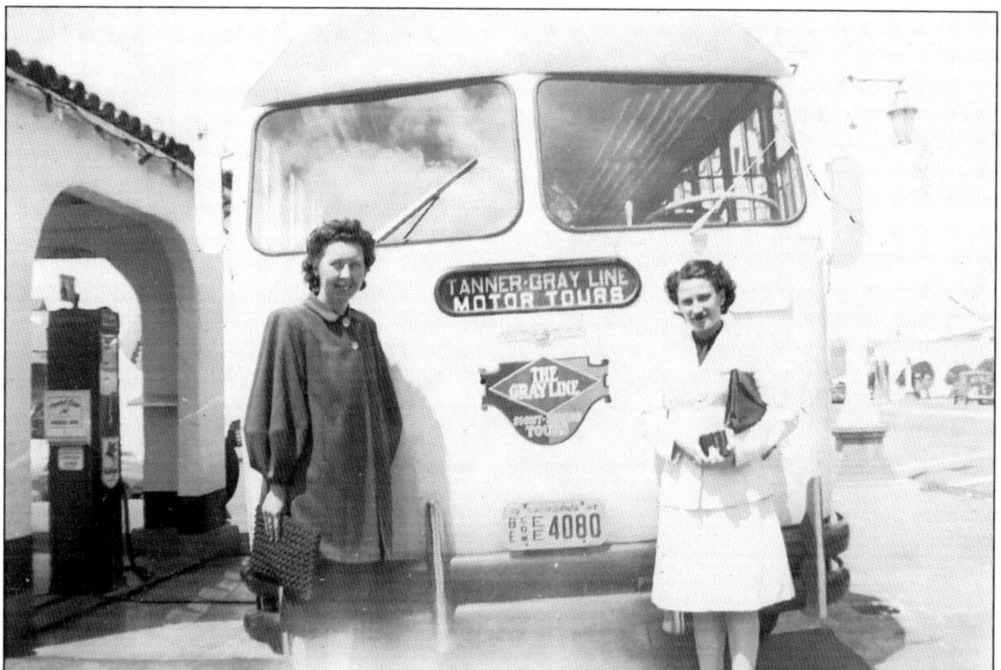

Dot Bethest and Virginia McKeown pose at the old bus depot on Broad Street before a long trip in 1947.

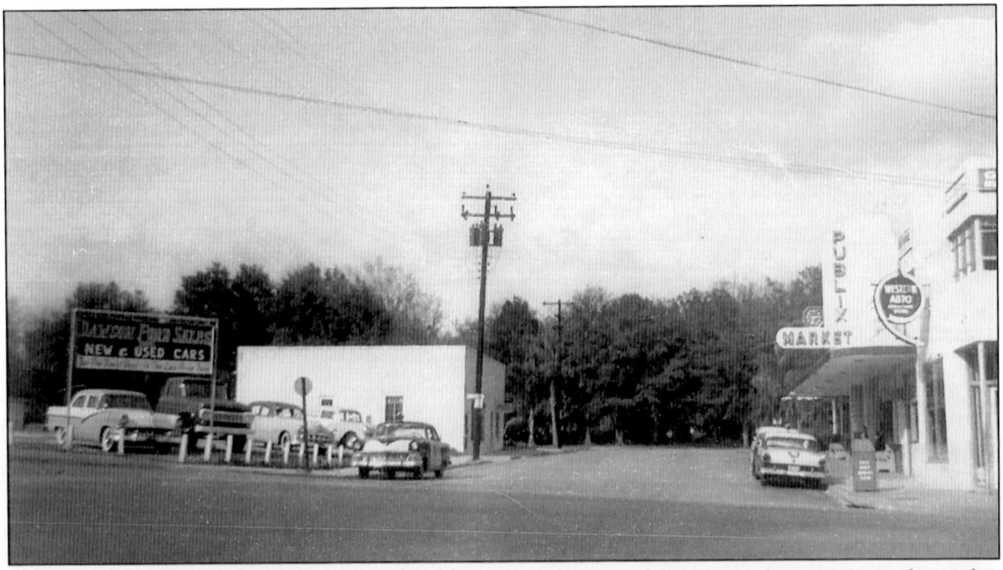

In this 1958 view of North Brooksville Avenue, Publix and Western Auto are on the right. This was the Publix location from 1950 to 1965.

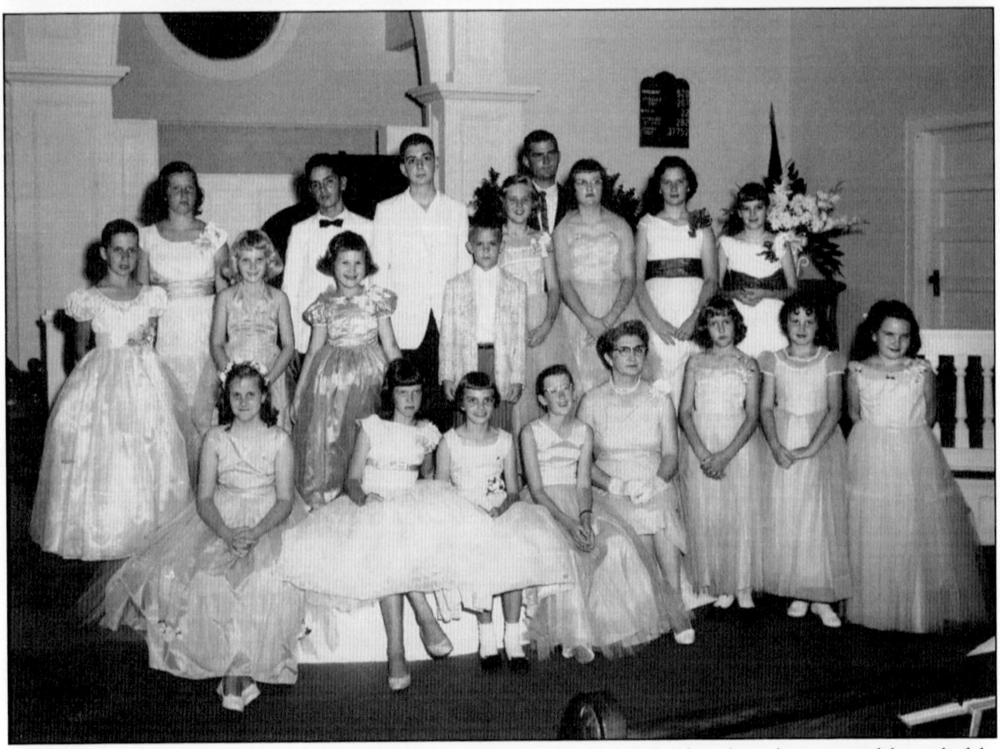
Though performing at Mrs. John Allen's 1959 piano recital, the four boys would probably rather be somewhere else. The pianists are, from left to right, (front row) Linda Stone, Linda Emerson, Tinsy Jane Hardy, Gaye Underwood, Mrs. John Allen, Sandra Loftin, Janie Varn, and Linda Treiman; (back row) Roberta Barton, Joy Emerson, Chrissie Vance, Bob Martinez, Carol Treiman, Dwight Allen, Eddie Webb, Barbara Bell, Paul Tucker, Edith Varn, Beth Ehlers, and Margie Varn.

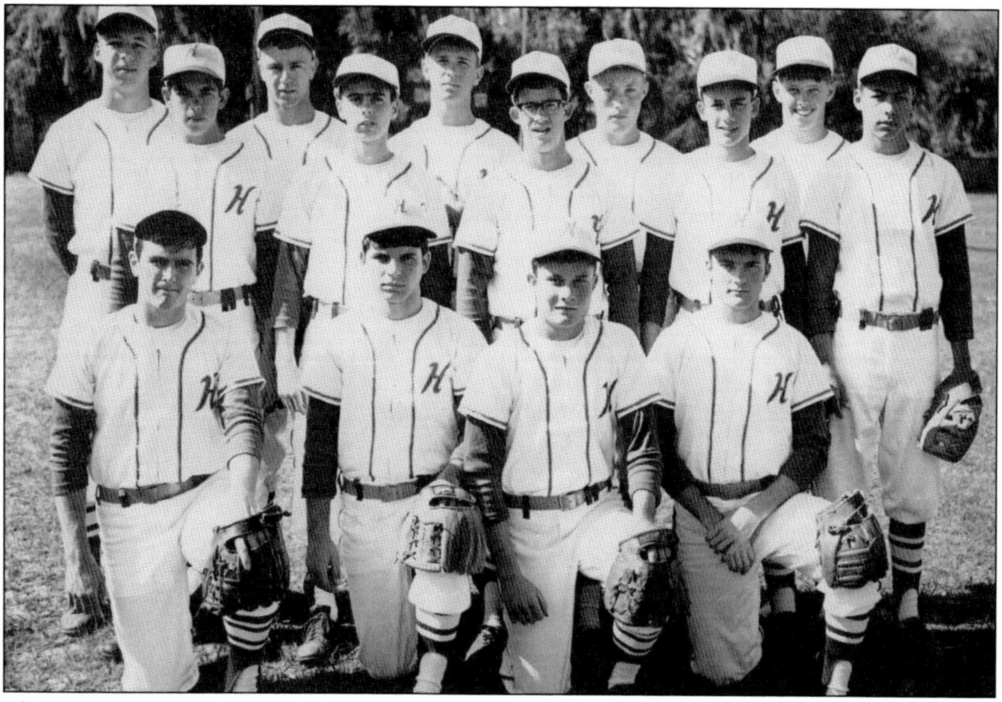

The 1966 Hernando High baseball team, just one year away from being state champs, is, from left to right, (front row) Larry Key, Bobby Chorvat, Buddy Hancock, and Lynn Thompson; (back row) Larry Lee, Donnie Varn, Terry Owens, Bruce Wilson, Charlie Barnett, Randy Raines, Thomas "Bubba" Varn, Donny Moen, and Hale Lee. Most of these boys would return the following year along with Grover Ellis, Larry Farmer, and Sam Sharp to win the 1967 Class B State Championship.

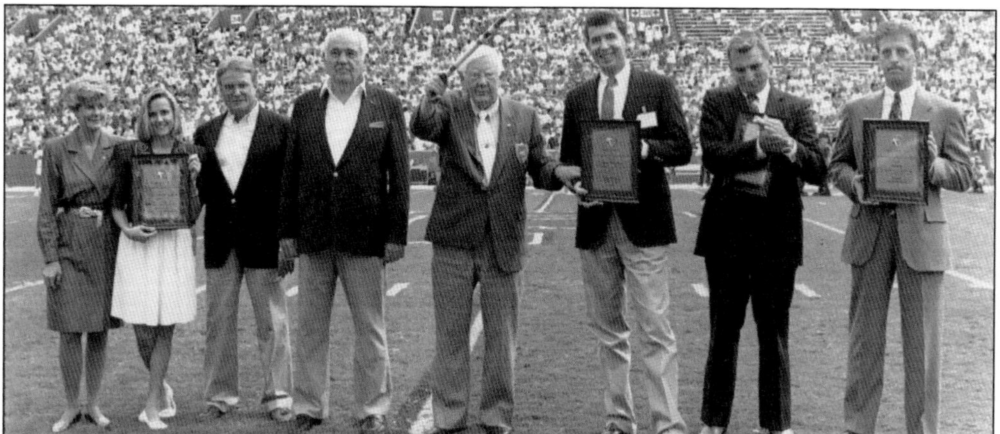

No other citizen in Hernando County had a more illustrious life than Alfred McKethan. Premier banker and businessman, he was also responsible for the development of roads throughout Hernando County and the growth of the mining industry; his political ties were most influential. Here he receives another award at Florida Field during a Florida Gators halftime in 1988. A noted philanthropist, his contributions to the University of Florida were legendary. He graduated from there in 1931 and remained an avid fan until his death at the age of 93 in 2002. The University of Florida baseball field bears his name.

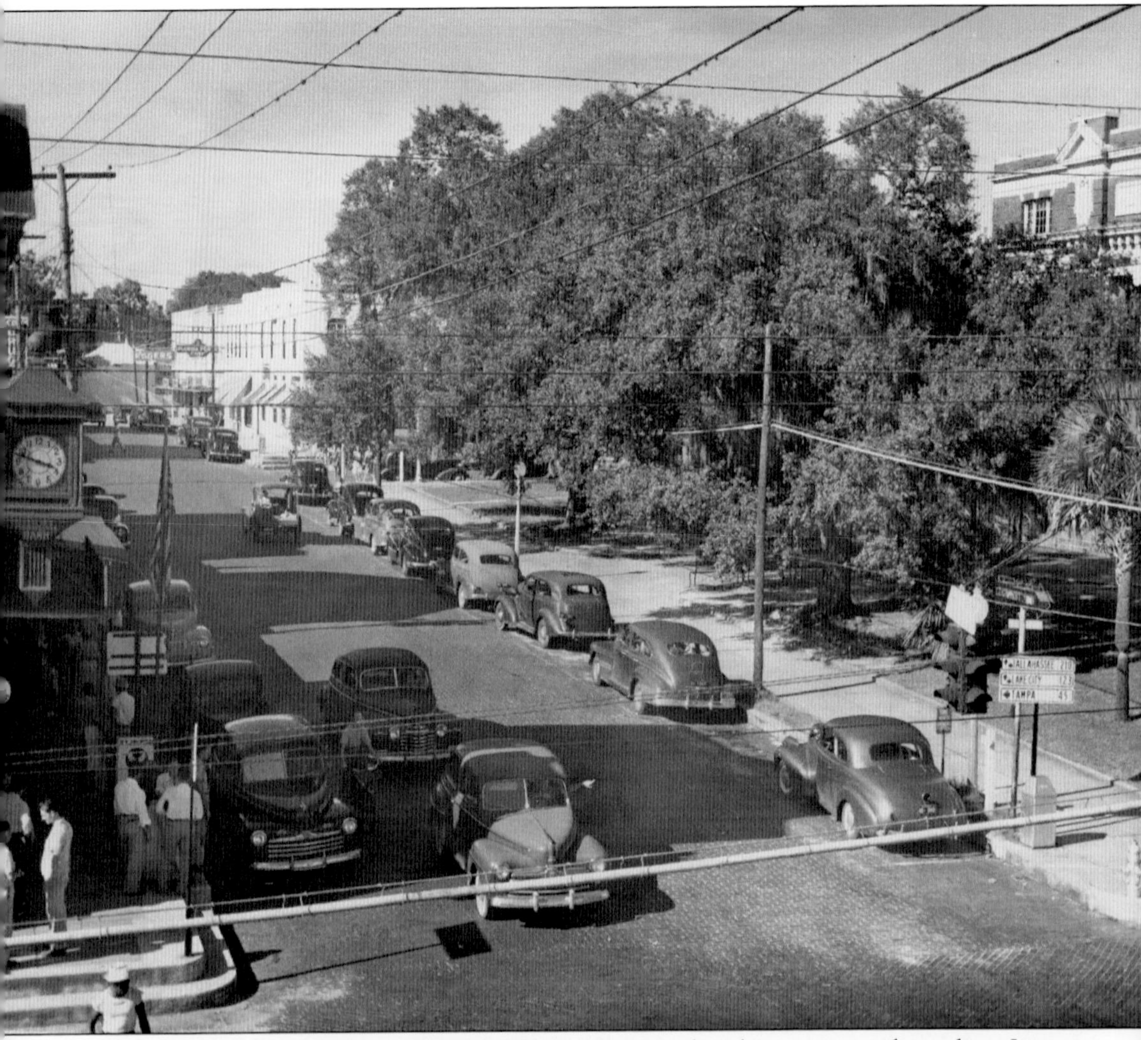

Here is a Saturday afternoon in 1948; downtown was the place to go in those days. It was a beehive of activity, where people gathered to meet friends and neighbors and talk about politics, sports, family, and the latest rumor.

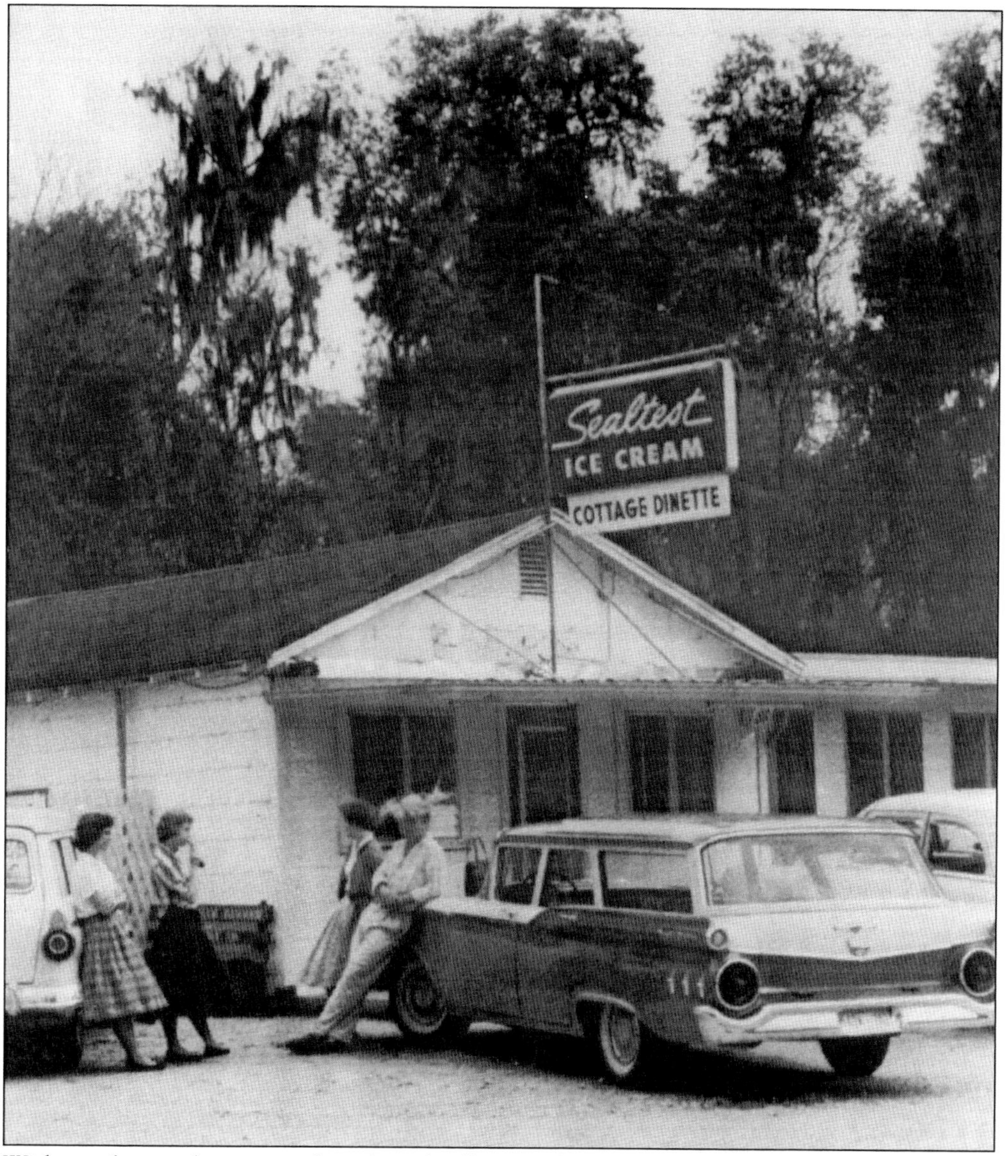

With its bunny burgers and rock-and-roll, seen here in 1959, the Cottage Dinette on U.S. Highway 41 was a big hit with all ages from its opening in 1953 until it closed 40 years later. Famous for its special burgers, fried chicken, and pies, it also featured a juke box and popular waitresses.

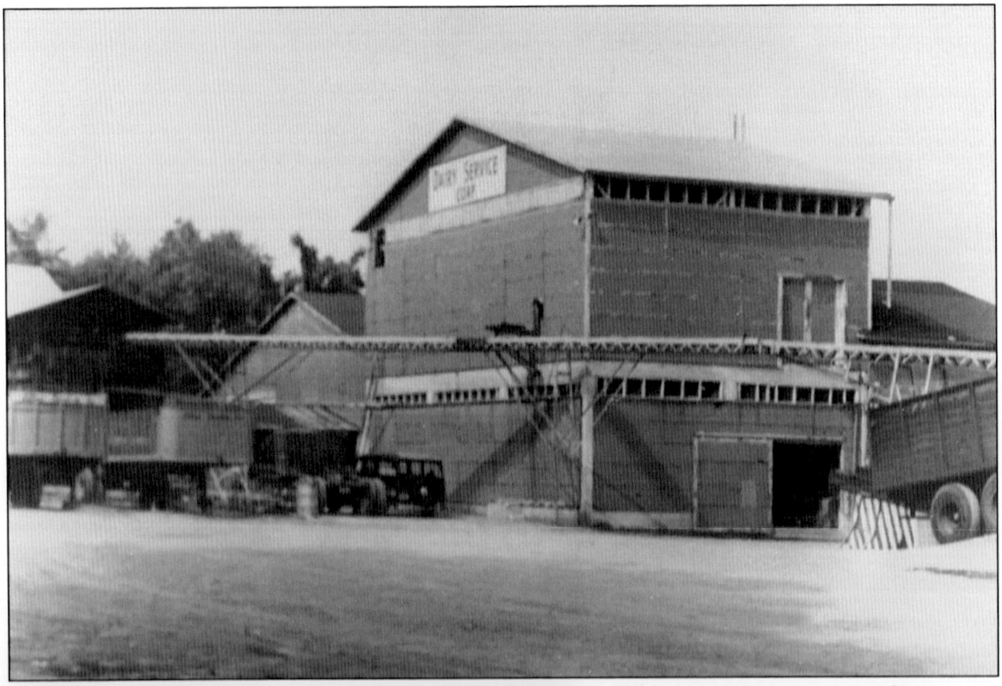

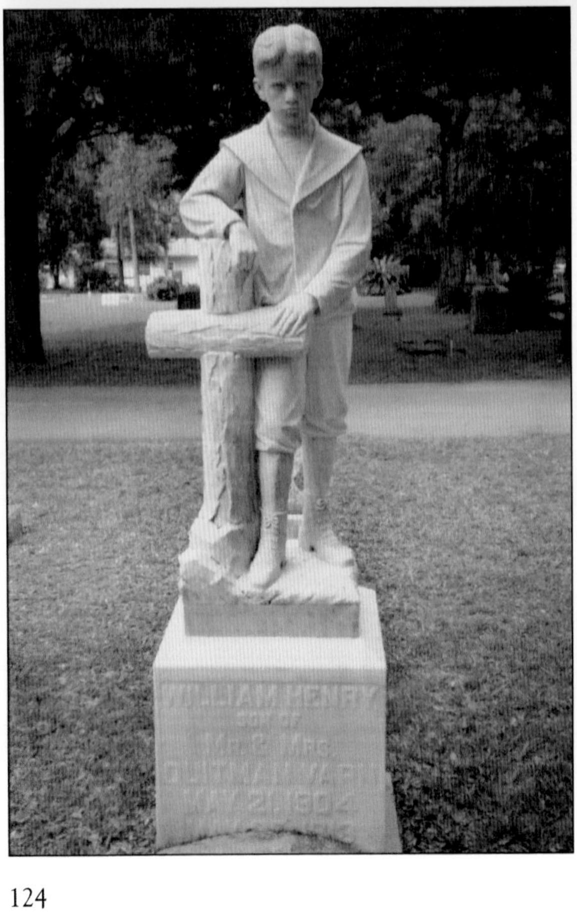

This citrus plant is pictured in 1954. Brooksville was known as "the Home of the Tangerine"; on certain days the smell of burnt oranges hung over the entire city. This plant was on what was then called Summit Drive, now known as Martin Luther King Boulevard.

If you really want to know Brooksville history, you must visit the Brooksville Cemetery. The earliest known tombstone in Hernando County is here—Jane Hope died on March 14, 1845. There are many other unique ones such as the one above of William Henry Varn, a young lad who passed away in 1913. It is about a mile east of the city, just off State Highway 50.

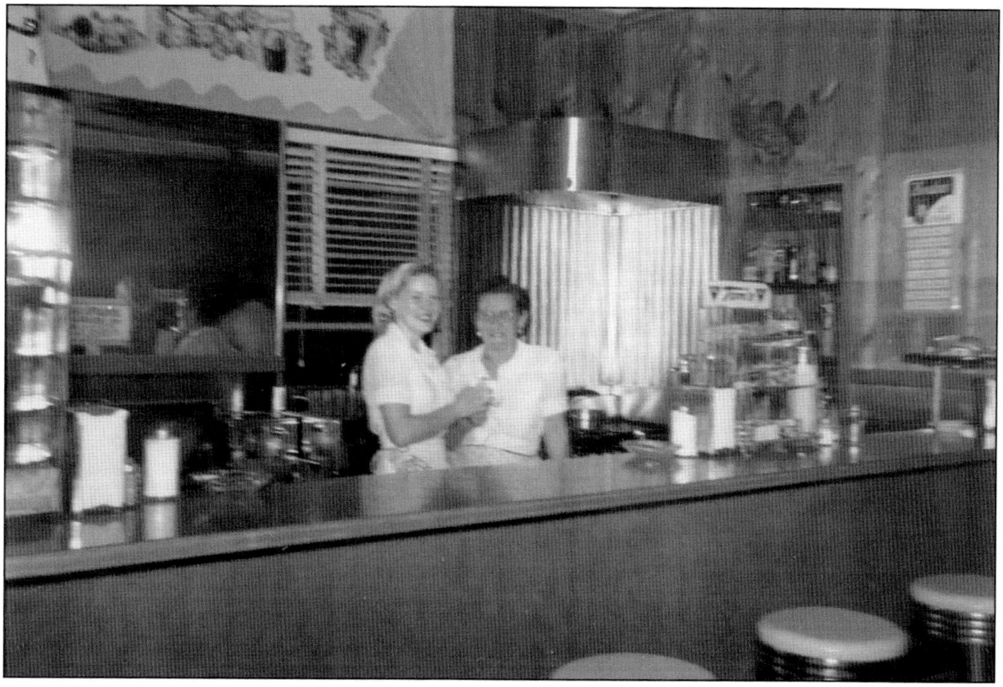

Two waitresses are pictured in 1953 at the old Sports Center restaurant on Jefferson Street, which featured pool tables around the back.

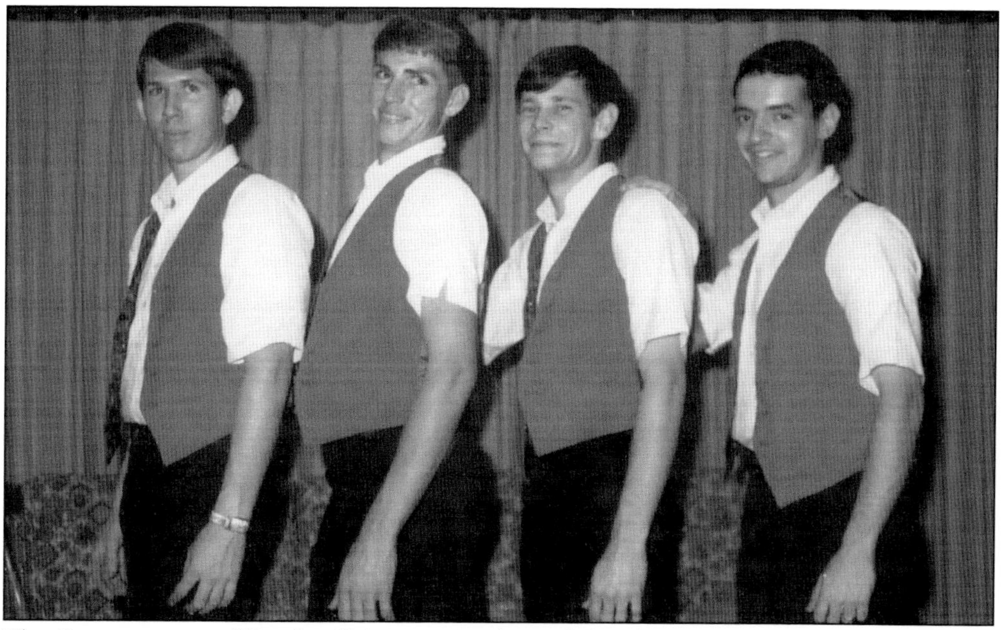

The Cavemen, one of Brooksville's most popular rock bands in 1965, played dances from St. Petersburg to Gainesville. "Garage" rock bands were quite common in those days with every town holding weekend dances and sock hops. Everyone had Beatlemania. Most bands like the one above had regular bookings every weekend. The band is, from left to right, Frankie Springstead, rhythm guitar; Alonzo Merritt, drums; Pete Shingleton, vocals/bass; and Bob Martinez, vocals/lead guitar.

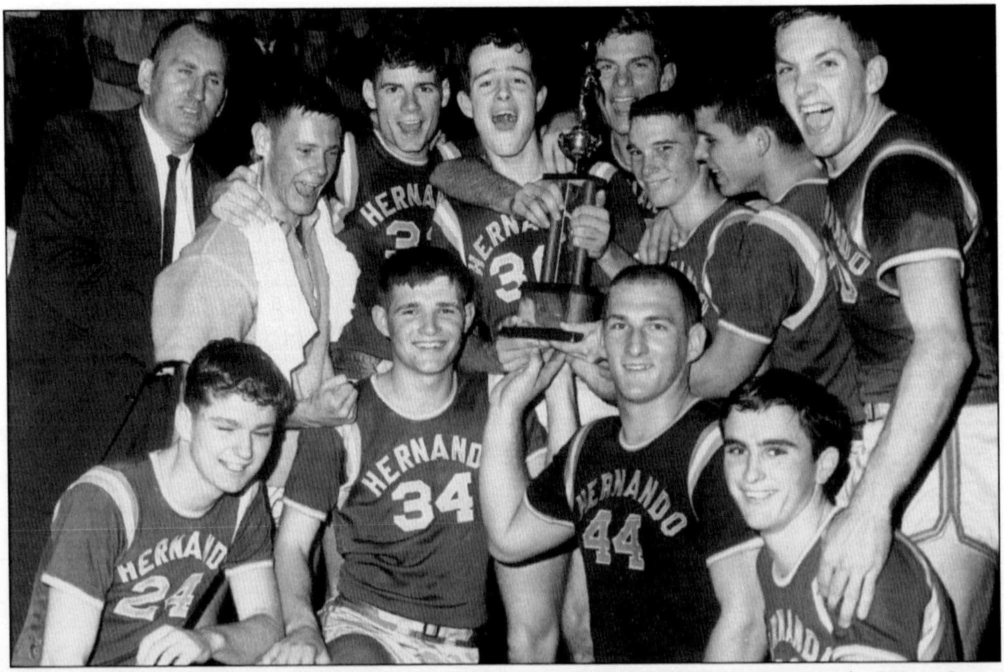

The 1964–1965 Hernando High basketball team won 22 games in a row to win the West Coast Conference Championship, only to lose the next two games in the state semifinals.

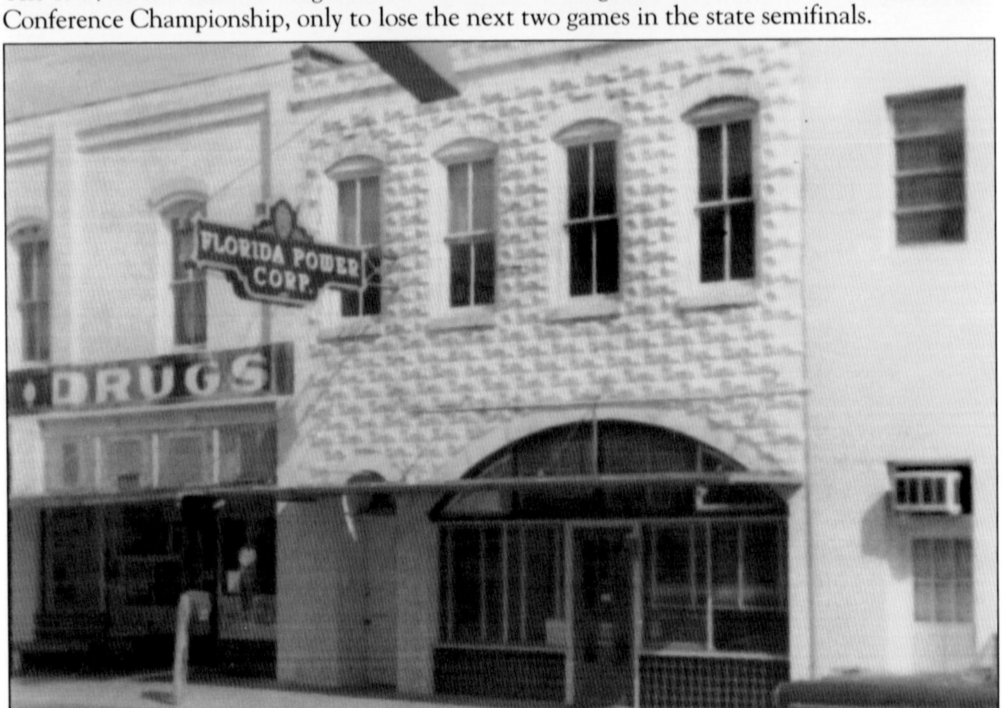

Hope's Drug Store and Florida Power Building, seen here in 1956, was located on North Main Street. Hope's was operated by Walter and Margie Hope and was one of those places fondly remembered by those who recall the cherry cokes, magazines, baseball cards, and even long-playing records and 45s for sale.

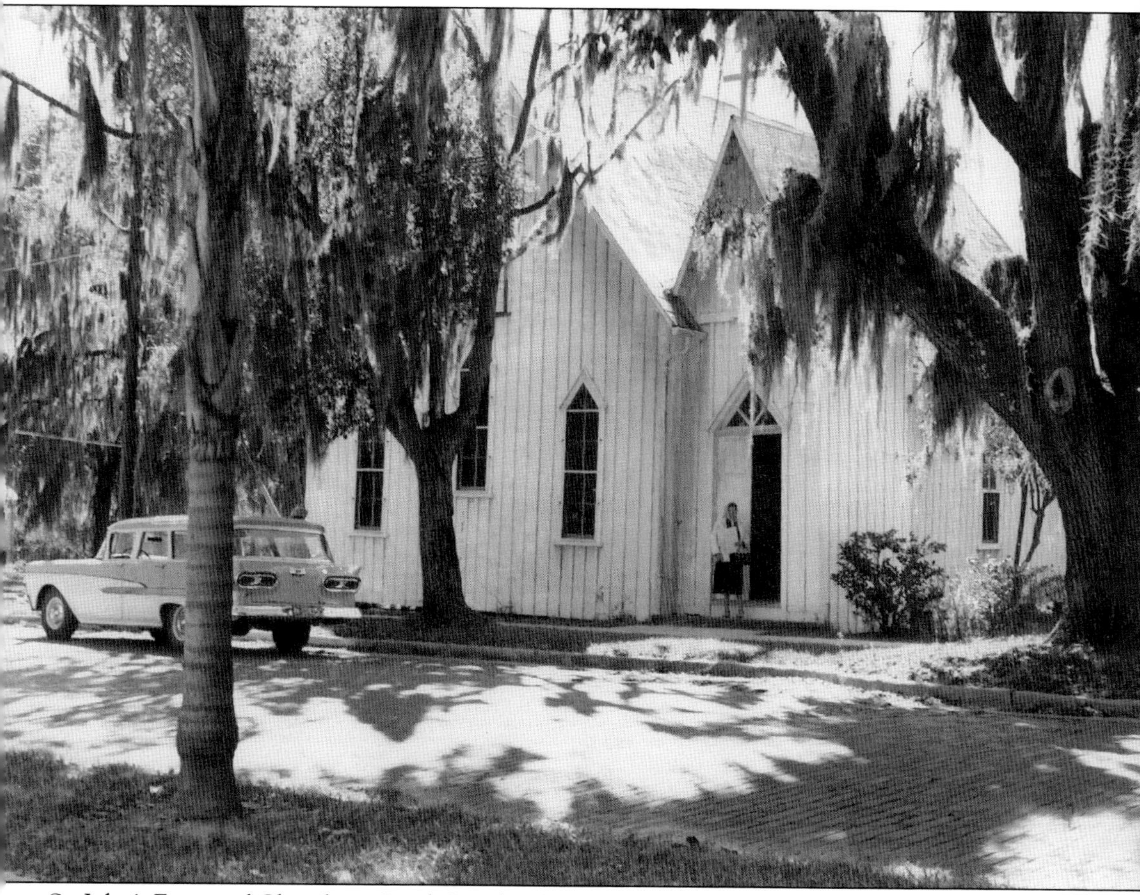

St. John's Episcopal Church on South Brooksville Avenue, pictured here in 1958, looked pretty much the same as when it first opened in 1885, with the exception of the 1958 Ford station wagon. Since then it has been completely renovated.

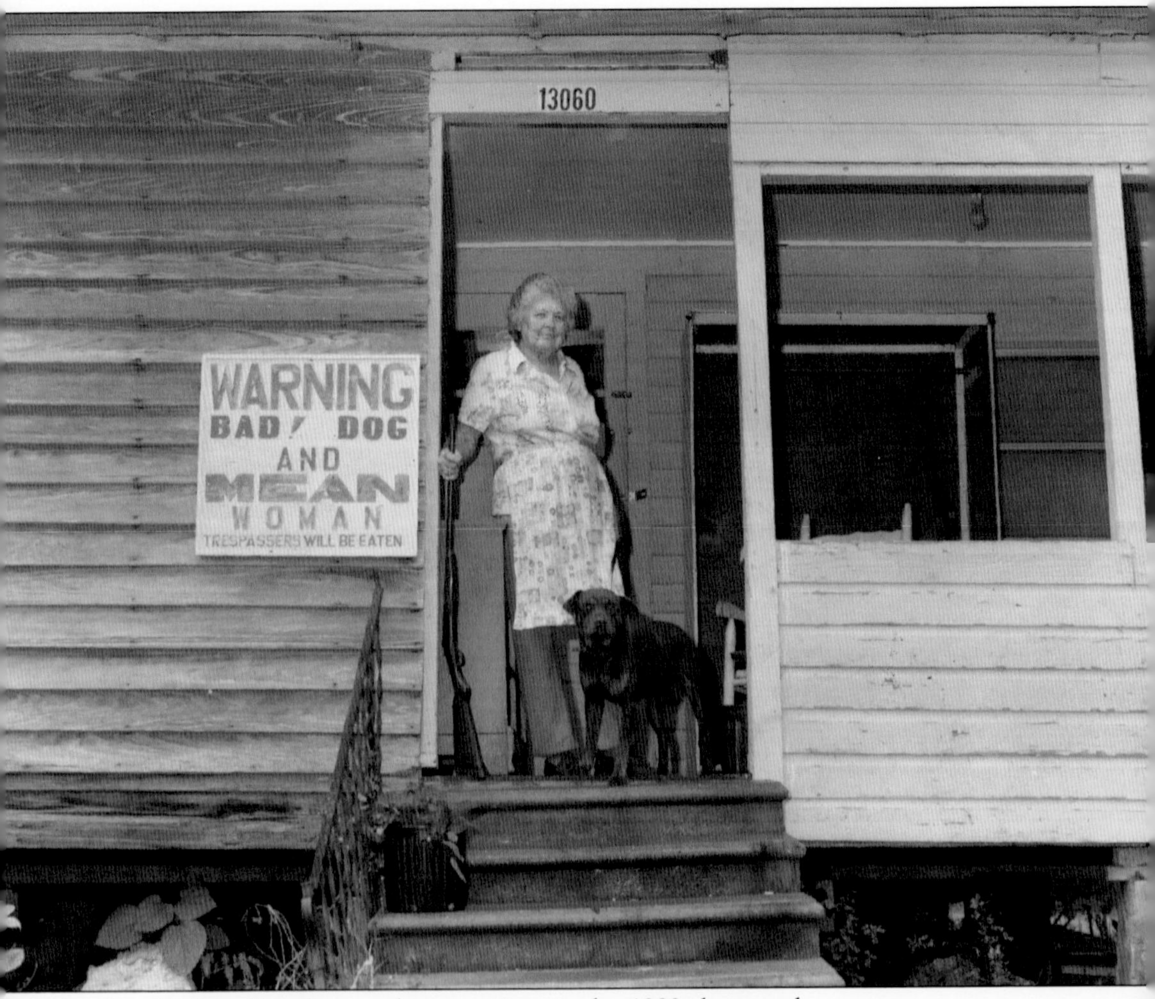

Lois Waller of Istachatta welcomes visitors in this 1980 photograph.